Pink Floyd

Bruno MacDonald

Pink Floyd

Through the eyes of . . .

the band, its fans, friends and foes

DA CAPO PRESS • NEW YORK

Library of Congress Cataloging-in-Publication Data

Pink Floyd: through the eyes of . . . the band, its fans, friends, and foes /
  Bruno MacDonald [editor].
     p.   cm.
  Originally published: London: Sidgwick & Jackson, 1996.
  Includes index.
  ISBN 0-306-80780-7 (alk. paper)
     1. Pink Floyd (Musical quartet)—Criticism and interpretation. I. Mac-
  Donald, Bruno.
  ML421.P6P56   1997
  782.42166′092′2—dc21
  [B]   97-5216
                                                                  CIP
                                                                   MN

The permission acknowledgements on p. 329–32 constitute
an extension to this copyright page.

First published in the United Kingdom in 1996 by Sidgwick & Jackson.

First published in the United States in 1997 by Da Capo Press, Inc.
by arrangement with Macmillan Publishers Ltd.

Published by Da Capo Press, Inc.
A Subsidiary of Plenum Publishing Corporation
233 Spring Street, New York, N.Y. 10013

Manufactured in the United States of America

Acknowledgements

For their help with this book, my thanks to Ingrid Connell, Dan Hawthorn, Claire Hector, Roberta Kurtz, Ian McCann, Mark Paytress, Mat Snow, Elizabeth Thomson and all the writers and publishers who kindly allowed their work to be reprinted.

For their support and tolerance, my love and thanks to Sue Innes, the MacDonald family, my friends at Smiths and RED, Ruth Walton and my coeditors on *The Amazing Pudding* – Andy Mabbett, Ivor Trueman and Dave and Carole Walker (details of *The Amazing Pudding* are available from 67 Cramlington Road, Birmingham B42 2EE, UK).

Invaluable assistance and encouragement was provided by Jeff Jensen, editor of the international Pink Floyd magazine *Brain Damage* (details from PO Box 109, Westmont, IL 60559, USA, or PO Box 385, Uxbridge, Middlesex UB9 5DZ, UK).

Thanks also to John Kelly, editor of the Syd Barrett magazine *Chapter 24* (101 Amersham Road, High Wycombe, Buckinghamshire HP13 5AD, UK) and Alan Jenkins, publisher of *Spot the Bear* (Cordelia Records, 25 Arnesby Crescent, Leicester LE2 6QZ, UK). A stamped addressed envelope or International Reply Coupon will improve your chances of a swift reply from all four publications.

Through the eyes of . . . is dedicated to Douglass MacDonald, without whom . . .

Bruno MacDonald

Preface

Of the numerous myths concerning Pink Floyd, among the most resilient is that they never give interviews. When, in 1987, Floyd embarked on a concert and promotional tour, more than one feature was trumpeted as the band's first interview in make-up-your-own-figure years.

The truth is naturally mundane. The Floyd – or, rather, Roger Waters – stopped flogging their wares around the music Press after *Dark Side of the Moon* went stellar, and platinum sales ceased to rely on media coverage. In contrast, in the late '60s and early '70s, Floyd could rarely be prised from the pages of *Melody Maker* or *Disc & Music Echo*, and even in the relative silence post-*Dark Side*, they would usually submit to interviews if solo albums needed a helping hand into the charts.

Capital Radio's Nicky Horne even persuaded all four members of the band to contribute to *The Pink Floyd Story* in 1976, the broadcast of which fortuitously coincided with the release of *Animals*. Waters explained: 'The thing about not speaking to people just came up because we did loads and loads and loads of interviews, loads and masses of them. And it's the usual thing: after the umpteenth time of somebody saying, "Why did you choose the name Pink Floyd?" you either say, "I'm gonna answer this question for the rest of my life," or you say, "I'm not interested in speaking to people who know nothing about us or music or anything else." So we decided not to do that bit. It was nothing to do with creating an image – it was purely personal response to people mucking us about, a lot.'[1]

Among those employed to guard the castle walls was publicity officer Gary Stromberg. 'His brief,' recalled Waters in 1990, 'was "No". That was it. We said, "Gary, we want you to come on the

1. Capital Radio, January 1977

whole tour and deal with the press and the media in every way possible and the answer is 'No'. 'Can we have tick—?' 'No.' 'Can we do an int—?' 'No.' 'Can we take pho—?' 'No.' 'Can—?' 'No.'"[2] A similar direction from Van Morrison to *his* Press officer had met with the response, 'Get yourself a fucking parrot then,' but Stromberg evidently obeyed (and, over and above the call of duty, introduced Waters to his second wife, Carolyne Christie).

The Floyd's aloofness cracked when particular criticisms riled them. Tussles between the Floyd and representatives of the *NME* and *Melody Maker* are included here, although the Floyd archives boast further examples of their media mudslinging.

In 1988, avid *Guardian* reader Roger Waters was sufficiently stung by accusations made by his ex-colleagues in the newspaper to write a point-by-point refutation; albeit not one distinguished by any great accuracy. Of *The Wall*, for example, he declared that: 'None of the band members other than myself were in any way involved in the creative aspects of the film.'[3] That David Gilmour had co-produced the entire soundtrack appeared temporarily to have escaped the battle-crazed bassist.

In 1991, a four-month correspondence in *Guitarist* magazine on the authorship of Pete Townshend's 'White City Fighting' and Roy Harper's 'Hope' – both Gilmour co-compositions – was terminated by a letter from the Floyd guitarist: 'I have instituted proceedings in the High Court against myself for blatant plagiarism, as I feel that this sort of thing must be stamped out.'[4]

Other digs, however, met only elegant apathy. 'The carpings of the likes of *Melody Maker* have been as gnats stamping on the back of a buffalo,' mourned writer David Bennun in a feature on Gilmour. 'All that time, all those insults, and he never gave a damn. How much more satisfying to wind up someone like Phil Collins, who obsessively collects every word written about him and

2. *The Album Network*, 1989
3. *Guardian*, 24 July 1988
4. *Guitarist*, January 1991

seemingly takes it to heart (although we haven't yet succeeded in putting him off making records). It's enough to make you lose faith in the power of the Press.'[5]

Typically, Roger Waters chose not to ignore those 'carpings'. Despite telling a Radio Clyde DJ in June '87 that 'what *Melody Maker* does, doesn't concern me', he was sufficiently stung by their trashing of his 'Radio Waves' single to reproduce the review on a promotional poster, adding his own prefix: 'Don't even think of listening to this record. Support free criticism.'

Rick Wright, whose lack of interest in Floyd's 'messages' led him to be portrayed as the playboy of the group (and subsequently contributed to his dismissal), took a more airy view. Having informed a BBC interviewer in 1974 that he didn't want to talk about his acquisition of a country home, he continued: 'It's the standard thing, isn't it? Group makes it: everyone disappears into the country. One reads about it every week in the music press.'[6]

Any lingering disappointment about the Floyd's reclusion may be swiftly assuaged by a scan of the interviews that *did* surface in the '70s. With a few notable exceptions – some of which appear here – such features scored high on the soporific scale. Rick Wright's shyness and David Gilmour's indifference meant that neither could be coaxed into saying anything very interesting. 'You're not used to giving interviews, are you?' remarked one writer to the latter, who was supposed to be promoting his first solo album. 'No,' came the reply.[7]

Nick Mason, in contrast, was and is an engaging raconteur. Even he, however, mourned the fact that 'quite a lot of our dialogue with the Press over the years has been a bit of a punch-up rather than a discussion'.[8] Moreover, his self-confessed distance from the creative centre of the band inevitably limited the extent to which

5. *Melody Maker*, 27 March 1993
6. Radio One, *Rockspeak*, October 1974
7. *Beat Instrumental*, July 1978
8. *The Amazing Pudding*, September 1985

he could shed light on the concepts in which the Floyd specialized (or indulged).

The man who could, didn't, by and large. Waters was by far the least PR-friendly Floyd; and, despite claiming that if 'you get any more serious than Lennon at his most serious', you 'fucking throw yourself under a train', he was rarely depicted as anything other than a depressed paranoiac. 'A gloomy, self-obsessed man,' concluded Michael Watts in a 1980 *Melody Maker* feature, 'such as one finds in a Bergman film.' Waters duly beat Morrissey and Leonard Cohen to the title Gloomiest Man in Rock, as awarded by *Punch* magazine in 1991.

By his own standards, Waters embarked on a punishing press schedule for *The Wall*. He gave in-depth explanations of the album to DJs Tommy Vance and Jim Ladd, obliged the former with a second chat about concerts, and promptly returned to the Floyd cocoon. Only one print reporter – *Newsweek*'s Janet Huck – elicited anything from him; the magazine, however, appeared not to recognize its own scoop, and printed mere snippets from the exclusive interview (Ms Huck's work appears, unedited, in this book).

Subsequent projects – *The Wall* movie, *The Final Cut, The Pros and Cons of Hitch Hiking* – were also embellished with the bare minimum of interviews. Waters did, however, make up for it in the late '80s, when ticket and album sales of distinctly non-Floydian proportions obliged him to tread the promotional path.

His former confidant Karl Dallas presaged this capitulation in 1986, suggesting that Floyd's history was significant 'because they tried to buck the power structure ... I suspect they failed to get people to *listen* to what they had to say, as opposed to how they said it [because] what they wanted to say was something you end up having to say outside and against the structures they were using'.[9]

9. Karl Dallas, *Bricks in the Wall,* Baton Press 1987

Preface

Waters seemed happy to embrace such contradictions – he has, for example, made videos for all his solo singles, despite blasting MTV and its stock in trade at every opportunity. 'I'm trying to bandage the hand that feeds me,' he announced once, although a rare admission to DJ Mary Turner suggests a more prosaic explanation: 'We're not ignored by the *Guinness Book of Records*, but we've been largely ignored by the media during our lifetime. If you read any article, no mention is ever made of Pink Floyd. We're never included in the same sentences as the Beatles, the Rolling Stones and The Who.'[10]

Their sheer lack of rock 'n' roll charisma, however, has prompted many column inches devoted to the paradoxical nature of their success. 'The relative obscurity Floyd have maintained as individuals,' observed *Q*'s Phil Sutcliffe, 'leaves a vacuum which human nature abhors.'[11] Indeed, to then-*NME* writers Nick Kent and Julie Burchill, the Floyd's detached facelessness was a red rag: they were a group who had betrayed both their roots and, by extension in the punk years, the whole spirit of rock 'n' roll.

Other senior scribes were less hostile but no more enthusiastic; 'boring beyond belief,' was Nic Cohn's verdict. New York journalist Nicholas Schaffner apologetically introduced one feature on the band with: 'For the most part, Pink Floyd's spectacular aural achievements speak for themselves, and little need be added about the self-effacing wizards lurking behind the, er, wall'[12]; a comment he no doubt regretted when engaged in writing a biography of the band some years later.

Floyd's sedate variation on rock 'n' roll, their musing on the shortcomings of education and finance and their somewhat woolly politics found a more equanimous home in the mainstream media. Of the band's 'Games For May' concert in 1967, the *Financial*

10. *Westwood One*, March 1985
11. *Q*, January 1988
12. *The British Invasion*, McGraw-Hill 1983, p. 139

Times concluded: '. . . when you add in the irrepressible Pink Floyd and a free authentic daffodil to take home, your cup of experience overflows.' Two decades later, the 'blowsy charms' of Floyd's Wembley Stadium gigs prompted a similarly bemused reaction: '[The] music . . . creates an anonymity which paradoxically carries its designer label like a badge.'[13]

Similar continuity can be found in the *Daily Mail*, most of whose Floydian coverage has sprung from Roger Waters' marriage to Lady Carolyne Christie. Their divorce in 1992 looked set to put paid to Waters' appearances in the *Mail*; happily, not least for those looking to shore up 'armchair socialist' accusations, her ladyship's replacement was Priscilla Philips, whose friendship with the Duchess of York promoted Waters from gossip column to front-page status.

The other members of the Floyd tended largely to escape the attention of gossip columnists, although Nick Mason's involvement with a photogenic blonde actress aroused the *Sun*'s interest, and David Gilmour's second marriage to journalist Polly Samson prompted wide-eyed naïvety from *The People*: 'Raven-haired Polly, who is a little under twenty years younger than the superstar guitarist, is a very popular girl on the *Sunday Times* and loves going to parties. That's something that old Dave has always enjoyed.'[14]

A couple of intrepid publications have attempted to sling sleaze at the Formica-smooth Floyd. The *Mail on Sunday* speculated on Gilmour's role in Kate Bush's career: 'Theirs was an unlikely encounter: she the shy fifteen-year-old violin-and-piano-playing doctor's daughter, he the wild and wicked lead guitarist with '70s supergroup Pink Floyd.'[15] Such hints of under-age passion were readily diffused by Bush's admission that she 'wasn't really into Pink Floyd at the time' – not to mention that in the 'wild and

---

13. *Financial Times*, 8 August 1988
14. *The People*, 15 November 1992
15. *Mail on Sunday*, c. October 1989

wicked' stakes, Gilmour rates several leagues below, to pick a name completely at random, Jimmy Page.

The *Sun* also got in on the act. True, it was first on the scene with the Floyd re-formation story in 1986, and was generous in its coverage both of their comeback and Waters' Berlin extravaganza. But more characteristically, it reported in 1988 that Waters had paid an artist to print toilet rolls with Gilmour's visage on each sheet: '. . . a very good idea,' commented the former, for whom the story was as much news as it was to everyone else.

The *Sun* also briefly hopped on the Syd-spotting bandwagon. On the word of TV Personalities' mainman Dan Treacy (author of 'I Know Where Syd Barrett Lives'), the paper reported that Barrett had painted everything in his mother's house green, including the fridge, cooker and television. '"You have to admit he's an intriguing figure," Dan says.'[16]

You won't, however, find those Syd Barrett legends here. With Mike Watkinson and Peter Anderson's scrupulously researched *Crazy Diamond* still in print, the Barrett story is there for anyone who wants it. We offer instead rare quotes in the A to Z of Floyd songs, an insight into *The Madcap Laughs* by producer Malcolm Jones, a refreshingly humane retrospective by Dave Thompson and Syd himself on the super, soaraway sounds of 1967. But if this anthology has any sort of agenda, it's to demonstrate that the post-Barrett Floyd were capable of generating – albeit involuntarily – engaging Press coverage of their own.

But *Through the eyes of . . .* should not be viewed as a biography. The Marquee to megadomes story is brilliantly covered in Nicholas Schaffner's *Saucerful of Secrets: The Pink Floyd Odyssey*, and doesn't need revisiting.

So what is it?

It is intended as a companion to the work of Pink Floyd; a little something to while away the hours as you spin one of their side-long epics. The contributors include familiar names from the rock

16. *Sun*, 8 June 1982

Pink Floyd

Press alongside some less predictable Floyd commentators: actor Robert Lindsay was so concerned that his thoughts be recorded accurately that he reworked a *Sunday Telegraph* piece for this book. Others took a more relaxed view: *Melody Maker* veteran Chris Welch reported that he 'was quite surprised to see the articles culled from the *MM* and even more so to read the flowery, laid-back style of the period!' Of his 'Floyd Joy' article that reappears here, Chris added: 'What I do remember is that the picture we used of Dave was probably the most flattering of any of a Floydian star. He was very good looking in those days, and his mum actually wrote to me and asked for a copy of the pic, as he looked so happy!'[17]

Chronologically, we range back and forth across the Floydazoic era, although the scattered album reviews in Part One are more or less in the right order. Shots at Top 40 success have been omitted because, as Waters conceded, they were 'no bloody good at it'. Despite fluke smashes with 'Money' and 'Another Brick in the Wall', Floyd remain rock's supreme 'albums-only' band (an honour that might rest with Led Zeppelin were their legend not constructed on rather more lurid foundations). Neither *Top of the Pops* nor the stage was their natural environment: hence occasional attempts at 'Greatest Hits' or live albums warrant only footnotes in even their own discography, let alone the grand scheme of rock 'n' roll things.

Accordingly, you will find nothing here on the 1988 live set *Delicate Sound of Thunder* ('Further proof that you can't listen to a light show,' *Musician*), the 1973 repackaging of *Piper at the Gates of Dawn* and *A Saucerful of Secrets* as *A Nice Pair* ('I see that somebody at EMI has found a use for their massive pressing plant,' *Sounds*), or 1981's post-*Wall* cash-in *A Collection of Great Dance Songs* ('Exactly what form of body-movement goes with Pink Floyd is anyone's guess – that slow, steady rocking motion that you see in people falling asleep on buses, I should think,' *NME*).

Eagle-eyed Gilmour fans will also lament the non-existent coverage of their hero's first solo album. Sadly, if anyone found

17. Personal correspondence

something interesting to say about this endeavour, they kept it to themselves. 'It's all a very Floyd-esque affair,' concluded *NME's* Neil Perry, wearily. 'I doubt if Gilmour's worried about it, and I don't think I am either.'[18] Amen.

Equally under-stimulating are most of the Floyd's adventures in celluloid. *Live at Pompeii, The Body, La Carrera Panamericana* ... for a band who prided themselves on their dynamics, they sure made some boring movies, which need detain us no further.

As for *Pulse* – at the time of writing, their latest release – this artificially enhanced *Delicate Sound of Thunder* was admirably presaged by a comment from Rick Wright in 1994: 'I'm still very aware of what we were doing back in the late '60s. We were very experimental and, because we were, we were playing a lot of bad things too; I mean, *not* good music. On the other hand, I sometimes miss that. What we do is very good, but it's not pushing boundaries as much as we used to.'[19]

And to give all this stuff some context, there are features on the members of Pink Floyd, not to mention Pink and Floyd themselves, in Part Three. There are no 'Moon the Loon' type rock star legends lurking here, but it is instructive to glimpse the men who made up 'the band who ate asteroids for breakfast' (thank you, Nick Kent).

So look on this as something to keep you awake through *Atom Heart Mother*, and you'll be fine. Hope you enjoy it.

18. *NME*, 17 June 1978
19. Radio One, *Saturday Live*, 15 October 1994

Contents

Contents

Cracking up

Return of the living dead

Contents

xix

Contents

Oh, by the way . . .

Welcome to the machine

David Fricke

Pink Floyd – the inside story

Rolling Stone, 19 November 1987

They simply refused to leave. The house lights were up, and the ushers were counting the minutes before they could knock off for the night. But even after three full hours of lasers in the face, trippy sound-in-the-round, brain-frying special effects and all those FM-radio classics – 'One of These Days', 'Time', 'Us and Them', 'Welcome to the Machine', 'Comfortably Numb' – the fifteen thousand kids in the Montreal Forum would not budge. For nearly twenty minutes, they stood at their seats, screaming themselves hoarse, determined not to move an inch until Pink Floyd came back on stage.

That this wasn't quite the same Pink Floyd – Roger Waters, the band's bassist, singer and dominant songwriter, was absent – that had transfixed potheads in the early, spacey '70s did not faze this audience, or the other two SRO crowds during the group's three-night stand in Montreal. Hell, they'd just seen the humungous inflatable pig from the '77 *Animals* tour and the crashing airplane from the old *Dark Side of the Moon* shows. And when the silvery chime of David Gilmour's guitar skated over Rick Wright's burbling Hammond organ and Nick Mason's heartbeat drumming in 'Echoes', with Gilmour and Wright's voices gliding together in feathery harmony, it definitely *sounded* like Pink Floyd. Veteran Floyd freaks had waited for this a long time, a whole decade since the full quartet's last major tour. Novices were here because of the Great Floyd Mystique, the tales of concert wonder passed down by elder brothers and old hippy uncles. And the crowd wasn't going to leave until it got one more shot.

Eventually, the Floyd relented, returning with its seven-member troupe of extra musicians and singers for a stab at 'Shine On You Crazy Diamond', which they'd tested only a couple of times in rehearsal. 'It was extraordinary,' said Gilmour later. 'The people were on their feet cheering so loudly that at a couple of points I couldn't even hear what I was playing.'

'There were a few mistakes,' said Wright, laughing, 'but we got through it. And the song is so Floydian. It was a perfect way to end the evening.' Gilmour had announced the song with peals of church-bell guitar over icy keyboards and a slow blues pulse, heightening the chill of the absent Waters' reflection on the eclipsing of genius by madness. Later, as the fans filed out, one of the big sellers at the merchandise stands was a T-shirt that said, on the front, PINK FLOYD, and, on the back, STILL FIRST IN SPACE.

Two weeks later, in the Oakland Coliseum, Roger Waters wasn't settling for second place. He didn't have the pig or the airplane. But as usual, he had a couple of heavy axes to grind, among them the threat of nuclear self-destruction and the potential of communications technology as a means to bring people together, two themes central to his latest album, *Radio KAOS*. Not surprisingly, Waters ground those axes with the same black humour, theatrical ingenuity and apocalyptic urgency that he brought to the staging of his musical autobiography *The Wall*, incorporating striking computer graphics, newsreel footage of Armageddon in the making and fictional telephone exchanges between a young spastic boy named Billy and a KAOS DJ, played by real-life radio pro Jim Ladd.

But there was also a matter of honour at stake here. When Waters poignantly reprised old songs like 'Welcome to the Machine', 'Money' and 'Another Brick in the Wall', he wasn't just doing the best of Floyd. Those were *his* songs, 'the words and music of Roger Waters', as Ladd declared at the end of an extended Floyd medley in the first half. The implication, of course, was unmistakable: anyone else out there playing these songs, claiming to be Floyd, is bogus.

'I would be terribly happy for you to like what I'm doing and to like what he's doing,' Waters said sharply the next day, referring to Gilmour, 'if it wasn't for the fact that he was calling himself Pink Floyd. He isn't. If one of us was going to be called Pink Floyd, it's me.' Even the old props in the current Floyd show, Waters insisted, were originally his idea. 'That's my pig up there,' he said, 'that's my plane crashing.' He snickered and added, 'It's their dry ice.'

The 'Which one's Pink?' debate has been a legal football kicked around by lawyers since last fall, when Waters sued Gilmour and Mason in an attempt to prevent them from using the name, claiming the group was 'a spent force creatively'. (Rick Wright, who quietly left the group in 1980 after the *Wall* shows, has unofficially returned for the new Floyd album and tour.) Both camps, however, have now taken their cases to the people in a vindictive Press war. Floyd fans are, in a sense, getting two state-of-the-art rock shows and records – Waters' *Radio KAOS*, the Floyd's *Momentary Lapse of Reason* – for the price of one band. But the price has been disastrously high. In their fight to determine who is the rightful heir to the Pink Floyd throne and the continuing fortune it's worth, Waters, Gilmour and Mason have destroyed whatever personal friendship, band camaraderie and musical unity first bonded them two decades ago. The musicians who created *The Wall* are now up against a wall of their own – the one separating them from one another.

When asked about the barrage of charges and countercharges flying between the other Floyds and him, Roger Waters quotes a lyric from Don Henley's 'Long Way Home': 'There's three sides to every story / Yours and mine and the cold, hard truth.' And in *Waters v. Floyd*, the cold, hard truth is that they can't stand each other. They resent what each has done to the other, what each has said publicly about the other, what each has exacted from the other emotionally, artistically and financially.

If you believe half of what Gilmour and Mason say about their former bassist, Waters is an arrogant, dictatorial egomaniac hungry for all the credit and the subsequent rewards. If you believe half of what Waters says of the surviving Floyds, they are lazy, greedy bastards hacking out a record and sleepwalking through a tour to build up a multimillion-dollar retirement nest egg using, in Waters' words, 'the goodwill and the name Pink Floyd'. It's as if they lived

5

in parallel universes, each battling visions of the other's monstrosity.

The fans, of course, are happy to be getting any Floyd, any Waters, at all. Twenty years of reclusive media silence and infrequent tours and albums have only increased the rock public's hunger for all things Floyd. Unfortunately, the public's joy and approval can't always be heard over the din of accusations and allegations and the brittle snap of lawyers' briefcases opening and closing.

David Gilmour, forty-one, has heard the snap of those briefcases a lot during the past year. While recording *A Momentary Lapse of Reason* and preparing for the current Floyd tour, he was either in conference or on the phone with lawyers nearly every day, planning responses to Waters' suit. Reclining on a hotel-room sofa one morning after one of the Montreal gigs, Gilmour talks about the Floyd feud with a combination of resignation and stubbornness. Rumours of the group's demise following the release of Waters' strident anti-war epic *The Final Cut*, in 1983, were premature, he claims. Waters' decision to hit the solo trail was not the end of the band, at least as Gilmour and Nick Mason knew it.

'We never assumed that it was defunct,' says Gilmour. 'But the growing tide of rumours and Roger's vocal output combined made it almost like an avalanche. We couldn't keep issuing Press statements saying, "No, we haven't split up." It wasn't worth the bother. Our assumption – my assumption, anyway – was that we wouldn't do another record.'

According to Gilmour and Mason, Waters officially announced his leaving in a letter to the Floyd's record companies, Columbia in America, EMI in the UK, in December 1985. 'We had had discussions,' Mason says. 'We sort of knew something was up.' Gilmour and Mason say that Waters thought his exit would mean the *de facto* end of the group.

'We'd been having these meetings in which Roger said, "I'm not working with you guys again,"' Gilmour says. 'He'd say to me, "Are you going to carry on?" And I'd say, quite honestly, "I don't know. But when we're good and ready, I'll tell everyone what the plan is. And we'll get on with it." I think partly his letter was to gear us up into doing something.'

'Because he believed very strongly that we wouldn't do it,' says Mason.

'Or couldn't do it,' Gilmour says, 'I remember meetings in which he said, "You'll never fucking do it." That's precisely what was said. Exactly that term.' He laughs wryly. 'Except slightly harder.'

Waters and the other Floyds, particularly Gilmour, had been on a collision course for years, as far back as the making of *Dark Side of the Moon*, in 1972. Producer Chris Thomas was brought in to supervise the mixing of that album, Gilmour says, because he and Waters were having 'a radical argument' over how the record should sound. Later, as Waters assumed greater responsibility for the group's conceptual direction and music, the acrimony increased.

'He forced his way to become that central figure,' Gilmour says. 'That's what he really wanted, to be that central figure. I felt, and I'm sure Nick did too, that it was not the best thing to happen. As productive as we were, we could have been making better records if Roger had been willing to back off a little bit, to be more open to other people's input. It wasn't like we were all sitting there leaning on him to look after us. It was a question of him having forced his way to that position, of him being very tough and having more energy for that sort of fighting.'

Bob Ezrin, who functioned as both co-producer and referee during the making of *The Wall* (he and Gilmour co-produced the new Floyd album as well), says the verbal brawling never escalated to fisticuffs. 'It was all done under that English smiling, left-handed, adversarial stance they take, with the smiles on their faces and soft voices. But basically they were saying, "I hate you, and I'm going to kill you." The war that existed between those two guys was unbelievable.'

They dropped the pretence of politeness, however, during the recording of *The Final Cut*, Waters' album-length meditation on the death of his father in World War II. Waters was, understandably, very possessive of the piece; it was a highly personal exorcism of his obsession with his loss as well as an expression of unbridled outrage at the politicians and generals who casually demand such pointless sacrifices. Gilmour didn't share Waters' enthusiasm for the record. He complained that some of the songs weren't up to snuff, pointing out that they were in fact rejects from the original *Wall* demos.

'Basically, he felt and says that I was being wilfully obstructive,' Gilmour says, visibly bristling. 'Which is absolutely not true. My criticisms and objections were constructive in the best possible way. They are the sort of constructive criticisms that made other albums, like *The Wall.*'

Waters didn't see it that way, Gilmour says. He threatened to scrap the whole record if the guitarist would not relinquish his position as co-producer. Gilmour agreed but refused to give up the extra producer's royalties that would have been due him. 'That's how it ended up, very miserable,' Gilmour says. 'Even Roger says what a miserable period it was. And he was the one who entirely made it miserable, in my opinion.'

Relaxing by the hotel pool under a bright, warm California sun the day after his Oakland show, Waters calmly but firmly refutes Gilmour's version of the *Final Cut* clashes. The album, he admits, was originally supposed to be songs left over from the movie version of *The Wall.* 'Then I got on a roll,' he says, 'and started writing this piece about my father. I was on a roll, and I was gone. The fact of the matter is that I was making this record. And Dave didn't like it. And he said so.'

But Waters, forty-three, dismisses as 'absolute bollocks' the notion that he forced *The Final Cut* on Gilmour and Mason. 'I said, "Perhaps this should be a solo record. I'll pay you guys the money we've spent, and I'll make this a solo album."' He smirks. 'No, they didn't want that, because they know songs don't grow on trees. They wanted it to be a Floyd record.'

The record came out as a Floyd effort. Any illusion, though, that this trio would or ever could work together again was shattered. Waters would have nothing else to do with Gilmour. Gilmour refused to be a mere sessionman in a Waters-led Floyd. Even Nick

Mason, who had maintained a personal friendship with Waters and shared his interest in theatrical presentation, allied himself with Gilmour. 'Dave found himself particularly picked on during *The Final Cut*,' Mason says. 'I found myself feeling that this was not fair.'

That was over three years ago. But the stage was set for the current legal imbroglio. Waters insisted that Pink Floyd as a band, as a musical partnership, was finished. Gilmour's position was that just because Waters said it was finished didn't make it so. Ironically, though, it wasn't the Pink Floyd name game that set the whole ugly mess in motion, but a tangentially related business matter. Waters' version of what happened is this.

In early 1985, he terminated his management deal with Steve O'Rourke, Pink Floyd's long-time manager, over a dispute regarding contractual obligations for future Pink Floyd product – how could there be future Pink Floyd records if there was no group? – and resultant royalty penalties if those commitments were not filled. Waters insists he gave O'Rourke six months' notice, as called for in his deal. O'Rourke says he was terminated illegally. Waters then offered Gilmour and Mason a series of compromise deals in which he essentially would let them have the name Pink Floyd if they ratified his dismissal of O'Rourke. In doing so, Waters was taking a calculated risk that Gilmour and Mason would not continue as the Floyd.

'Don't ask me why they never took that deal,' Waters says. In June 1986, O'Rourke prepared to sue Waters over the management deal and back royalties. At that point, Waters claims, he told the other Floyds, 'Listen, guys, if those papers come through my door, we all go to court. I am not going to be hung out in court for years and years while you guys are calling yourselves Pink Floyd.' The following 31 October, Waters made good his threat, filing suit in London against Gilmour and Mason to prevent them from using the name Pink Floyd.

Waters admits there is a certain inconsistency in his current stand against Gilmour and Mason's use of the Floyd name and his earlier willingness to let them have the name. But it was, he contends, 'for the sake of a quiet life. This was two years ago. Believe me, my life has been anything but quiet for the last two years. I thought it was wrong. I still think it's completely wrong. I don't think they should be called Pink Floyd.

'It's taken me two years to make some fundamental connections. There is the legal issue, which is the only thing that can be resolved in court. And that is, who owns the piece of property that is the name Pink Floyd? That is a legal issue; you go to court and fight over it.

'The other issue is completely separate, the whole issue about what is or isn't a rock group. What is the Beatles? Are Paul McCartney and Ringo Starr the Beatles? My view now is they're not, any more than The Firm should have been called Led Zeppelin, even if John Paul Jones had been there.'

Gilmour counters Waters' logic with a very simple statement. 'I had an awful lot of time invested in the group,' he declares. 'It was an intolerable situation, but I was damned if I was going to be forced out. I am an extremely stubborn person, and I will not be forced out of something I consider to be partly mine.' As to whether he and Mason do or do not qualify as Pink Floyd without Waters, Gilmour says *A Momentary Lapse of Reason* is all the proof he needs.

'We never sat down at any point during this record and said, "It doesn't sound Floyd enough. Make this more Floyd." We just worked on the songs until they sounded right. When they sounded great and right, that's when it became Pink Floyd.'

It's unlikely that any judge or jury, if the suit comes to trial, will decide the rightful ownership of the name Pink Floyd by listening to a record. And both Waters and Gilmour realize that, legally or otherwise, any settlement or judgement will probably fall short of their demands. 'The ideal settlement would have happened years ago when we could have all shaken hands,' says Waters. 'I've finally understood that no court in the world is interested in this airy-fairy nonsense of what is or isn't Pink Floyd. All I'm likely to get out of it – or could possibly get out of it – is a slice.'

'It will never be solved to everyone's satisfaction,' Gilmour says wearily. 'But it will be solved to the point of reality. And soon, I hope.'

In the beginning, there was Syd Barrett, and in London's Paisley underground of 1966–67, it was commonly accepted that *he* was Pink. An art student from Cambridge, he co-founded Pink Floyd in late '65 with Waters, a schoolboy chum from Cambridge who was studying architecture in London, and two other architecture students, Rick Wright and Nick Mason. It was Barrett who named the group (combining the names of two old bluesmen, Pink Anderson and Floyd Council); he also sang most of the songs and gave the group its charisma. Driven by his eccentric muse and regular excursions on LSD, he steeped the fledgeling Floyd in a heady synthesis of English teapot whimsy, riveting melodic invention and freak-rock tumult, all captured vividly for posterity on the group's 1967 début album, *Piper at the Gates of Dawn*.

Another surviving artefact of Barrett's errant genius is a captivating 1967 black-and-white promo video of the original Floyd cavorting to its first single, 'Arnold Layne', a film clip Waters shows in his *Radio KAOS* concerts every night, always announcing at the end, 'The great Syd Barrett, lest we forget.' Waters says he still likes to sing old Barrett gems like 'Bike' and 'Dark Globe' in the bath.

'What was so stunning about Syd's songs,' he says, 'was, through the whimsy and the crazy juxtaposition of ideas and words, there was a very powerful grasp of humanity. They were quintessentially human songs. And that is what I've always attempted to aspire to. In that sense, I feel a strong connection to him.'

That connection took a darker turn toward the end of '67 as Barrett – unable to shoulder the burdens of fame and his own acid-accelerated mental instability – withdrew into a debilitating madness. He never recovered. David Gilmour, also from Cambridge, was soon recruited to pick up Syd's guitar and vocal duties. At that point, despite two English hits ('Arnold Layne' and 'See Emily Play'), the Floyd was at its lowest ebb, adrift without a songwriter or a direction.

'It was an open page,' Gilmour says. 'My initial ambition was just to get the band into some sort of shape. It seems ridiculous now, but I thought the band was awfully bad at the time when I joined. The gigs I'd seen with Syd were incredibly undisciplined. The leader figure was falling apart, and so was the band.'

Pink Floyd spent the next four years in space, so to speak. On transitional records like *A Saucerful of Secrets*, *Ummagumma*, *Atom Heart Mother* and *Meddle*, the band developed a compositional style based on long exploratory jams from which melodic themes and pivotal riffs would emerge and, in turn, be spread across lengthy suite-like canvases. Although the band's vigorously anti-pop aesthetic and imaginative sonic architecture was in large part responsible for the rise of English progressive rock in the '70s, Waters – who gradually assumed responsibility for writing the band's lyrics after Barrett's psychological collapse – scoffs at the 'space music' tag frequently applied to the Floyd records of that period.

'The space thing was a joke,' he says. 'None of those pieces were about outer space. They were about *inner* space. That's all it's ever been about – human beings and their insides, whether it was Syd's writing or mine. They were both about the same thing.'

The group's exploration of inner space reached its artistic and commercial apex in 1973 with the release of *Dark Side of the Moon*, one of the biggest-selling LPs of all time; as of this writing, it has spent six hundred and ninety-eight weeks on the *Billboard* album charts. Conceptually unified, immaculately recorded, *Dark Side of the Moon* found the Floyd grafting the rigours of formal songwriting onto its muralistic style of composition – and succeeding beyond its wildest expectations. It was also one of the last genuinely collaborative Floyd records, highlighted not just by Waters' incisive observations of alienation, schizophrenia and death but by the strong instrumental brushstrokes of Gilmour and Wright, particularly the latter's love of jazzy minor-seventh and flattened-second chord changes (Wright's chorus for 'Time' was based, in part, on 'So What', from Miles Davis' album *Kind of Blue*).

'Occasionally, people would come in with a complete song,' says Wright. 'For example, "Us and Them" was a little piano piece I had worked out. I played it for them; they liked it. Roger went into another room and started working on the lyrics. Whereas things like "Echoes" would be all of us in a rehearsal room, just sitting there thinking, playing, working out ideas to see if they went anywhere. It's a nice way to work, and I think, in a way, the most Floydian material we ever did came about that way.'

Dark Side of the Moon had two important effects on Pink Floyd. One was stardom; overnight they went from being highly respected psychedelic artisans and FM-radio cult heroes to being the objects of fanatic adolescent male adoration. 'It took me until ten years ago to stop being upset that people whistled through the quiet numbers,' says Waters. 'I used to stop and go, "Right! Who's whistling? C'mon, be quiet!"'

The other major consequence was Waters' increased interest in narrative songwriting, big themes and grand theatrical gestures, culminating in *The Wall* and *The Final Cut*. 'I was always trying to push the band into more specific areas of subject matter,' he says, 'always trying to be more direct. Visually, I was always trying to get away from the blobs. I wanted to work with visual material that meant something, where there isn't much left for you to interpret.'

'I don't think any of us differed all the way through on the subjects Roger approached,' says Gilmour. 'We were pretty much of a like mind. On *The Wall*, although I didn't agree with that part of the concept – the wall between us and the audience – I still thought it was a good subject to do. My father didn't go off to the war and get killed in it. So that area of it did not apply to me. But I could get into it as fiction.'

Which is about as far as Waters would let any of the other Floyds get. 'There wasn't any room for anyone else to be writing,' he states frankly. 'If there were chord sequences there, I would always use them. There was no point in Gilmour, Mason or Wright trying to write lyrics. Because they'll never be as good as mine.

Gilmour's lyrics are very third-rate. They always will be. And in comparison with what I do, I'm sure he'd agree. He's just not as good. I didn't play the guitar solos; he didn't write any lyrics.'

In short, Pink Floyd was now, as Bob Ezrin puts it, 'Roger Waters Presents'. He wrote the material, ran the rehearsals, worked on the concert presentations and judged the contributions of the others by the same rigid artistic standards he applied to his own work. He also took the initiative in firing Rick Wright, during the recording of *The Wall.*

Not surprisingly, there are differing accounts of Wright's exit from the group. 'The story that gets out,' Waters says, 'is that it was a personal whim of mine, which is absolute bollocks.' He argues that Wright's performance in the studio was substandard, that he was making no musical contribution and hadn't been for years (Wright had not been listed in Floyd songwriting credits since 1975's *Wish You Were Here*). Bob Ezrin describes Wright as 'a victim of Roger's almost Teutonic cruelty. No matter what Rick did, it didn't seem to be good enough for Roger. It was clear to me that Roger wasn't interested in his succeeding.'

Wright diplomatically attributes the friction between Waters and him to 'a heavy personality problem' – so heavy that Waters threatened to pull the *Wall* album and make it into a solo effort if Wright was not dismissed after the conclusion of the project. 'I wasn't particularly happy with the band anyway,' Wright says. 'The way it was going, the feeling. I'm in no way trying to put this man down. I think he has great ideas. But he is an extremely difficult man to work with.'

By this time, Pink Floyd was an extremely difficult context to work within for anybody, something even Waters does not deny. 'I suppose it comes down to the fact that we are people in rock 'n' roll bands,' he says, 'and people in rock 'n' roll bands are greedy for attention. We never managed to come to a common view of the dynamic that existed within the band, of who did what and whether or not it was right. It was an irritation to start with, and it became an impossible irritation towards the end.'

Waters has learned, to his chagrin, that many long-time Pink

Floyd fans are also mystified by the creative dynamic that existed within the band, a negative side-effect of the Floyd's shadowy public profile throughout the '70s. 'It is frustrating to find out how many people don't know who I am or what I actually did in Pink Floyd. We get on a plane, and people ask what band we're in. I tell 'em I'm Roger Waters, and it doesn't mean a thing to them. Then I mention Pink Floyd, and they go, "Yeah, 'Money'. I love *The Wall*."

'Oh, I wanted anonymity. I treasured it. And somehow we made it big and stayed private and anonymous. It was the best of both worlds. But now it's as if the past twenty years have meant nothing.'

Funny he should say that. Nick Mason did a phone interview with a reporter from a daily newspaper recently in which he answered all the usual questions about Waters, the lawsuit and the new Floyd album. In the course of this, he happened to mention Syd Barrett.

'And this reporter said, "Hold on a minute. Who's Syd Barrett?" It was quite touching, actually. She had just started writing about pop music. She had no idea about Syd or our early history.

'Maybe in another twenty years,' Mason says, tongue firmly in cheek, 'if we're still around, people will be asking, "Who's Roger Waters?"'

One of the titles David Gilmour considered for the first Waters-less Pink Floyd album was *Delusions of Maturity*. Waters would have liked that. When asked his opinion of the new Floyd record, he is characteristically blunt.

'I think it's a very facile but quite clever forgery. If you don't listen to it too closely, it does *sound* like Pink Floyd. It's got Dave Gilmour playing guitar. And with the considered intention of setting out to make something that sounds like everyone's conception of a Pink Floyd record, it's inevitable that you will achieve that limited goal.

'I think the songs are poor in general. The lyrics I can't believe.' He chuckles ironically. 'I'm sure it will do very well.'

Pink Floyd

It is hardly an embarrassment to Floyd's post-*Dark Side* chart tradition. Within three weeks of release, *A Momentary Lapse of Reason* was in *Billboard*'s Top 10, while Waters' *Radio KAOS* was on the bottom rungs of the Top 100. There is, of course, more to this than numbers. A healthy percentage of *Momentary Lapse*'s immediate sales are certainly attributable to the trust rock fans place in the brand name Pink Floyd. The album was leaping off the racks before many people had even heard a single note.

Nevertheless, in accepting the challenge of making a new record under the Floyd banner, Gilmour and Mason were faced with the daunting task of measuring up to public anticipation based in great part on the standards set by Waters. That they made an album lacking the strident, pedagogical edge of *The Wall* or *The Final Cut* is no surprise. That the album is aurally sumptuous and texturally seductive will be reassuring to anyone who was spellbound by the glacial grandeur of *Meddle* or the extended instrumental passages of 'Shine On You Crazy Diamond'. With 'On the Turning Away', the reconstituted Floyd may also have a hit single of 'Money' proportions on its hands. A caressing ballad with a glowing chorus and climactic Gilmour guitar, it is more openly hopeful and loving than anything Waters allowed himself to write for the Floyd.

The question of just who is Pink Floyd is complicated by the fact that Gilmour and Mason are out-numbered eighteen to two on this record by the assorted session musicians, background singers and lyricists who were recruited to make *Lapse* – and that's not counting Rick Wright, who returned to contribute keyboards part way through the recording of the album, and Bob Ezrin, who played additional keyboards and percussion. But Gilmour does not try to disguise the fact that he could not do it alone, that he needed and wanted help.

'You can't go back,' he says. 'You have to find a new way of working, of operating, and getting on with it. We didn't make this remotely like we've made any other Floyd record. It was different systems, everything.'

For one thing, he dispensed with the idea of making a concept album early on. 'We thought, "Sod this, we don't *have* to make a concept album. If we work on making everything great, then maybe it will show itself to have some sort of linear form later."'

'It's not our *métier*,' says Ezrin. 'We're not kidding ourselves. We're not Roger Waters. But we do other things, and we do them very well. We decided the atmosphere was the most important thing. The concept really just had to be a feeling that was pervasive. The atmosphere of the album is best defined by the environment in which we were working.'

That environment was the River Thames, on the *Astoria*, Gilmour's lavish turn-of-the-century houseboat, which he has turned into a recording studio. Ezrin and the Floyd spent seven months on the *Astoria*, which is docked sixteen miles outside of London, recording most of *A Momentary Lapse*. 'The river became the motif,' Ezrin says. 'It came up in all the songs. The river imposed itself.' Also imposing itself on the sessions was the spectre of Waters and his repeated assertions that a Gilmour-led Floyd was no Floyd at all.

'It's like a challenge in public,' says Ezrin. 'By virtue of Roger saying, "I did it all, and if I leave, it doesn't exist," basically what he's saying is that David is a nonentity artistically. That's not fair. But if someone puts that message across long enough and hard enough, then you have to prove yourself. My perception was that Dave was torn between an angry posture that says, "Goddamnit, I've been here for twenty years, and I have a right to be here," and having a little voice in there that says, "Maybe I'm not good any more."'

Waters suffered no such misgivings with *Radio KAOS*, although he admits that the *KAOS* stage production – which incorporated pertinent old Floyd songs and graphically illustrated the album's apocalyptic theme – transmits his message a lot more effectively than the album alone. 'I accepted halfway through the record that as a narrative form the album was doomed to failure. You just get a taste of the narrative. I made the decision to go with it anyway and allow the project to develop if it was going or stop if it's not.'

Unfortunately, Waters isn't exactly doing Floyd-like business on the road. While Floyd is packing arenas and stadiums, he's having trouble selling out one-nighters.

'The connections one makes in quality make up for the ones you make in quantity,' he declares. 'In Indianapolis and San Diego, we had like four thousand people in twelve thousand seat halls. And strangely enough, at those shows, I got a fantastic affirmation from the audience, that not only did they want to grasp some of this stuff, but that they actually do. And that helps me get over the moments, the knockers who sit at their typewriters and say, "This is all liberal airy-fairy bullshit."'

The affirmation of his audiences has been therapeutic during the War of the Floyds. 'This tour has really helped me to junk a lot of this,' Waters says. 'I feel like I'm leaving a lot of this crap on the side of the road. And I'm very grateful for that.'

Waters and the other Floyds aren't exactly sitting around waiting to be declared the victor. Waters was so heartened by the reaction to his *KAOS* roadshow that immediately after the first leg of the tour, he flew to Compass Point Studios, in Nassau, the Bahamas, with his live band to cut songs for a *KAOS II* album. The Gilmour–Mason–Wright Floyd will be on the road for nearly a year; plans include a second swing through the US in 1988.

Yet both sides are haunted by the loss of the spirit that united them once upon a time. 'I can't tell you how sorry I am about all this,' sighs Mason. 'It's so pointless. I'm sorry that I've fallen out with a friend.'

'I regret Nick Mason, yeah,' says Waters, pausing thoughtfully. 'I feel very betrayed by him.'

Meanwhile, the lawyers keep racking up those fees, and the fans shop and compare. And when the dust finally settles, you can bet *Dark Side of the Moon* will still be on the charts.

David Griffiths

Pinkos return from United States

Record Mirror, 21 September 1968

The Pink Floyd were just back from riot-torn America, a proud nation they'd been touring for seven weeks. Asked for their impressions, Roger Waters said: 'We saw mainly the insides of hotels.' Dave Gilmour was equally evasive: 'It's quite a big country.' Rick Wright said nothing and Nick Mason was on holiday.

Strained silence. A few flip remarks until Roger began to comment more or less as follows: 'We saw two different worlds. On our level – the people who came to hear us – everything was fine. But outside – the capitalist society – was, er, tatty. It works all right so long as you don't look too closely. But they are scared, really scared, of the new young Americans and that's why they are reacting very violently. And it doesn't work. Police clubbings and the beatings and shootings that are going on – they won't have the desired effect, simply because there are so many young people. They aren't just weekend ravers. Many of them have dropped out completely.'

The three Pinkos were in agreement that Britain is an entirely different social and musical scene. 'The situation is much less immediate here because hippies are not being beaten,' said Roger. 'It's all a bit of a laugh, something to discuss over a Scotch and dry ginger. There isn't, therefore, the same emotional involvement. I don't feel any more menaced by a British policeman than by a milkman. The police here, on the whole, are public servants trying to do a job. About the musical difference – well, Rick should answer that. He's our musician.'

Rick: 'In America the audience comes to listen. In England they come to pick up scrubbers, though I should make an exception of a few places such as Middle Earth.'

Pink Floyd

Roger: 'We don't play any longer at places where people go to booze and pick each other up.'

Oh, you're doing well enough to be able to pick and choose, then? Roger: 'We're not making our fortunes but we're doing all right. We can survive by playing the kind of music, and recording the kind of LPs, that we like – and there are enough customers to make it worthwhile.'

Dave: 'We're beginning to find that we're booked on concerts – particularly on the Continent – where we get top billing over famous groups that we looked up to as the Big Stars when we were starting. It's not easy to adjust to this. We keep thinking there must be some embarrassing mistake.'

Talking of America, Rick pointed out: 'They don't go to dances to fight. You never see yobbos in a dancehall – they go to street corners.'

Roger: 'If our American listeners don't like our music they go away, they don't stand around booing.'

Rick: 'Yes, but they're prepared to listen to a whole set in case there's *something* they can enjoy.'

Roger: 'They wouldn't dream of shouting at you in a million years.'

Which is not always the case in Britain, even though there is far less serious violence here. But then the Floyd no longer spend much time touring around Britain. 'We can only really speak about England,' added Roger, 'And only the south of England at that. We don't know what goes on up north. London is our scene.'

Debbi Smith

The Pink Floyd is London's answer to West Coast Sound

GO, 4 August 1967

If you can imagine a completely 'West Coast' group flourishing in the heart of London, a group that have never left England and have never heard of Country Joe and the Fish, then you have a vivid imagination.

You have also found the Pink Floyd, who are fast making quite a reputation in Britain with their sinister records and eye-crossing stage effects.

Garbed in the multi-coloured, shiny shirts that seem to be the uniform in London at the moment, Syd, the Floyd's lead guitarist, padded around the studio, barefoot. And between 'takes' of weird sounds, Syd tried to give *GO* some insight into what makes the Floyd tick.

'We use lights to get the audience used to the type of music we play. It's hard to get used to it, actually, because it's a new type of idea; a loose, free-form music. But because it *is* a new type of music, we realize that it takes a lot more time to get used to it. The crazy lights help, I think. Anyway, I like looking at them.'

Unlike most British groups, the Pink Floyd believe in 'total absorption'.

'You just can't come into a place where we're playing and order a drink and have a chat. You have to concentrate on what we're trying to say,' explained Rick.

Still, three out of four Floyds object to the term psychedelic being applied to their music. The fourth, Syd, has adopted an attitude of tolerance.

'People can call it anything they like,' mused Syd. 'We don't like labels to be stuck on things, but as long as they listen, I don't object.'

Pink Floyd

Still, Rick, the group's organist and weird sound expert, may have a valid reason for objecting to the psychedelic label.

'The word psychedelic means mind-expanding, or at least it did when they started it out,' he said. 'But in Britain if you say "psychedelic" you mean "drug-taking", and that's a scene we wouldn't want to be identified with.'

Yet the Pink Floyd look and seem to act as if they had just stepped out of a show at the Fillmore Auditorium. There is no question that the love and flowers scene has hit them – hard.

'We are working on our manager to get us over to the West Coast,' added Roger. 'We don't get many records of those groups over here and we do want to see it for ourselves.'

Basically freewheeling, like the music they create, the Pink Floyd have no set goals yet.

Nick, the group's drummer, said: 'I can't imagine myself doing this in forty-five years' time. But then, I can't generalize, can I?'

Syd said: 'It's better not having a set goal. You'd be very narrow-minded if you did. All I know is that I'm beginning to think less now. It's getting better.'

I pointed out that if he were to stop thinking entirely, Syd might as well be a vegetable. 'Yeah!' was the startling comeback.

Anyone for broccoli?

Pete Frame

The Year of Love including the birth of the Pink Floyd

Zigzag

Introduction

(you can skip this bit if you want to . . . you won't miss much).

I lay back in the sumptuous luxury of velvet upholstery and gazed across the panoramic skyline from the penthouse suite of the Blackhill Enterprises' Mayfair offices as a gorgeous nymphet poured coffee into bone-china cups and offered After Eight mints. I casually mentioned the Pink Floyd, and the words seemed to cut through the vapid atmosphere like razor blades. Jenner's face, his clean-cut features aglow with interest, paled as he ground his cigar butt into the big diamond-studded ashtray resting on the polished mahogany desktop. 'The Pink Floyd?' he repeated, as he casually straightened his tie and picked a stray hair off his mohair suit . . .

That had you all going, didn't it? In actual fact, the way it happened was a little different. I had stumbled up to Blackhill's crumbling Bayswater office to meet Peter Jenner as arranged, but had to wait on the doorstep for almost an hour before Jenner (half of Blackhill Enterprises) and Andrew King (the other half) arrived, as usual, on their tandem. As Andrew began to unload rain-sodden contracts and documents from the panniers, Peter hustled me through the chaotic mountain of strewn papers into 'the back room', where he invited me to make myself comfortable on one of the most austerely designed wooden chairs in the history of furniture. He disappeared, leaving me to stare out of the window at the mass of leaking drainpipes clinging to the wall of the tenement block which backed on to the yard, and returned with a cracked Woolworth's mug of tepid radiator flushings.

Pink Floyd

'Here's some coffee,' he grunted, plonking it down on the Formica kitchen table which served as his desk. He took a worn tobacco tin from his pocket, selected the half-smoked remains of a Park Drive tipped, and peered at me through his cracked National Health spectacles. 'Now then,' he wheezed with considerable hostility, 'What is it you want? Make it snappy, I'm a busy man.'

'It's the Pink Floyd,' I stammered, 'I want to know how the underground started . . . I was told that no one in England knew as much about it as you do; that you're the acknowledged authority on the subject.'

His chest swelled with pride below the holey vest which hung on his bony frame, as his disposition changed to one of great charm. 'They say that, do they? Well, er, yes, of course I'd be delighted to tell you all about it . . . but it's a long story.'

'That's OK,' I replied, 'just give me all the facts as well as you can remember, and I'll go back home to distort and rehash your words into a vaguely coherent article.'

The List of Players

Mr Underground .... John Hopkins
An underground journalist .... Miles
A shady LSE drop-out .... Peter Jenner
A pirate disc jockey .... John Peel
A psychedelic music ensemble ....The Pink Floyd
An unemployed person .... Andrew King
A finger in various pies .... Joe Boyd
An East End pixie .... Marc Bolan
All other parts played by Mick Farren.

The Discovery of the Pink Floyd

If you can cast your mind back to the dying days of 1965 (which most underground stalwarts find impossible because their drug-

24

addled memories can't remember any further back than last week), you'll recall that the chartbound sounds were 'We Can Work It Out', 'Eve of Destruction', 'Get Off Of My Cloud' and 'Turn, Turn, Turn'. Around that time, too, Smithy had just declared UDI in Rhodesia, President Johnson was showing his gall bladder operation scar to the waiting world, the Post Office tower had recently been opened and the Government had just abolished the death penalty.

Right, now that we've established some sort of departure point we can begin our narrative.

Peter Jenner had been set for a very distinguished career in the field of education; an assistant lecturer in the Department of Social Administration at the London School of Economics ... but he was bored with that. He was also a passionate avant-garde jazz freak ... but he was bored with that, too: 'Most of it was becoming so unpleasant on the ear that I just couldn't get off on it. John Coltrane and Ornette Coleman were the last two to really interest me.' His tastes changed towards R&B (of the Bo Diddley type) where they remained for some time ... approximately up until this end-of-'65 period.

Apart from music, his head was buzzing with ambitious notions of founding a free school and a record label, on which to record his freaky jazz musician mates whose virtuosity offended the ears of all civilized record company executives. His partner in crime in cooking up these wild schemes was a bloke called John Hopkins (later to be known as Hoppy), who he had known for years. Now, Elektra Records had just set up an English office under the astute auspices of Joe Boyd, who Hoppy got to know, and a deal was worked out whereby Elektra would assist them in matters of finance, pressing and distribution.

Subsequently, an album by AMM was released (on the Elektra label rather than their bizarre DNA label, the logo for which Mike McInhery – later a well-known poster artist – had taken great pains to design), featuring Keith Rowe, Cornelius Cardew and various other musicians in the 'avant-garde/classical/weirdo scene ... and it was a very, very good, far out record.'

It sold about a thousand copies, but nevertheless turned out to be the first and last album they made. However, not only did it re-open the madcap Jenner's head to electronic music, but it also set his economics-orientated mind to work on the facts, figures and percentages of the record industry. He did his sums and came to the momentous conclusion that the only way to come out of things with a profit was to get hold of a smash hit – and even a person of his musical illiteracy (he could hardly differentiate between the Dave Clark Five and the London Symphony Orchestra) knew that freaky sax-blowing weirdies were not about to set the singles chart on fire. The problem caused a great deal of anxiety and he was on the point of consulting a psychiatrist, when it happened.

At 3 a.m. one morning, it came to him in a blinding flash. He threw the blankets from the crude framework of his camp-bed and rushed downstairs to make a drink. He could hardly control his excitement as his trembling hands cupped the steaming Bovril ... 'A pop group,' he finally ejaculated (not a pretty sight).

The fact had been staring him in the face for several months, but it was not until early 1966 that he recognized it ... the ideal vehicle to strap his energies to. The previous summer, one of his closest friends had been Eric Clapton, but Jenner at that time was totally disinterested in English pop music; compared with jazz and *bona-fide* American blues, it was just a load of trite, ephemeral rubbish – and, to a degree, I suppose his bigoted opinion was just about right; there was very little integrity in pop.

Clapton (though this has nothing to do with our story) had suddenly decided to leave John Mayall's Bluesbreakers (in August '66, though he rejoined three months later) and had formed a new band which he was going to take to Europe to get it together in a Greek country cottage, man; there was Jake Milton on drums (now in Quintessence), Ben Palmer on piano (later Cream's roadie), a sax player called Bernie, a bass player who subsequently became leader of the Communist party in Birmingham and John Bailey (who was in McGuinness Flint for a while). They all went off from Jenner's flat in a big American car.

Anyway, to revert to the main body of the narrative, Jenner began to look for a tasteful pop group. No, that's a lie ... he wasn't that enthusiastic. He still had his secure job at LSE and he merely decided to wait until the right group presented itself to him.

His first probings were abortive – and little wonder. Hoppy had got hold of a tape of one of the Velvet Underground's first gigs in New York and it was concluded that if the Velvets played their cards right, they could enjoy the patronage of Messrs Jenner and Hopkins. Such naïvety! (This story is true, by the way.) They phoned New York and spoke to John Cale, who tactfully pointed out that a Mr Warhol was already handling their affairs.

Now inevitably the sequence of events is going to get a bit blurred and jumbled if we don't stick to the music, but let me just mention a few other things. In these early months of 1966, the thoughts of various poets, painters, writers, musicians, etc., were all funnelling in the same direction. The seeds of the underground were sown and everybody was waiting for the harvest, so to speak. The Free School idea had taken root and was being set up in Notting Hill, and the All Saints Hall was becoming the central meeting place during this fermentation period. To finance the school, which was run on donations, it was decided to put on a few concerts, and these developed into the odd gig at the Marquee in Wardour Street.

Jenner: 'It was in June, I remember, because I was in the middle of the crucifyingly boring chore of marking examination papers. I always used to leave it until the last minute so that I'd be impelled to rush through them rather than go through the laborious agonies of wondering if a paper merited an A or B+. Anyway, I decided to pack it in for the evening and go along to this mad gig at the Marquee, which was being run by people like Steve Stollman (whose brother had started the ESP label in New York) and Hoppy. Well, I arrived there around ten thirty and there on the stage was this strange band, who were playing a mixture of R&B and electronic noises ... and I was really intrigued because in between the routine stuff like "Louie Louie" and "Roadrunner", they were

27

playing these very weird breaks; so weird that I couldn't even work out which instrument the sound was coming from. It was all very bizarre and just what I was looking for – a far out, electronic, freaky, pop group ... and there, across the bass amp, was their name: The Pink Floyd Sound.'

How to make a mountain out of a Blackhill

'I didn't know *anything* about pop music,' recalls Jenner. 'I just can't tell you how little I knew. I mean, I hardly knew about the Beatles even, and I didn't know anything about the Stones – and it was only at that time that I started trying to become aware of what was happening in pop music. Anyway, after thinking about it, I decided I'd like to record these Floyd geezers, and I finally tracked down Roger and Nicky, who were living in an obscure flat in Highgate. It was the typical student scene – they'd bought a £20 J2 van and some gear with their grant money but were on the point of splitting the band because 1) they weren't getting any gigs, 2) they were going on their summer holidays and 3) it was interfering with their studies. Roger and Nick were training to become architects, Rick was going to a music school and Syd was at art school and more interested in painting than music.'

Peter merely introduced himself, said hello and said he'd be interested in talking to them when they reconvened after their holidays. It was only at this stage that he discovered what an amateur set-up The Pink Floyd was: no contracts, no agency or management, no gigs, and very little gear, most of which was either extremely decrepit or else encased in home-made cabinets – but still, the seeds were there.

Enter Andrew King, a lifelong friend of Jenner's, who had resigned from his position as an educational cyberneticist (I don't know what one of them is either); he too had become bored and found it much more gratifying to hang out on street corners. He entered into loose partnership with Jenner and jointly, as Blackhill Enterprises, they took on the management of the Floyd, which was more than they'd planned to do because the original idea was merely to find a group for their label idea ... but now they determined to go the whole hog and make The Pink Floyd into a top band.

Carnival time arrived at the Free School and part of the festivities included a rock concert at the All Saints Hall – and what better choice for the group than ... The Pink Floyd. As well as that, some American friends of Hoppy's came along and projected coloured slides on the group as they played – not moving whirlpools of colour, just static slides, but it was the beginning of the 'mixed media' idea, and it started Jenner thinking. Snippets of information about the San Francisco scene had been filtering over the ocean; the West Coast psychedelic scene was much more together and advanced than its Notting Hill counterpart, so why not try to find out about the sophistications such as acid, light shows, peace and love, flowers and all the rest of the paraphernalia and implement some of them here?

The light show idea really appealed, but as no one could tell them about the refinements, they had to improvise. Peter and Andrew, a right pair of mechanical duffers, took instruction on the way to hold a hand saw and constructed a very primitive, Heath Robinson device consisting of domestic spotlights from British Home Stores, operated by domestic light switches, shining through coloured Perspex pinned to this crude framework they'd nailed up out of lumps of wood. (This remarkable triumph of carpentry is now an exhibit in the sculpture hall of the National Museum of Early Psychedelic Art in Chicago.)

The Floyd needed help. They needed encouragement, equipment, rehearsal, roadies, work, recording contracts, direction and all the rest of it, and their new managers didn't have the first idea about the roles and attitudes of the established managers, but they waded in at the deep end. Now, there's an old adage which says: 'Fools rush in, and get the best seats' – and that, by a strange quirk of good fortune, is exactly what happened. Over the next few months, the Floyd seemed to waltz into the charts, onto the television and into clubs and theatres without any problems at all.

Here's an example of their luck: Peter was still at work, so Andrew did most of the day-to-day management and also, from the remnants of an inheritance, paid for a thousand quid's worth of gear ... which was promptly stolen. So they had to get another load of new gear, this time on hire purchase.

By this time, things were happening fast. In October 1966, the *International Times* (later shortened to *IT*) was launched and the Roundhouse was taken over for a celebration party, where two thousand-odd people (most of them were odd) were given free sugar cubes and assailed with the raw sounds of the evolving Underground's two top groups, The Pink Floyd and the Soft Machine, both of whose reputations had spread via regular gigs at the All Saints Hall. All the different factions of the underground were represented and it was as if the net had suddenly tightened round all the loose ends, bringing them together, literally under one roof.

'At that time, the Roundhouse hadn't ever been used as an entertainment venue and it was just FILTHY. On top of that, there was virtually no electricity other than an ordinary domestic supply and wires dangled here and there ... so our puny light show looked magnificent in all the darkness.'

Celebrities abounded: Antonioni was there, Paul McCartney was there – to name but two, and it was 'an incredibly fashionable affair ... probably the most epochal party you could ever see, and the bands got noticed, particularly the Floyd who blew up the power during their set and consequently ended the evening's entertainment. That in itself, to be cut off in the middle of "Interstellar Overdrive", was a bummer, but at the same time it was incredibly dramatic.'

The Floyd had, by this time, dropped most of their R&B repertoire in favour of the more electronic/freaky stuff and I, in my blissful ignorance, had assumed that this was a result of acid experimentation and the like, but this was not so. It was done at Jenner's insistence; he directed them off the 'Louie Louie' trip towards the 'Saucerful of Secrets' style, and it turned out to be the perfect managerial move – although it was done largely out of ignorance ... Jenner merely thought the electronic stuff sounded better than the American imitations which he'd never really been keen on. Also, thinking that there was nothing difficult in composing new numbers, he impressed on them that they should write more original material of a 'weird' nature, but at the same time bearing the requirements of the singles market in mind. So, their style evolved to the satisfaction of their managers, who thought it was good but had no idea how radically different it was from anything else that was happening in pop music.

IT rapidly became the official organ of the underground (supplemented by *Oz*, which started up a couple of months later) and then, in December '66, Hoppy and his associates opened UFO, the first regular underground club (and the best). Here's a brief description of what went on, borrowed from *IT* #29 and written by Miles, whose interviews and reviews had become so influential:

> December 23rd saw 'Night Tripper' at Tottenham Court Road, advertised by a poster and a display ad in *IT* #5. There was no indication as to who would be there performing; the audience attended because they 'knew' who would be there and 'knew' what was happening. The name change to UFO occurred the next week and the first UFO advertised The Pink Floyd, Fanta and Ood, the Giant Sun Trolley and Dave Tomlin improvising to government propaganda.
>
> UFO was created by and for the original 'underground', posters from Messrs. English & Weymouth and an *IT* stall by the cloakrooms. The first UFO also had a Marilyn Monroe movie, karate and light shows. It was a club in the sense that most people knew each other, met there to do their business, arrange their week's appointments, dinners and lunches and hatch out issues of *IT*, plans for Arts Lab, SOMA, and various schemes for turning the Thames yellow and removing all the fences in Notting Hill. The activity and energy was thicker than the incense ...

Miles also ran Indica Bookshop in Southampton Row, a veritable goldmine of goodies; a whole new world to be discovered by emerging hippies (like me) ... full of books, underground papers like the *San Francisco Oracle* and the *East Village Other*, magazines, posters, Marvel comics. Phew! And the *International Times* was born out of and published from their basement, which for a while was the nerve centre of the underground.

By the beginning of 1967, UFO was already bulging to the walls with freaks – and The Pink Floyd, their music becoming increasingly strange by pop music standards, were the big musical draw. Jenner: 'At the first two or three UFOs, the Floyd were on sixty per cent of the gross to provide music and lights, and my first managerial blunder was allowing that to be altered so that we got straight bread instead of a percentage, because the place instantly became very fashionable – I've never seen anything like it, before or since. And the band had become even more fashionable; without any records or any exposure outside of a couple of places in London, we got a centre-page spread in the *Melody Maker*.'

If you know anything about the workings of the pop music industry, you'll know that any manager or publicist would sell his boyfriend to get a centre spread in *MM*, but Jenner wasn't at all surprised ... He assumed that this was the normal routine thing to happen to any band. But the Floyd were becoming red hot; the word was spreading like a forest fire – all the record companies were interested and suited executives were lured into the addict-infested filth of UFO to see the band in action. Eventually they signed with EMI, who offered them the best deal, including an advance of £5,000, which was just unbelievably astronomical in those days; more like a telephone number than a sum of money – and, surprisingly, EMI really did get behind them and did an incomparable promotion job.

Welcome to the machine

1967 . . . what a year!

Back to the scene in general. The media was latching on to the more sensational aspects of hippieism/flower power/beautiful people, and what was going down in San Francisco was now on everybody's lips. There were more gatherings here too; on 29 January *IT* sponsored an Uncommon Market spontaneous happening thing at the Roundhouse and a little later came THE ULTIMATE in drawing together the Underground . . . the 14 Hour Technicolor Dream, held at Alexandra Palace. The Uncommon Market's main attraction was a fifty-six gallon jelly (if you rolled around naked in jelly, you were considered very far out and groovy and gained great esteem and fame), but the Dream, which took place during the night of 29 April and was originally to be a benefit for *IT* which had been busted for obscenity the previous month, not only attracted five thousand longhairs, but featured almost every underground group in England.

I remember it well; the whole thing just burned into my memory for ever . . . it hit you as soon as you walked into the place – lights and films all over the walls and blitzing volume from two stages with bands playing simultaneously! On one stage you had the completely unknown Arthur Brown, this crazy whirling painted lunatic accompanied by a hunched-up speeding organist and a thrashing drummer, and on the other you had the Soft Machine, with Daevid Allen wearing a miner's helmet and staring like a weird zombie and Kevin Ayers wearing rouge on his cheeks and a black cowboy hat surmounted by giant model glider wings. I just couldn't believe it; outside, the straights of Wood Green were watching their tellies and sipping their tea, and inside this huge time machine were five thousand stoned, tripping, mad, friendly, festive hippies . . . talk about two different worlds!

At the time, one of the things that immediately impressed me most was the lack of any sort of physical or mental barrier between performers and audience; when a band finished its set, the members got off the stage and wandered into the crowd to sit on the floor. It was all so unlike the usual pop gig where a group arrived on stage via a back passage, played and went off by the same route – never mixing with the inferior rabble.

What else did I see? The Purple Gang, with mandolins, washboards and amplification troubles, bashing out their 'Granny Takes A Trip' – one of the early hippie classics, Dick Gregory and Pete Townshend and Yoko Ono were there, Savoy Brown, the Social Deviants with Mick Farren singing Chuck Berry standards against a monstrous cacophony of discordant rock and Denny Laine was there too – but, though he had his guitar and Viv Prince with him, he didn't play (which was sad, because 1967 was his supreme year of creativity).

Hoppy was there, never without a smile, and Suzi Creamcheese, and they were giving out free bananas (because it was around the time of the US underground great banana hoax; they conned everyone into believing that you could get high by scraping the pith from the inside skin, baking it and smoking it).

As dawn started to shine a shimmering eerie light at the windows, The Pink Floyd came on: 'It was a perfect setting,' says Jenner. 'Everyone had been waiting for them and everybody was on acid; that event was the peak of acid use in England ... everybody was on it – the bands, the organizers, the audience – and I certainly was.' Of course, the Floyd blew everybody's mind.

But this was a special occasion; the Floyd, though '*the* psychedelic band', were not really into psychedelics at all – they were much more booze orientated ... and this was generally the case with the early underground bands; it was the pop groups of the time, the teenybop raves like the Small Faces, who were doing the drugs.

Around this time, the pirate radio stations, whose lifespan was already being limited to months by the Marine Offences Act which was being rushed through the Commons, were at their most influential in shaping the pop charts: 'We start 'em, others chart 'em.' Radio London, by far and away the best, refused to play 'Arnold Layne', the Floyd's first single, because it was about a transvestite, but Radio Caroline, once the payola had been handed over, got behind it and supplemented EMI's big promotional campaign. Before long, it had got to number 23 in the national chart, which, of course, was no surprise to Peter Jenner, who thought it was only natural for a single to go into the charts. But due possibly to the 'dirty song' ban, it never quite reached the Top 20 and thus the essential *Top of the Pops* boost eluded them.

Their second single, they were sure, would be even more successful, but there were doubts. Joe Boyd, who had left his Elektra job to become involved in a variety of enterprises including record production, running UFO and group management, had produced and made an excellent job of 'Arnold Layne', but EMI decided to rub him out in favour of Norman ('Hurricane') Smith, who had just been promoted from engineer to staff producer. It was a very unpopular move; everybody, including the fuming Joe Boyd, was choked off and Norman knew it, but his experience with the Beatles, his exacting demands, his ideas and ambitions, turned up trumps and it turned out to be a very productive combination.

The song they selected was 'See Emily Play', which Syd had written (as 'Games For May') specially for a concert which our intrepid managers mounted at the Queen Elizabeth Hall. It was a staggeringly successful event – a solo performance, which was totally unheard of, because the big groups of the time would never do more than a thirty-minute set – 'and we got this guy from EMI to erect speakers at the back of the hall, too, which was like the predecessor of the azimuth coordinator. We had an incredible light show by then as well, and the concert, which was the first pop show ever held in the hall, was just unbelievable. At one stage, one of the roadies came on dressed in admiral's gear and tossed armfuls of daffodils up in the air ... It was just amazing, and everybody went berserk.' Everyone except the owners of the hall, who went absolutely bananas because the bubbles which had filled the place had left marks all over their posh leather chairs, and some of the flowers which had been handed out to the audience had been trodden into the carpets.

Anyway, everybody was knocked out with 'Emily', especially Radio London, who felt that they were missing out on the flower power scene. They went crazy; the first week out, it was number one on the *Big L* Top 40, a chart which bore no relation to anything other than the fevered imagination of the programme director.

In actual fact, far from 'missing out on the hippie scene', Radio London was a distinct pioneer in that area, with John Peel's *Perfumed Garden*, transmitted two weeks out of every three (as far as I can remember) between midnight and 2 a.m. Prior to getting this programme, Peel's 'climber of the week' was always worth hearing (among those that stick in my mind are 'Tiny Goddess' by Nirvana and 'Somebody to Love' by the Airplane), but once he got this midnight thing going, it was compulsive listening. It was for me anyway; I used to lie there listening to the Doors, the Incredibles, Donovan and all the others, and arrive at work the next day with great bags under my eyes – and he used to get hold of imports and play unheard-of grist like Captain Beefheart and his Magic Band and Country Joe and the Fish. It was an amazing period – one I wouldn't have missed for the world.

By the time June rolled around, the unity of the underground was already disintegrating, with the different sections criticizing the ethics of each other, and the bread-minded entrepreneurs had begun to step in and promote flower-power festivals and happenings on a very obviously commercial basis. There were so many 'underground bands' that you couldn't move for them, but the thing that caused most discomfort to the hard core of the old school was the arrest and sentencing of Hoppy for dope possession; he got nine months.

Though many avant-garde musicians (not to mention people in other spheres) had been smoking marijuana for years, the public image of drugs was the wicked black man prosecuted for selling reefers to unsuspecting teenagers. But all of a sudden, all the mods were gulping down handfuls of pills, and the longhairs were either getting stoned or else trying out this incredible new acid stuff which had newly arrived from the laboratories of America, where it was still legal until late 1966.

The Sunday papers feared for the future of the nation's youth, the police got pressured into paranoia and they went berserk with their arrests; Jagger, Richard, Lennon, Georgie Fame and Joe Cocker were all busted for possession, but the first really big purge came in the early hours of 3 March 1968, when a hundred and fifty police suddenly plunged into the depths of Middle Earth, which had opened as a rival to UFO in early '67. They took five hours to search seven hundred and fifty people and made only eleven arrests, though one heard grapevine reports of the vast tonnage of hash that was swept up from the floor afterwards.

Back to the Floyd, who were now just about world famous due to a combination of luck, talent and a miraculous series of events. 'If we had started out with just any old banger group, we'd have been finished within a year, because we had so little idea of what we were doing, but fortunately, the Floyd had all this talent. Andrew and I just played everything by ear; goodness only knows what the established record-biz poseurs must've thought about us ... I suppose that when we left their offices they just looked at each other and collapsed in disbelief at our naïvety.'

They cut their first album in studio 3 at EMI while the Beatles were constructing *Sgt. Pepper* next door in studio 2, and that sold well too – so everything was going along smoothly – but at the London School of Economics, where Peter still taught, he was one of the junior staff in favour of the student revolution which was beginning to erupt and he eventually got a sharp reprimand; either he curbed the nature of his extra-curricular activities or else he could tender his resignation. So he compromised, and took a year's leave of absence ... which has so far extended itself to five years.

It was around this time that the pressures of the world started exerting themselves on Syd Barrett, who was really the genius of the group; he was writing, arranging, creating the sounds, singing – but he was, as everybody who ever followed the Floyd knows – cracking up a little. Peter accepts some of the responsibility for what was happening; he was always demanding greater effort, more productivity, more songs for future singles and so forth, but the gig scene was probably more to blame.

Pink Floyd

In the London longhair haunts, everything was fine – perfect vibes between audience and group – but once they got out into the world they found that their music had hardly been accepted; gigs were disastrous. Kids who turned up purely to hear a 'Top 20 group' could not come to terms with feedback and the like – so they booed and threw pennies ... Jenner's face contorts in agony as he recalls the general miseries of touring in that summer of '67.

Finding a suitable chartbuster to follow 'Emily' proved impossible; loads of material (much of it amazing classics like 'Scream Your Last Scream Old Woman With a Basket' and 'Vegetable Man' which have yet to be released) was recorded, but no obvious single surfaced to keep them buoyant, and a tour interrupted the proceedings. It was an epic theatre package tour of the type we'll never see again – seven groups in one show ... and they did two shows a night! A roadie's nightmare! Jimi Hendrix had forty minutes, the Move had thirty, the Floyd had seventeen, Amen Corner fifteen, The Nice twelve and so on, and it was all bound together by compère Pete Drummond, whose main success lay in alienating the fans.

That tour did wonders in popularizing them, but a subsequent tour of America was decidedly very strange; they'd arrive at a gig and someone backstage would invariably induce them to sample the latest line in synthetic drugs and some extraordinary music would ensue. One of the aims of the early Floyd was to achieve the San Francisco/psychedelic stance, which they thought they were doing quite well, but it transpired that their music was far removed from anything the Americans had ever seen before. With few examples of the West Coast sound to take their lead from, they had just guessed and assumed what the more progressive groups might be trying, and in doing so had evolved a style entirely of their own.

The end of an era (and the start of another)

Within a year of the first stirrings of love, peace and brotherhood, the underground had passed through its period of togetherness.

UFO, under the control of Joe Boyd, had closed down, and Hoppy, just out of prison, was now much quieter and there was no one to assume his pivotal role as coordinator of underground activities. Jenner: 'I think it was a tragedy for the hip community when Hoppy was put in gaol and I don't think it ever recovered, because it was his energy which fired so many schemes. He held everything together and helped to maintain a unity.'

Everyone withdrew into his own camp rather than think about the underground as a whole ... a very harrowing bandwagon period during which hypocrisy was around on a very big scale.

Meanwhile, the Floyd was falling apart too; the pop Press were coming out with rapturous accounts of how Syd would do a whole number strumming just one chord, but the other three weren't so much amused as troubled, and they decided to make a few changes. They could never be sure if Syd was suddenly going to change the rhythm or structure of a piece – and things stretched just a little too far ...

Syd stayed with Blackhill, who had plans for a solo career, and the Floyd recruited Dave Gilmour and went off to a new management in March 1968. The end of an amazing, but very weird era.

'We were always convinced that they were going to be as big as the Beatles – we were sure of that – but the way we ran things was so haphazard. For instance, at one time we had the Floyd, Andrew and me, June Child [who worked in the office and later became Mrs Bolan], two roadies and two lights people – they were all on salary, and we didn't keep any sort of control over expenditure ... Ludicrous amounts were spent on ridiculous things, and the money scene got very unstable as a result of no hit record and no gigs, a situation which had arisen because of the reputation they'd gained for being unreliable.

'Basically, the Floyd left us because they thought we'd have no confidence in them without Syd, which was true, even though it was a mistake for us to think like that. We just couldn't conceive how they would be able to make it without Syd, who put all the creativity in the group.'

So off they went, leaving the financial position approximately as it had been eighteen months earlier ... everybody was broke. Jenner: 'If I'd known then what I know now, things would've been very different. The Floyd would have made a lot of money much sooner than they did, and I'd be a very rich man.'

By this time, however, Blackhill had just taken on the management of an unrecorded duo who had no gigs and survived mainly because of John Peel's interest and help ... they were called Tyrannosaurus Rex, but that's another story altogether.

References For a fuller picture, read *Play Power* by Richard Neville and *Bomb Culture* by Jeff Nuttall. Also see Glen Sweeney in *Zigzag* 4 and Mick Farren in *Zigzag* 5. Old copies of *IT* and *Oz* are interesting, and a snoop around Compendium Books in Camden Town is always worthwhile.

Art and architecture

Lisa Mehlman

The trouble with
Pink Floyd's hits

Disc, November 1971

'We're really making emotional music. I wouldn't say it's intellectual,' said David Gilmour when I talked to him this week about
Pink Floyd. None the less, the group has a devoted, more or less
cultist audience here in New York who think that they are more
intellectual than not, and the audience treated their Carnegie Hall
concert this week as if it were almost a religious event.

The incredibly loud, spacey music, accompanied by those great
sound effects, created an atmosphere that was really cosmic. Pink
Floyd played for almost three hours, and despite some minor
problems, they were a huge success with a totally sold out crowd
of two thousand nine hundred people.

It was almost the end of their tour, one that consisted of many
one-nights in different cities. When I spoke with David, he
emphasized also that the band was getting a bit tired of having to
play the same material night after night. 'In England it's different,'
he said. 'We can do anything we like, really. We've often gone on
stage and done material that we've never done before and the
audiences are used to us and they love it. But in the States, it's
more or less like we have to play our "hits".'

And indeed, the typically rude New York audience did shout
out for 'Astronomy Domine' and, unbelievably enough, 'See Emily
Play'. To that, Roger Waters just sneered and said, 'You must be
joking!'

Richard Middleton

Piper at the Gates of Dawn

Pop Music and the Blues, 1972

An important characteristic of psychedelic pop is the use of electronic effects and electronically-created noise. One of the best examples of this is the work of the Pink Floyd, a British group well known for their multi-media shows and the vast amount of electronic equipment which they use. The Pink Floyd have developed an improvisational, 'free-form' style, in which traditional pop techniques are mixed with a multitude of electronic effects. It is significant that they share Jimi Hendrix's interest in space and astronomy, many of their songs carrying his obsession much further, both in explicitness and musical implications. So it is not surprising that in their music pop reaches possibly its most 'inhuman' form, man all but disappearing in the vastness of the cosmos.

They are not always quite so extreme as this. 'Pow R Toc H' alternates sections of chaotic noise with sections of expressive blues piano. Man is set in a non-human context but still exists – though chaos wins in the end. 'Take Up Thy Stethoscope And Walk' seems to be a medical allegory, in which humanity is 'operated on' by horrific electronics and brain-battering noise, beat and ostinato. But here, at the end of the piece, vocal music appears and the patient asserts 'I'm alive'. And 'Astronomy Domine', as the title implies, goes so far as to explore man's control of his environment, his superiority to the cosmos.

Even here, however, the 'human' aspects of the music are not distinguished by much intelligence, feeling or order. Moreover, the more extreme of the Pink Floyd's pieces make not even these concessions. In the very long, entirely 'instrumental' 'Interstellar Overdrive', for example, the disordered, apparently random, electronically-dominated noise displays signs of coherence – a drone or an ostinato – very rarely indeed.

Art and architecture

Most of 'A Saucerful of Secrets' is similar, only the brief appearance of a drum-beat disturbing the general chaos. Man is all but swallowed up in the inhuman vastness of space. The music could almost be that of a randomly programmed computer after the end of the world. It is comparable to no other music except 'serious' electronic music, particularly the use of live electronics by some *avant-garde* composers. Here, then, pop and modern art display their fundamental similarity of developmental direction most clearly – already mutual influence between groups like the Pink Floyd and young, 'serious' composers exists – for here pop, generally culturally 'behind' *avant-garde* art, takes the unusual step of travelling as far away from the traditions of Western culture as the most extreme artists of the *avant garde*. In this (admittedly relatively esoteric) music, the parallel developments of the modern artist and the adolescent meet . . .

Returning to the Pink Floyd, it is interesting – and significant – to find that at the end of their recording of 'Interstellar Overdrive', 'The Gnome', a song of another kind, follows without a break. This song's folk-like lyricism, whose combination of sweetly tonal construction and pentatonic touches reminds one of Dylan and the Beatles, its clear, simple texture and structure, and its 'innocent' use of triadic harmony, which again is reminiscent of the Beatles, indicate that here indeed is a rebirth of order, humanity and beauty out of the cosmic chaos of the preceding music.

The spirit of the song is one of childlike wonder and naïve happiness, making it clear that out of destruction has come new life. Order issues out of disorder, harmony out of chaos, time out of eternity; space-age man is reborn out of the cosmic wastes. And the impressive thing is how the implications of space, explored in 'Interstellar Overdrive', are neither neglected nor surrendered to, but accepted and transcended: the cosmos is humanized.

Miles

A Saucerful of Secrets

International Times, 8 August 1968

The Floyd have developed a distinctive sound for themselves, the result of experiments with new 'electronic' techniques in live performance. However, the result of most of these experiments was presented particularly well on their first album; there is little new here.

The electronic collage on 'Jugband Blues', though it uses stereo well, has been done much better by The United States Of America. The unimaginative use of a strings arrangement spoils 'See Saw'. The use of electronic effects on 'A Saucerful of Secrets' is poorly handled and does not add up to music. It is too long, too boring, and totally uninventive, particularly when compared to a similar electronic composition such as 'Metamorphosis' by Vladimir Ussachevsky, which was done in 1957, eleven years ago.

The introduction of drums doesn't help either and just reminds me of the twelve and a half minute unfinished backing track 'The Return of the Son of Monster Magnet' which somehow got onto side four of The Mothers of Invention's *Freak Out* album, much to Zappa's horror and which was left off the British version. In the same way as bad sitar playing is initially attractive, electronic music turns people on at first – then as one hears more, the listener demands that something be made and done with these 'new' sounds, something more than 'psychedelic mood music'.

'Let There Be More Light' presents the Floyd at their best as does most of side one. They are really good at this and outshine all the pale imitations of their style. With their 'Saucers' track, experiments have a historical place and should be preserved, but only the results should be on record, at least until they bring out one a month and are much cheaper. A record well worth buying!

Mick Farren

Ummagumma

International Times, c. October 1969

This double album package is above all an essential purchase for anyone who has ever got into the Floyd at any time. I must confess I came to dig the Floyd somewhat late in their career but, having made that step, I can only say that these two albums are a really magnificent package.

The first disc comprises four pieces from their live repertoire, beautifully played and really well produced by Norman Smith. I think it is probably one of the best live recordings I have ever heard.

The second disc consists of a section by each member of the group. The first side starts with Richard Wright's 'Sysyphus', which begins with a slow, dignified theme, goes through some rather strange progressions on piano, then harpsichord, Mellotron (?) and finally returns to the first organ theme.

Roger Waters' section is split into two tracks: the first a song accompanied by guitar and simulated birds and bees; while the second is an amazing piece of lunacy which can be described as a literal interpretation of the title, 'Several Species of Small Furry Animals Gathered Together in a Cave and Grooving With a Pict'.

The second side opens with Dave Gilmour's track, which is much more what one would expect from the Floyd, except with a great bias towards guitar.

The final piece, Nick Mason's, opens with a baroque flute theme, which is followed by a long percussion sequence with extremely effective use of stereo and a final return, in true Floyd manner, to the original theme.

Syd Barrett of The Pink Floyd

Blind Date

Melody Maker, 22 July 1967

Art – 'What's That Sound (For What It's Worth)' (Island)

Good. I don't recognize it and I've no idea who it is, but it drives along. Liked the instrumental sound. A medium hit. I suspect it to be American. I dug.

Gene Latter – 'A Little Piece Of Leather' (CBS)

It's a great song. That's nice. It's on the soul scene and I think people will go on digging the soul scene. I hope the people who listen to us will listen to this as well. The new wave of music is all-embracing. It gets across and makes everybody feel good. I don't think this will do well in the chart but it'll be OK for the clubs. I nearly guessed who it was – Gene Latter?

Jim Reeves – 'Trying To Forget' (RCA Victor)

Very way out record. I think I tapped my foot to that one. I don't know who it was. Well, let me think – who's dead? It must be Jim Reeves. I don't think it will be a hit. It doesn't matter if an artist is dead or alive about records being released. But if you're trendy, this doesn't quite fit the bill. It's another that would sound better at $33\frac{1}{3}$.

Barry Fantoni – 'Nothing Today' (Columbia)

Very negative. The middle jazzy bit was nice. Apart from the saxophone bit, it was morbid. I don't know what it was all about. It seemed to be about somebody kissing somebody's feet. I don't want to hear it again. Maybe it should be played at 78.

Alex Harvey – 'The Sunday Song' (Decca)

Nice sounds – yeah. Wow. Lots of drums, but it avoids being cluttered. The people in the background seem to be raving a bit more than the people in front. English? One of those young groups like John's Children? It moved me a little bit, but I don't think it will be a hit. Very snappy.

Tom Jones – 'I'll Never Fall In Love Again' (Decca)
I detect a Welsh influence in the strings. I feel it's one of those numbers you should play at slow speed, or backwards or upside down. It's Sandy McPherson. Everyone knows who it is. It won't be a hit because it's too emotional. It'll sell a lot, but I won't buy one.

Blues Magoos – 'One By One' (Fontana)
It's got a message, but it didn't really seem to branch out anywhere. It's nice, and I dug it, but it won't do anything. No idea who it was. You're going to tell me it's the Byrds. I really dig the Byrds, Mothers of Invention and Fugs. We have drawn quite a bit from those groups. I don't see any reason for this record being a big flop or a big hit. It was a nice record.

Oliver Nelson – 'Drowning In My Own Despair' (Polydor)
Crazy – yeah. If pressed to think about it, I would suggest it was The Four Tops. So, it's not The Four Tops. If you want a hit, it's best to make your own sounds. The label is a pretty colour.

Vince Hill – 'When The World Is Ready' (Columbia)
Fade it out. Vince Hill. I didn't understand the lyrics at all. It's very well produced and very well sung. It may be a hit, but I shouldn't think so, because the lyrics are so unconvincing.

David Bowie – 'Love You Till Tuesday' (Deram)
Yeah, it's a joke number. Jokes are good. Everybody likes jokes. The Pink Floyd like jokes. It's very casual. If you play it a second time, it might be even more of a joke. Jokes are good. The Pink Floyd like jokes. I think that was a funny joke. I think people will like the bit about it being Monday, when in fact it was Tuesday. Very chirpy, but I don't think my toes were tapping at all.

Malcolm Jones

The Madcap Laughs

The Making of *The Madcap Laughs*, 1986

One day, late in March 1969, I received a message that Syd Barrett had phoned EMI's studio booking office to ask if he could go back into the studios and start recording again. It was over a year since Syd had parted company with the Pink Floyd and, as head of Harvest [records], the request was referred to me.

I had never met Syd, although he had apparently been in the studio with Peter Jenner a year previously, just after I had joined EMI. Needless to say, I was familiar with his past successes with the Floyd, and I knew as much as anyone about the circumstances surrounding his leaving. It had occurred to me on several occasions to ask what had become of Syd's own solo career. Peter Jenner and Andrew King, the original Floyd management team, managed many artists on Harvest.

Dark references were made to 'broken microphones in the studio and general disorder' by EMI management, and this had resulted in a period when, if not actually banned, Syd's presence at Abbey Road was not particularly encouraged. None of Peter Jenner's recordings of Syd had turned out releasable, and no one in EMI's A&R department had gone out of his way to encourage Syd back. Now that I had A&R responsibility for Harvest, I was determined to make the most of this contact with Syd and I rang him back immediately.

Syd explained that he had lots more material for a new album, and since he had not recorded for more or less two years there was no reason to doubt him. He was also keen to try and salvage some of Peter Jenner's sessions, and in all seemed very together – in contrast to all the rumours circulating at the time.

There was, he said, a song called 'Opel', another called 'Terra-pin', a song about an Indian girl called 'Swan Lee', and one called

'Clowns and Jugglers'. Plus he had started work at Abbey Road on a James Joyce poem, 'Golden Hair', which he was most anxious to complete. It all sounded too good for words!

Michael West

Two more of a kind

Opel – the Syd Barrett magazine, May 1985

One question has perplexed eminent Barrettologists for literally weeks – ever since, in fact, the 'new' tape surfaced. This question is, of course, when the fuck was 'Milky Way' recorded? As anyone who has heard it (and I'm sure most of you have) knows, it is an out-and-out classic and the person responsible for its non-release deserves to be hung, drawn and quartered. With this worthy question in mind, I decided to ring the number that had been thrust in my greasy mitt by an equally greasy friend with the comment, 'It's EMI's phone number.'

After myriad switchboard changes (most of them wrong), my call was routed correctly.

'Hello?'

'Hello.' I was nervous but trying my best not to show it. 'Er, hello, I was wondering if you could help me. Er, could you tell me what tracks Syd Barrett recorded in 1975?'

A pregnant pause of expectancy.

'Syd who?'

'Syd Barrett. You know, the guy from Pink Floyd.'

'Not again, we get loads of calls about him. You aren't the guy who called up last week, are you?'

'No.'

'What do you want now? Could you tell me your reasons for enquiring?'

Oh shit – my excuse was flimsy, but it worked:

'Er . . . I, er, believe it's been issued in Japan, as a twelve-inch single.'

'From 1975, you say?' There was a whine of microfilm and then the voice came back.

'I'm sorry, we have no Syd Barrett entry for 1975. There was a session in '74. That's the last we've got.'

Art and architecture

'Can you tell me what the tracks were that were recorded then?'

'Certainly, just hold on ... Oh, I'm sorry: it doesn't say. It just says "various bits and pieces – details inside tape box". Sorry.'

'Well, do you have access to the box? Could you tell me what it says inside?'

'I'm afraid not. It'll be down with all the other stuff, down in the archives.'

'And when were the last sessions before '74?'

'In 1970 ... just hold on, there it is. "Milky Way", "She Was A Millionaire", "Rats": all seventh of June, 1970.'

'"She Was A Millionaire"? June 1970? Can you read me out the rest of the sessions? From the beginning?'

'Of course: "Baby Lemonade", "Maisie", "Gigolo Aunt"...'

'Slow down ...'

'"Wolfpack", "Milky Way", "She Was A Millionaire", "Rats', "Love Song", "Untitled", "It Is Obvious", "Effervescent Elephant"...'

'"Effervescent Elephant"? Isn't that "Effervescing Elephant"?'

'That's what it says here: "Effervescent Elephant", "Dolly Rocker", "Dominoes", "Let's Split"...'

'"Dolly Rocker"? "Let's Split"?'

'Yes, that's right, "Let's Split", "Wined And Dined"... They're not in any order, you know.'

'Can you start again?'

Barrett

Beat Instrumental, January 1971

Syd Barrett is capable of much greater things than this. He sounds flat on most of his vocals and the instruments give the impression that only one track of the stereo is actually working. 'Gigolo Aunt' borders on early Floyd but that is the best thing to be said about the entire album.

Atom Heart Mother

Beat Instrumental, December 1970

With this utterly fantastic record, the Floyd have moved out into totally new ground. Basically a concept album, the A-side title track utilizes Pink Floyd, orchestral brass and mixed choir. All blend to form a totally integrated theme which is the great strength of this LP. Great, great, great and I'd love to hear it in quadrophonic!

Michael Watts

Pink's muddled Meddle

Melody Maker, November 1971

One can't help but feel that Pink Floyd are so much sound and fury, signifying nothing. Their achievement has been to create a space rock sound, which revolves around the use of electronic effects combined with the usual musical instrumentation of four-piece rock bands, i.e. drums, guitar, bass and organ.

Frequently, they have utilized this concept to good effect, right from the early days of 'Interstellar Overdrive' and 'Astronomy Domine' to the *Atom Heart Mother* and *Ummagumma* albums, but how much of this, in fact, has been pure effect?

Stripped of the sense of etherea, the music hardly stands up as more than competent rhythmic rock, while even the use of electronics and spacey atmospherics is not as adventurous as it may seem at first hearing, especially when considered alongside such as 'Zero Times' by Tonto's Expanding Headband.

Meddle exhibits all their faults, as well as their most successful points. The first side is taken up with songs, as opposed to long instrumental pieces, and it's in this area that they most expose themselves to criticism. Since Syd Barrett left, there has been no one in the band able to cope with the sort of pithy statement that is necessary to the five-minute pop track, which undoubtedly explains why they have ceased to work to the single format. The vocals verge on the drippy, and the instrumental work-outs, which rely heavily on Dave Gilmour's guitar, are decidedly old hat. Listen to 'One of These Days'; it's a throwback to 'Telstar' by the Tornados.

The second side, 'Echoes', is the one where the concept comes in. It encompasses the whole side, starts off with a passage of Asdic pings and lots of soaring guitar before settling into a genuinely funky organ riff, and then there is introduced some wind effects and the sound of cawing rooks (or it could be cows; that's how it comes across). It follows on with some beautiful cello set against further use of the Asdic, before the whole piece crashes out in a crescendo of volume and rattling cymbals.

Far out, you may say. Not really. Although there appears to be some continuity in the work – the Asdic echoes, get it? – my basic impression was of a series of effects without any underlying depth. Interesting, even aesthetic, they may be, but superficial ultimately, like background noises in a Radio Three play. When there is little real musical substance to sustain those effects, how can the result be anything but a soundtrack to a non-existent movie?

Roy Shipston

Are spacemen Floyd on their way back to Earth?

Disc & Music Echo, 22 November 1969

OK, you can come out now! Pink Floyd only want to communicate – not frighten or destroy people with an overdose of decibels as they appeared to be trying to do in the early days of the psychedelic thing.

I first saw them about four years ago, before they made those two hit singles – the very mention of which makes them visibly sick these days. Then, their music seemed limited to playing in one key. Lyrics were practically non-existent, and I was convinced that the beautifully coloured bacteria shapes on the backcloth were there only to draw attention from the row they were making.

They don't need light shows now. Their music has matured to become acutely interesting and exciting. But what are their aims and ambitions? What is the point of the Pink Floyd?

'We just want to get on and get through to people with the things we do. We want to get through to every person in the country, to every person in the world even. It's just communication; that's what it's all about,' says guitarist Dave Gilmour.

'I suppose we all want to improve the world, make it a better place to live in, like everyone else. There is a great revolution taking place at the moment, which seems to have emerged from the pop movement, the underground scene. The same thing is happening in all the arts.

'We all have very strong views – differing views – but we try to keep it out of our music. Some of it comes through in our writing, obviously, but we are mainly concerned with just communicating with people through our songs.

'I don't think it's wrong if someone well-known uses his position to get over his beliefs, or influence people. Why shouldn't he? It could be wrong if it is a bad belief. We're just not very good at writing that sort of song. We never really set out to protest about violence or anything. We don't want to come across with some incredible message.'

How does he define their music?

'There's not really much to explain. I don't know why it works out like it does. There's no special thing that we deliberately work at. We are just trying to move ahead, to get things done – for enjoyment and soul.

'We find that people dig what we are doing, and the way we work is to do things that we like at the time, rather than things they will like us to do. It's always been that way and it seems to work. Of course, you have to do some numbers that they know, but they're ones that we still enjoy doing.'

Why is so much of Pink Floyd's music space-orientated?

'We don't deliberately try and make everything come out like that. It just works out that things happen that way. We all read science fiction and groove to *2001*; it's all very good. But some of our things happen completely accidentally.'

It is difficult to imagine what kind of music Floyd will create in, say, a year's time. Their style has not changed much since the beginning; it has evolved significantly, but a style can only be exploited so far. If perfection is ever reached, the Pink Floyd, in their field, are probably as near to it as possible. So how will they progress?

'I don't know how it's going to go. It's tended to get a little less "spacey" lately. It's just a matter of doing new things, new pieces of music, and seeing what happens. You can have an idea, then when the whole group gets together it will change completely. How a song is originally and how it eventually turns out may be two different things.

'The group has changed a lot since the early days, and come a long way. The worst period was after the two hit singles: we went right down then, because people expected us to do them and we wouldn't. Now we are as busy as we want to be. We do two or three gigs a week, and that keeps us going. But I never seem to have any cash – it's such an expensive business. We are also a bit slow, especially on recording. It takes us months to get out an LP.

'We get in the studio for a couple of days, then someone else, like the Beatles, wants to record and we get shoved out. So a couple of weeks later we go back and we've forgotten the mood. It takes a lot of time getting back into the thing.

'What we really need is a block session to get something done in one go. We have great fun in the studios, mucking about. But I don't think I could go on recording without doing appearances. It's great to do a live gig, but we can do so much more recording. I don't see why we should limit ourselves on record to what we do on stage.

'There are a lot of things we haven't really touched on yet. Television, for instance, which is good publicity. We have been approached about doing programmes but nothing's ever come of it. I thought we had some nice ideas for a TV show – they'd probably still be OK. But TV generally is so boring.

'I suppose everybody's ego would be satisfied by a lot of fame, but it seems that if you have a record in the charts, you are rejected by the so-called underground movement. Hit parades do spell death for our sort of group, but if we did a single, I'd be quite happy if it got into the charts.

'Our main thing is to improve, and we are trying all the time. We are striving to improve our amplification; on stage and in the studios, we want to clean up the sound equipment. But I don't foresee any drastic changes. We've used a choir and brass section and we tend to play any strange instruments that happen to be lying around. We don't feel limited.

'One of our hang-ups is that people who haven't seen us come along believing that we're going to be good before we start. And we're not always quite what they expected.

'Myself, I don't think we'll ever get through to the masses . . .'

Robert Christgau

Dark Side of the Moon

Rock Albums of the '70s, 1981

With its technological mastery and its conventional wisdom once-removed, this is a kitsch masterpiece – taken too seriously by definition, but not without charm. It may sell on sheer aural sensationalism, but the studio effects do transmute David Gilmour's guitar solos into something more than they were when he played them. Its taped speech fragments may be old hat, but for once they cohere musically. And if its pessimism is received, that doesn't make the ideas untrue – there are even times, especially when Dick Parry's saxophone undercuts the electronic pomp, when this record brings its clichés to life, which is what pop is supposed to do, even the kind with delusions of grandeur.

Robert Christgau

Syd Barrett

Rock Albums of the '70s, 1981

Syd Barrett comprises the two albums Barrett made after leaving Pink Floyd in early 1968. The second was released in England just before *Atom Heart Mother* in 1970, which must have made a striking contrast; in the wake of Floyd's triumph with *Dark Side of the Moon* the contrast is even sharper.

Barrett coughs when he's not wheezing, he can hardly strum his guitar and his lyrics are off-the-wall in a modest workaday way. David Gilmour and Roger Waters back him up (good for them), but sloppily (good for them again); there's no hint of their engineering-student expertise.

Admittedly, a lot of what results is worthy of the wimp-turned-acid-casualty Barrett is. But a lot of it is funny, charming, catchy – whimsy at its best. I love most of side one, especially 'Terrapin' and 'Here I Go'. And while my superego insists I grade it a notch lower, I know damn well it gives me more pleasure than *Dark Side of the Moon*.

Cracking up

Steve Peacock

A pre-season report on Pink Floyd

Sounds, 17 August 1974

Headmaster's report, summer term, 1974 – or 'Hullo, Nick, what have the Pink Floyd been up to recently?'

'We are pleased to say that this year's experiment in introducing the Summerhill approach to the sixth form has been successful. It is something for which the boys have been clamouring for some years now, and the introduction of a system where there are no deadlines, where they don't have to do anything unless they feel like it, has produced the desired result. After the initial rush of inactivity, boredom set in and the chaps have decided that they really do want to work after all.

'Big projects are planned for the autumn term. The boys have learnt from their experience with the last set piece – which has been extremely popular with the examiners – and are planning to approach the next project in the same way. This may be a more time-consuming way of working – preparing their set pieces thoroughly before taking them to the studio for a finished version – but it seems more productive in the end.

'Extra-curricular activities seem to have been more productive this year – particularly Mason's out-of-hours projects with Robert Wyatt, who we are extremely pleased to have back – and the sports master has been pleased with the football team's progress as well as with a variety of minor sports.'

What a silly concept – all due to a trauma I suffered as a schoolboy, and a curious conversation with Nick Mason at a party. I'm sorry, I'll start again. Or rather I'll let Nick do it.

'In the studio, we haven't really been doing anything, because there was a general feeling after *Dark Side of the Moon* that that was a preferable way of working – to get the pieces organized first on the road before recording them.'

So the next album will be a while yet. They have been making some progress on the continuing saga of the Household Objects album though – this was first mooted early in 1971, a kind of extension to 'Alan's Psychedelic Breakfast' on *Atom Heart Mother*. This idea is to make an album using sounds produced from anything that is not a conventional musical instrument – wine-glasses, felling axes, buckets of water, rolls of Sellotape – and they've been working on it as their ideas have cropped up.

'I think it will happen one day, because most of the ideas we've tried seem to work really well so far … it's in very random form at the moment, not in pieces. There are things like sixteen tracks of glasses tuned to a scale across the 16-track: it can be played across the faders, but what it really needs is each one going through a VCS3 or something, and then coming in to a keyboard. I suppose really it's a very, very, very, very crude Mellotron. There's a whole load of things we've done – some of them just down as sounds that work, others as base lines, tunes.'

But that won't be the next album: so far they've got two pieces – one a Roger Waters song, one a group piece – which they've been working on. 'We've taken them to France to road test them.' Those pieces will 'almost definitely be part of whatever we do next'.

A British tour is planned for November – planned in as much as the group want to do it, but with the attendant problems that they haven't yet found suitable places to play, nor even a suitable theatre in which to rehearse the show. Doubtless, these are problems which can be overcome, but perhaps one shouldn't bank on November; still, they are keen to work.

There are new 'tricks and jerks' for the presentation of *Dark Side of the Moon* in the offing for the tour too. What are they? 'Wouldn't really like to say – I suppose they'll be roughly along the lines of what we did in France, which was use a lot of back-projection films, but it's mostly ideas at the moment and I don't want to discuss them and then be very embarrassed to find that they don't exist.'

The French dates – five cities and then three shows in Paris – were the first gigs for a year. How did they go? 'I think very well, all things considered. It was a bit thrown together at the last minute for the usual reasons – not because we didn't know about it well beforehand, but because until it's close it doesn't seem very real.'

One rather less savoury feature of the tour – and God alone knows how they got involved – was that they agreed to help sell some brand of French bitter lemon in return for the bitter lemon people underwriting the tour, so they could keep the prices down. Sounds unlikely?

'It all sounded so sort of once-removed that in a fit of madness we all agreed that we'd do it – we thought we'd rip them off for loads of cash, when in fact, of course, that didn't happen, and it was us who lost. It just got so confused – we'd intended them to subsidize the tour so we could make the tickets cheaper, and in the end no one could work out whether the tickets were cheaper or not. It was all such an unnecessary complication.

'It was quite interesting in what it brought out, though – we expected much more aggravation, from people saying, "What the hell do you think you're doing?" than there in fact was, which was rather disappointing in a way because we'd got so worked up about it by then. We ended up giving all the money away to some French charity, which made it all the more confusing.'

This year has also seen the release – at long last – of the *Pompeii* film. Nick has the usual reservations about it: 'I don't think we perhaps took quite the interest in it that we should have done, although Adrian, the guy who made it, was quite interested in having us say what we thought about it all along. It's not bad, but I'm not entirely happy with it. With the interviews particularly, I think perhaps we should have got more involved in trying to really say something about what's happening and what we do as a group – something that would be interesting and would last.'

Why did it take so long to get to the cinemas (for once the slowness is nothing to do with the band)? 'God knows – I think it was because everyone thought rock and roll films were not very good news, but in fact it has turned out to be very good news.

'And then, you get this ridiculous thing of everyone ringing up saying, "Great, fantastic, it worked, let's do another one exactly the same, immediately." There really is this thing of when something is successful, people always want to do the same again as near as damn it – a different song or two, but essentially the same idea, the chaps playing.'

To which the inevitable Floyd reply is . . .

'How much?'

Treadmills on my mind (one of these days . . .)

Ever since I've known them, the Floyd have been saying that from now on they're not going to bash around, hurrying things: they're going to take their time and get it right.

Nick Mason, January 1971: 'I must admit it is slightly alarming, although it is what we've always said we've wanted.'

Dave Gilmour, May 1971: 'We don't seem to be worried about what other people would see as wasting time in the studio. We spent about a month in the studio in January, playing around with various ideas and recording them all. Then we went away to think about them. Now we are letting things take their natural pace.'

Those sessions became the *Meddle* album.

Roger Waters, December 1971: 'I think a mistake on our last two albums has been to bend to external pressures . . . to get the thing out. I think those tracks on *Meddle*, apart from "Echoes" and "One of These Days", turned out a bit weak because of it. But on the other hand it could be a mistake to try to make everything perfect . . . you're fighting a losing battle because you're never going to do it.

'When I go on the road I go into a kind of limbo – most of my mind stops working completely, because if it didn't I'd go crazy.

'There is a feeling in the group that we've let things slide horribly – and it's beginning to drive me crazy . . .

'There's this realization that one has, to a large extent, got hooked on a successful treadmill – you reach a point where you can't bear to turn the gigs down.

'Maybe it's something to do with age [*he was 28 at the time*] . . . When I was at school and all through college, I always looked upon my life as something that was about to start. It would be possible, if you got hooked on the next stage, and then the next, to live your whole life not really living it. I'm beginning to feel more and more that it is more and more important to really evaluate – as far as one can with the information available – what's going on and make the right decisions.

'We've got to step back from that career/money thing . . . take as little notice of those pressures as possible. And I think that will cause us to make better music.'

Rick Wright, June 1972: 'I just feel like I've been rushing around not knowing where I am – living in hotels, in planes, on American tours. It all got highly confusing.'

Nick Mason, October 1972: 'Whenever we finish an album, I always think it could have been better, but with things like *More* and *Obscured by Clouds*, I tend to think it's really not bad for the time – perhaps it's just there's more excuses . . .

'It's one of the annoying things in a way that the difference between something we've spent a week on and something that takes nine months isn't that great. I mean the thing that takes nine months isn't thirty-six times as good. Obviously, nine months doesn't mean nine months solid recording, but even so . . .

'It's true that we do get stale if we work too much. It's very simple really – if we work too hard then we all get very tired and we stop doing anything creative. We go into a sort of zombie, bash-it-out state which is really dangerous. It's the easiest way, possibly, of blowing up a band because the whole thing becomes pointless and you lose all interest in what you're doing.

'We try to work live as much as we can, and record, which takes so long, and so it gets really heavy to try to find long periods of time to write new things without rushing them. Like for *Dark Side of the Moon*, we did give ourselves a reasonable amount of time and it still wasn't long enough. We could always use more time.'

Meddle was released in November 1971. *Dark Side of the Moon* was first performed live in early 1972. They took it on the road first, and then recorded it. It was released in March 1973.

Roger Waters, May 1973, just before the Earl's Court show, in answer to a question about what he's been doing: 'I occasionally pick up a guitar and strum a few chords, or jot a few words down. But when I say occasionally, I mean occasionally. No, there aren't any concrete plans.'

It is now August 1974: there hasn't been an album since March last year, nor is one ready. Time, at last.

Nick Mason: 'Except that it's now too relaxed. We've found that working at our own pace gets so little done that we all get a bit frustrated. I certainly feel that as the sort of non-writer, because I can't retire to the studio and knock out a few songs. I think we all feel now that we'd like to have done more in the last . . . well, we're glad we checked it out, but I think that next year we're going to do a lot more work and struggle in a sense to meet deadlines.

'The thing is not to swing back madly, but to try to hit a balance, and the balance does lie somewhere in between the two. You've got to find out for yourself how much you want to work, and the only way is to stop, and then see if you want to go back working. Which we do.'

Bo Diddley with psychedelic squeaks

Peter Jenner saw The Pink Floyd Sound playing in devilishly amateur poverty at London's Marquee: they were a British R&B band with electronic squeakery built in – not, you might think, the obvious sort of thing to catch a potential manager's attention in June 1966. But Jenner wasn't a man to fall for the obvious.

Working as an assistant lecturer at the London School of Economics, he was also a disenchanted avant-garde jazz freak with a passion for Bo Diddley. He fancied managing a pop group, but knew nothing whatsoever about it . . .

The rest is well known in the annals of British psychedelia: the group became merely the Pink Floyd, pivoting at the time around the talents of singer, writer and guitarist Syd Barrett, had hit singles, appeared on *Top of the Pops*, and became one of the strongest symbols of the British – how you say – 'underground'. Jenner and Andrew King, as Blackhill Enterprises, managed them with a combination of flair, blind faith and extraordinary luck. The band produced the inspired album *Piper at the Gates of Dawn* – and hit the charts with singles like 'See Emily Play' and 'Arnold Layne'.

Alongside the Soft Machine, they became the focus of London underground events – stuff like the Alexandra Palace festival and their own 'Games For May' production at the Queen Elizabeth Hall – although they were less well received as they moved further away from London. This was after their chart success, when the audience were not stoned followers of London's answer to West Coast lunacy, but kids who'd seen them on the telly: their stage act – definitely not single material – was at odds with what was expected, and more often than not missiles were thrown. I remember seeing them at the bowling alley at Bedford – it must have been late 1967/early '68 – play an aggressive set to a cowed audience. They seemed to take a gloomy kind of pleasure in it: in the dressing-cupboard afterwards, Roger Waters made the grim comment: 'At least we frightened a few people tonight.'

But with their lights, their music and the company they kept, they were the first and only band – no, Arthur Brown perhaps – to achieve the twin status of darlings of the UFO club and hit singlers. It was a strange time.

Perhaps curiously, but quite logically when you think about it, Nick Mason says that they didn't really feel part of any drug-cultured social revolution: certainly they didn't feel that as much as they felt part of a new musical wave.

'I didn't know what the fuck was going on. Peter and Andrew and the kind of Joe Boyd figures that were around then were probably part of it in a way that I certainly wasn't. All four of us ... we were the band, that's all. Rather bizarre, sometimes very inward looking people who lived in a world of our own. There was no community spirit whatsoever; all we were interested in was our EMI recording contract, making a record, being a hit.

'At UFO we felt like the house band, and it was by far the nicest gig and it was what everyone asked about in interviews and so on, but I certainly wasn't into the lifestyle of the whole thing. I don't think I felt part of the new movement, because I was too busy being part of the new rock and roll movement, which was a different thing.'

A far out, electronic, freaky pop group ... in a way that was what they were, and certainly in the eyes of the radio-listening public that is what they became. But there was a great deal more to it than that, especially as the stresses and strains began to tell – particularly on Syd Barrett. The schizophrenic torture of being at the Roundhouse one day and at Shepherd's Bush for the BBC the next – and especially the hot/cold audience reaction – must have been appalling.

Nick: 'Obviously there was an amazing difference, but you just took it in your stride then. I think today I'd probably have a nervous breakdown ... but then it just seemed all part of your life.'

But whatever the reasons – and many of them are said to be of a chemical nature – Syd began to contribute less and less to the group. Dave Gilmour – a friend of Syd's from Cambridge – joined the group while they were recording *Saucerful of Secrets*.

'I didn't do much for a long time,' he explained later. 'I just sat there and played rhythm to help it all along. For a good six months – maybe more – I didn't do a single thing. I was pretty paranoid.

'I hadn't worked out how my playing would fit in and I wasn't at all confident of it in any way at all. It was mostly me and paranoia. I don't think they – the rest of the band – had fixed ideas of what I should do or any fixed ideas of how I should do it. I was more conscious of knowing I had something specific to do and thinking that I had something to follow. I guess I thought they had a more rigid idea of what they wanted me to do and be than they in fact had. I was frightened to stick my neck out and change what they were doing, 'cos the way I would naturally play guitar would obviously have changed it quite a lot.'

The change wasn't that sudden, or that unnatural. 'Even before I joined there was an attempt to do the big production thing. There was always the idea of having a really high-fidelity sound and putting on a fully produced show with quadraphonic sound. I mean, it was basically an audio idea then – lighting and effects came into it, but not so much as they do now.'

Syd left. He and Dave were in the band together for a couple of weeks. The changes for Pink Floyd were not so much musical – to my ears at least they followed a fairly natural path. It was their fortunes that changed. Peter Jenner admitted in *Zigzag*: 'If I'd known then what I know now, things would've been very different. The Floyd would have made a lot of money much sooner than they did, and I'd be a very rich man.'

Instead, the rich man is Steve O'Rourke, their new manager. In 1974, both the Floyd and Steve have earned a lot of money, and total album sales around the world now top ten million. It wasn't achieved without hard times and hard work.

When the four left Blackhill, they went to Brian Morrison for management. Steve O'Rourke worked for Morrison at the time, and when things didn't work out too well, he took over.

'It was a strange period,' says Nick Mason, 'with Syd leaving and us leaving Blackhill, and then us being on what was really a bit of a downhill slope. Dave was settling in ... I don't think that musically we were down. I think musically we started again, higher up, but there was the whole thing about our standing with Syd gone, and it all was ... fairly boring. Not much happened for six months – we were working quite a lot, but not really getting anywhere. We were working on *Saucer* and then what was really nice was we played the free concert in Hyde Park where we played *Saucer* and that was a lovely launch. It re-introduced us ... it was one of our lucky breaks.

'Then we went to America and started on all that business ...

which actually was another thing Brian Morrison did for us. Then Steve took over – and we never looked back.'

How long was it before they began to make money – really make money? 'I suppose it was about two years ago. We began to make it before then but we also started spending. Essentially the only way to make big money is by big hit records, so really I suppose it was *Dark Side of the Moon* – that made a real difference. The trouble is that we're now launching into yet another multi-million-dollar magnificence.

'But there's no way we could have done a whole lot of other things without *Dark Side of the Moon*. Everything else had sold OK, but it was the first big American seller – that's the real difference. There's also the extraordinary thing of *Dark Side of the Moon* doing a million, and then the others – like *Meddle* and *Ummagumma* – start catching up again.'

Writer bashing: the pack instinct

How did you get your name?

It isn't a question I've ever wanted to ask because ... well, actually I'm not very interested and anyway I read it somewhere when I was a mere stripling of a youth (even though I've since forgotten). Lucky really – people who ask that tend to arouse the basest instincts in the normally mild-mannered gentlemen of the Floyd.

Nick once talked about the psychology of group life – the way people behave in that situation: 'It's equivalent to families and various things I've never been in but I'd imagine would be similar – one being a small army unit and another a prep school.

'You can oscillate so easily between love and hate – real love and real hate. At one moment you can feel incredibly close to them, or to one of them, or you can hate them. It's never two against two either – it's always three against one. It really is amazing to watch sometimes. Jokes, and the way they become teasing, and bullying – that's what it gets down to.

'I think we've been lucky in that we've used our managers when there's been a lot of aggression, instead of always ganging up on each other. Steve can take a lot from us; we can be incredibly spiteful, and he can channel a lot of that from us without actually breaking and beating us around the head with clubs.'

To a lesser extent, dumb journalists perhaps perform the same function – the gang instinct certainly comes into play when someone makes the mistake of trying to interview the band together: they have a certain reputation for journalist-terrorizing. A question about the name or 'How would you describe your music?' can be like the scent of blood to a pack of dogs.

'I've been really ashamed of myself,' admits Nick, 'but unable to stop myself joining in. It's partly this thing of being with the band together – yes, the gang syndrome – but it definitely makes me behave in a way that I wouldn't normally do as an individual.'

Do they adopt defined roles? 'I'm an egger-onner: I sit there encouraging Roger or Dave to get in there.'

Who takes the lead? 'It depends what it's all about and it depends where we are. If it's a restaurant scene then Dave probably takes the golden biscuit for making trouble, if trouble is in the offing. But really it comes back to this old thing about being asked the same question all the time, which tends to happen when you've been at it for a couple of years.

'What really builds up these terrific scenes is when you get a reporter who doesn't really know when to drop it, and thinks that perhaps if he pressures it, he might get something important. So you get:

'How would you describe your music?'
'Grunt, don't wanna discuss it, grumble, grumble.'
'Well, sort of folk/jazz, or psychedelic jazz or the new classical music . . .'

'There's a whole range of questions interconnected with that, and we're off. But I think sometimes an interview can be a really good thing and it can help you to sort out things in your brain that perhaps you hadn't particularly thought about. Either that or a few good jokes.'

Pink Floyd

Still on the Press – is this narcissism, an unhealthy obsession with the trade? – how do they react to the things which are written about them? They've had their fair share of slags in the past, particularly from Barrett fanatics, also from people who enjoy a big target.

'It depends – if I'm with the band we all go, "Errh, remember 'is name ... bloody cheek, what does he know about music?" – but if I'm just reading it, I tend to think, Oh dear, wonder if he's right? I think I tend to worry about it more than the rest of the group. They're more hard-bitten probably.

'People always pay lip-service to the idea that if it's good criticism they don't mind, but it is true – I remember one occasion where everybody said they liked a show and one guy said it was pretty shabby, which was what we all felt as well. It was really nice to think that he was interested enough and knew us well enough to grade it – especially when you get to the point where people see you so rarely, particularly abroad, that as long as it more or less works it's OK.'

Over-praise is dismissed as easily as over-criticism then. But they do seem from the outside to be particularly impervious to attacks.

'That might be because we had our worst attacks during our first year of existence – attacks from the audience as well as everything else, which is the worst thing. I can't imagine how we got through that first year. I think that might have something to do with it.

'The other thing is that it's quite often patently obvious that these attacks are mounted by people who patently don't know what they're talking about – they praise things that are terrible and so on – and there's the thing of stirring up the readers' letters. Often they're based on this extraordinary thing of there's only one right way of making music; it's either "progressive" or it's "pop". You get articles opening, "In this era of pretentious music, how nice to get a fresh glitter-rock artist ..." and obviously vice versa.

'I remember this particularly related to my heroes of yesteryear, especially Cream: there was a thing where they were the golden group and then ... Well, it does seem to move in phases, really.

Cracking up

Stevie Wonder seems constantly to be going up and down, often quite unrelated to what he's actually turning out – to my ears anyway.'

Lunar dark side: great leap forward

The first album was recorded on a four-track machine, as was *Saucerful of Secrets* – both the original album version and the live version on *Ummagumma*; it wasn't until *Atom Heart Mother* that the Floyd had the luxury of eight tracks, and *Meddle* was the first on which they had sixteen.

Atom Heart really established the Pink Floyd as a band with not only the vision to create monster-scale rock music, but the technology – as always we hear the 'If only we'd spent more time' cries – yet *Ummagumma* remains *the* Floyd cultists' album. It's a curious state of affairs which does its best to puzzle the band. 'I never thought it was that good an album,' Dave Gilmour has said. 'I thought it was quite a nicely balanced little thing for live and the odd little bits of . . . ego-trips, whatever.'

Why the mystique? 'Beats me.'

We'll leave it at that; one man's meat chokes the vegetarian, don'tcha know. Everyone who cares, knows what he thinks about various Floyd musics, so let's leave the retrospectives. Except for *Dark Side of the Moon*, because in every sense that album has been A Milestone, A Turning Point, A Great Leap Forward – all that stuff.

There's the selling angle – we've done that. There's the artistic concept: after *Meddle*, Roger Waters expressed a desire to get away from the epic sound poems and 'come down to earth a bit, get a bit less involved with flights of fancy and get a bit more involved with what we as people are actually involved in'.

Perhaps just as important, it was a revolution in their technique: normally the band would record a piece – as much by trial and error as anything – and then learn it for the road. After playing it live for a while, they would begin to regret all the things they hadn't done in the studio. With *Dark Side*, they took it on the road first – for quite a while – and then took it to the studio. That way, they had a much clearer idea of the potential of the piece by the time they got as far as committing a note of it to record. For a band so renowned for their use of studio technology, it was quite a change.

At the distance of sixteen months since the release of *Dark Side*, Nick says: 'It was a huge jump forward in the organization of making an album. If we made it again today, I'm sure we'd do a better job, but all the right ingredients were there – i.e. the concept is clear and the songs ... the songs are all there. Probably Roger and Dave and Rick feel they could write better songs now, that's the feeling I get, but it's still a huge step forward in construction from our previous albums.

'I think also the message got across to quite a few people what it was about. Messages from rock and roll stars have to be – not exactly taken with a pinch of salt, but it is difficult telling people to watch out when you're sitting there making a million dollars and having a wonderful time. But it's not a hype. Roger, who did most of the writing, definitely means what he says in the words.'

And next time? Dave has been quoted as saying, 'Strategically, our best thing to do next would be something weird, far out that nobody could possibly understand.' Yes?

'We haven't had a tactical command meeting recently. That would suggest that the Household Objects album would have been the wittiest thing to do next, and it would have been if we could have knocked it out. But I think what we'll do is what we've always done in the past, which is to struggle away at whatever we've got and see how it comes out.'

An insular band, out on a funny limb

As a group, and to an extent as individuals, the Floyd have always seemed set apart from their contemporaries – a band with their own ideas of How It Should Be Done, however vague those ideas might seem when put into words, who work away on their own island producing Pink Floyd music which is ... not so much instantly recognizable, considering all their changes, but owing very little to contemporary fashion.

Dave Gilmour: 'Changes in fashion of playing and so on do affect us a little, but I guess we assimilate them quite well. I'm sure we do pick up on things and use them, plagiarize them – no, sorry, forge them into our own inimitable style.'

Would insular be a correct word? Nick Mason: 'Yes, I think that's quite a good word, and in fact I think it's rather a pity. We have allowed ourselves to be out on a funny limb of our own, and also not had too much contact ... Dave is a bit more involved with other bands, knows a few more people. I'd really like to do that more – just recently I've been thinking that – but I think for me it's partly paranoia.'

Did the insularity develop because of the kind of people they are, the style of music for which they were known? 'I think partly because of the kind of people we are, and also at the time we started doing solo concerts it was not the normal thing to do. Most of the musicians I know I got to know five years ago, when we used to share gigs with people. You'd all be on the road, and you'd turn up at some university and there would be Fairport Convention.

'The other day this was brought home to me fantastically strongly when a friend of mine was over from America and invited us over to tea, and it developed into a kind of soirée, and Richard Thompson was there, who I hadn't seen for five years or something. It was really nice to see him again ... but unless a similar thing happens, I probably won't see him for another five years.

'It's partly because one gets hung up for time, partly laziness I suppose, and partly all the other activities you get involved with. Also, I'm not a Speakeasy raver, which is the other place you come into contact with people.'

Have his production ventures, with Principal Edwards and more particularly with Robert Wyatt – listen incidentally for Robert's Mason-produced single, an incredible version of 'I'm a Believer', as well as the album – been conscious attempts to spread his wings a bit?

'No, not conscious. I was just delighted to have the chance – partly because you learn a lot and partly because it is nice to work outside group decisions. If it works out, everyone gains a lot from it.

'It's really good because everyone learns more about the trade.'

Nick Kent

Floyd juggernaut . . . the road to *Nineteen Eighty-Four*?

NME, 23 November 1974

On 14 November 1974, approximately seven thousand people washed their hair and travelled down to the Empire Pool, Wembley, to witness the Pink Floyd live. Almost everyone, that is, except Dave Gilmour – his hair looked filthy there on stage, seemingly anchored down by a surfeit of scalp grease and tapering off below the shoulders with a spectacular festooning of split ends.

Rather like Bill's locks, in fact.

Bill was sitting next to me throughout the concert y'see. Said he came from Hayward's Heath, Sussex – and well, anyway he *did* have something of the patent Gilmour style about him: stringy unwashed hair parted in the middle and furrowed behind the ears, an earnest complement of peach-fuzz masquerading as facial hair, plimsolls – the lot, in fact, even though his face lacked Gilmour's bully-boy well-formed features, substituting a kind of bleary-eyed doggedness which wrinkled up every time he took a blast off one of a constant series of 'cool jays'.

'Good stuff, this,' Bill muttered. 'We get it from this spade guy, down in Brighton. Straight off the boat it comes.'

Bill said he didn't go much on any other kinds of stimulant.

He also didn't like much music. Said it almost boastfully. Only a few albums. And the Floyd, of course. 'I've got a good stereo, mind. Big speakers.'

So what does he do with it?

'I'll tell you. I mean I like to get really, y'know *really* stoned – spaced, y'know, and I put on me Floyd . . . ah, *Meddle* or *Dark Side of the Moon* – that track "Great Gig in the Sky", and I'm laying there between the speakers really spaced, getting off on the stereo crossovers.'

Stereo crossovers?

'Yeah, y'know, when the sound goes from channel to channel. Phasing and that. Those are the bits I like best.'

Bill's girlfriend 'Jiff' thinks the Pink Floyd are the best group in the whole world. 'They're taking music to this whole new level. It's really . . .'

Cosmic?

'Yes, that's just what I was going to say.'

'One thing I've always taken into consideration, and which sums up, for me anyway, the fundamental personality crisis inherent in the old Floyd is that Syd was an artist and the other three were all student architects. I think that says an awful lot, particularly when you study the kind of music the Floyd have gone on to play since that time.'

That quote came courtesy of Peter Jenner, who confided the same to me some months ago. I'd almost forgotten it until about halfway through the Floyd's Wembley set, straight after the three new numbers had been performed.

At 7.55 p.m. I'd entered the Empire Pool toting healthy expectations for a thoroughly enjoyable evening of entertainment at the very least, already.

At 10.45 p.m. I left the same hall possibly more infuriated over what I'd just witnessed than I can ever remember being over any other similar event. Angry and rather depressed.

It was hell. But let's begin at the beginning.

At 8.20 p.m. or thereabouts the four members of Floyd saunter on stage. It is not a spectacular entrance. In fact they wander on rather like four navvies who've just finished their tea break and are about to return slowly to the task of tarring a section of main road.

After approximately five minutes of slightly laboured tuning up, the band start their first number of the set – a new composition entitled 'Shine On You Crazy Diamond'. It is very slow, rather low on melodic inventiveness, each note hanging in that archetypally ominous stunted fashion that tends to typify the Floyd at their most uninspired. The song itself is duly revealed to be of very slight mettle: the chords used are dull, as is the pace.

The song distinctly lacks 'form'. And then there are the lyrics.

'Come on you raver, you seer of visions / Come on you painter, you piper, you prophet, and shine,' sings Roger Waters at one point, his voice mottled by a slightly squeamish, self-consciousness of timbre, not to mention the fact that he also appears at this point to be somewhat flat. The lyrics are not very good, you see. Pretty much like sixth-form poetry – prissy, self-conscious and pretentious.

'You were caught in the crossfire of childhood and stardom / Blown on the steel breeze / Come on, you target for far-away laughter / Come on you stranger, you legend, you martyr and shine.'

The song is for and about Syd Barrett. He could have deserved better.

This thoroughly unimpressive beginning is duly followed by the second of the three new numbers to be showcased in this section. 'Raving and Drooling' is motivated by a rhythm somewhat akin to that of the human heartbeat with further references gathered from numerous Floyd stylized devices.

Wright drags some suitably Moog-orientated 'primal screams' from one of a mighty arsenal of keyboard instruments, Waters manipulates a stolid, simplistic bass-pattern, Mason plays one of the two or three standard rhythms he habitually employs – usually incorporating much emphasis on the tom-toms and cymbals – while Gilmour blithely chunks out a 'One Of These Days' rhythm stab on his guitar.

The song is again of incredibly minor import, Waters doing his whole 'Careful With That Axe, Eugene' tormented horse-faced routine – 'Raving and drooling I fell on his neck with a scream / He had a whole lotta terminal shock in his eyes / That's what you get for pretending the rest are not real,' etc., etc.

Pretty undistinguished stuff except for the fact that yours truly noted that the first line was wrenched out in much the same way that Barrett sung 'Wolfpack' on his second solo album. Otherwise, more identikit Floyd bereft of any real originality or inspired conceptualized *connaissance*.

So then there was 'Gotta Be Crazy', the magnum opus of this dubious triumvirate for which Waters had regurgitated the old *Dark Side of the Moon* study of society-and-its-destructive-pressures gruel to even more facile conclusions.

One could of course begin by pointing out that the song features a fairly decent melody – a fetching minor chord progression strummed out by Gilmour who also sings Waters' lyrics – 'You gotta be crazy, you gotta be mean / You gotta keep your kids and your car clean / You gotta keep climbing, you gotta keep fit / You got to keep smiling, you gotta eat shit!'

Boy, what an indictment on the whole bourgeois high-pressured schism of our time!

But then again, who better than the Floyd to commandeer such a grievous lambasting of the aforestated lifestyle when after all I can't think of another rock group who live a more desperately bourgeois existence in the privacy of their own homes.

And whaddyamean, people in glass houses shouldn't throw stones ... Waters hasn't even begun yet! I mean, here he is concluding this mighty epic with a potent line of bland psychological causes for his hapless victim's doomed condition – 'Who was born in a house full of pain / Who was sent out to play on his own' – when only a few verses prior to this he avidly gloats over the poor bastard's decline and fall – 'And when you lose control, you'll reap the harvest you have sown ... So have a good drown and you go down alone.'

There's obviously something here that doesn't, how you say, *correlate*. Not to mention a very perverse sense of morality at work.

So there are the lyrics – which I personally find quite offensive – and I still haven't mentioned the song's musical construction beyond that pleasing opening strum section which I forgot to mention sounded like the kind of chord structure the old Wyatt–Hopper–Ratledge Soft Machine used to do wonders with way back when.

Unfortunately, the Floyd, as always, let the song sprawl out to last twice as long as it should, summoning the aid of some of the most laboured bouts of aural padding imaginable. I mean, the very least one would expect from a song like this would be a tight, incisive structure, but then again incisiveness has never been something the post-Syd Floyd have prided themselves on, and so one has to wade through laboured sections of indolent musical driftwood before, lo, the plot is resumed and one is sent careering back to our Roger's bloated denunciation:

'Gotta be sure, you gotta be quick / Gotta divide the tame from the sick / Gotta keep some of us docile and fit / You gotta keep everyone buying this shit.'

'Buying this shit'???

Explain, Mr Waters, if you please. The song ends, as I stated earlier on, with a mildly potent '*J'accuse*' blast of postured psychological cause-and-effect ranting, leaving the audience with a twenty-minute interval in order to gather themselves for a further assault.

The second half is, of course, taken up by the whole *Dark Side of the Moon* presentation. Visuals for the new numbers had been muted to a minimum: two sets of spotlights tastefully flanking the stage throughout, while three mirror-balls were put into operation during 'Raving and Drooling'. But *Dark Side* was to be graced by the projection of a special film made as a visual complement to the music.

Again the Floyd light into the first section of the effort. More assured . . . but God, they look and sound so uninspired.

Wright's solo Moog doodling signals the first reel of the film being unleashed on the audience – random shots of a plane taking off, viewed from the cockpit, a garish cartoon segment of touchdown on an alien planet ending with a section of total incendiary destruction.

S'all right, mind you. Very obvious and that, but it keeps you engaged if not enthralled. It's only when you're informed by an intimate of the Floyd's entourage that the likes of Lindsay Anderson

85

and Nicholas Roeg – i.e., the best film directors in the country – were at the outset interested in helping out on the film until they actually came up against the Floyd and immediately made their excuses in order to opt out that it all starts to fall into perspective again.

It's also around this time that you start realizing how incredibly *limited* the band seem to be as musicians. As a rhythm section, Mason and Waters are perhaps the dullest I've ever witnessed filling a large auditorium, the former going through his tedious tricks most of the time, and falling apart at those unscripted junctures when the band are forced to involve themselves in attempts at spontaneity (these junctures of course are very few and far between, due to the situation of the whole show being moulded around the constrictive dictates of the visual presentation which depends ultimately on stop-gap timing).

Waters is not a very imaginative bass player, and doesn't improve things by incorporating a tone akin to the dull atonal thud one gets when hitting the strings of a piano with a rubber hammer.

Rick Wright is merely an adequate keyboard player, and always seems uncomfortable when forced to take action (at one point he attempted some gospel-tinged pianistics to complement the fine performance of Vanetta Fields and Carlena Williams' 'Great Gig in the Sky' segment and muffed it badly).

This weakness creates numerous watersheds in the music which just scream for some inspired interjection, whether in the form of a Ratledge-styled piece of inspired doodling or even one of those quasi-Herbie Hancock soft-jazz flurries which every young dolt in an up-and-coming progressive unit seems perfectly adept at pulling off these days.

Wright really hasn't improved that much since the old Floyd days; only the arsenal of keyboards has been added to.

Finally there's Gilmour – who, although an adequate guitarist, projects little personality into his playing, well doused as his solos are in the blues guitar school traditions.

Here again a lack of inspiration fails to perceive vast holes in the music which could so easily be cemented in by some tasteful rhythm work or a short, tight solo such as he is capable of.

So anyway the Floyd battle on with their films (more obvious footage of currency for 'Money' plus some shots of 'political leaders' for 'Brain Damage' – is this a political statement, boys?) and their tapes and their perfect PA system, and the audience are loving it.

Those still awake, that is. Our Mr Erskine was being flanked by somnambulant corpses on his side of the fence while I noticed a few bedraggled-looking souls dozing off in my corner.

Even our old mate Bill – remember him? – was rendered inert for some ten minutes until the applause for 'Money' brought him around.

Finally the *Moon* set is completed and the band walk off to ecstatic applause. They eventually return for an encore – no 'thank-yous' or anything ... I mean that would be just too much to ask, now wouldn't it – and the band do 'Echoes'.

Visuals are now relegated to luminous green orbs of circular light projected on the big screen (they never seem to really be spinning properly), while towards the end the band's ankles are engulfed in – wait for it – 'dry ice'.

The above constituted what could easily be the most boring concert I've ever been forced to sit through for review purposes. Mind you, the Floyds themselves were reportedly none too enamoured by the event either: apparently there was a nasty fight between the band after the set which culminated in a sound man being sacked and some guy from Island Studios being brought in at short notice to replace him.

Having been informed of this, we decided to curb the venom long enough to give the band a second chance and go back on the Friday night. This time the sound had indeed improved beyond all recognition and the first half went pretty smoothly until there arose some 'contretemps' betwixt Roger Waters at his most morose and someone who dared yell out 'Get on with it!' during yet more laboured tuning up in order to preface 'Gotta Be Crazy'.

Pink Floyd

'We're going as fast as we can,' muttered Waters derisively, sounding amazed that this young upstart actually dare criticize them.

If that weren't bad enough, someone yelped out, of all things, '1967,' straight afterwards.

This was too much for Waters. 'It's not 1967, it's 1974,' he snapped back.

Anyway, Friday's show still pinpointed how poor the band are at jamming or really sustaining either drama or dramatics, flailing around to little avail in their attempts to pad out what are at the best of times minor works. And the band's musicianship was, as before, questionably mediocre.

OK, boys, now this is really going to hurt.

What the two Floyd shows I witnessed on Thursday and Friday amounted to in the final analysis was not merely a kind of utterly morose laziness which is ultimately even more obnoxious than callow superstar 'flash', but a pallid excuse for creative music which comes dangerously close to the Orwellian mean for a facile, soulless music that would doubtless rule the airwaves and moreover be touted as fine art in the latter's vision of *Nineteen Eighty-Four*.

David Bowie, on his *Diamond Dogs*, unwittingly (as far as I can see, anyway) hit upon something which totally invalidates the rest of his similarly facile theorizing on a computerized cruel future planet when he plays, of all things, 'Rebel Rebel'.

'Rebel Rebel', you see, is the ultimate identikit diluted series of computerized rock gestures – the mechanical Stones riff, the brainless lyrics – real *Nineteen Eighty-Four* rock. The Pink Floyd are even closer to that, though. Over the last few years the band have in fact come to establish themselves as the total antithesis of what they started out representing: the whole Brave New World school of rock musicianship which broke loose back in '66–'67 and brought about real masterpieces like 'Eight Miles High', *Revolver* and *Piper at the Gates of Dawn.*

The Floyd in fact now seem so incredibly tired and seemingly bereft of true creative ideas one wonders if they really care about their music at all any more.

Cracking up

I mean, one can easily envisage a Floyd concert in the future consisting of the band simply wandering on stage, setting all their tapes into action, putting their instruments on remote control and then walking off behind the amps in order to talk about football or play billiards.

I'd almost prefer to see them do that. At least it would be honest.

Still, the Floyd can content themselves on one score. They are definitely the quintessential English band. No other combine quite sums up the rampant sense of doomed mediocrity inherent in this country's current outlook right now. 'Hanging on in quiet desperation is the English way.' Just delete 'quiet desperation' (Thoreau, for one, will be pleased) and choose your own depreciative little phrase as an amendment and we've got it all pigeonholed very nicely, thank you, squire. And there's absolutely nothing 'cosmic' about any of it, really, now is there?

[The second half of this feature, an iterview with Dave Gilmour by Pete Erskine, has been omitted to avoid repetition in the following piece.]

Pete Erskine

Dirty hair denied

NME, 11 January 1975

'Hi, Dave, have you washed your hair?'

'No.' Gilmour flashes a thin-lipped grin as he takes his seat. 'And if *he* can find any split ends in here (lifting clump of hair) then ...'

'Then *what*, DAVE?'

But he's already scanning the menu and doesn't hear. His free hand, however, is worrying over a plastic teaspoon. Unconsciously, he gradually crushes it, letting the pieces slip through his fingers and fall onto the tabletop. Gilmour is nothing if not self-controlled. Placid, even. But not quite.

His anger is of the sullen, smouldering variety and yet the weird thing is that even during such moments he'll often make way for a broad smile which can be utterly disarming because it might, just *might*, be a harbinger of doom, the herald for a personal close-up of one of the robust Gilmour flails. Although I can't imagine it ever happening.

He is angry, though. He told me so on the phone a couple of minutes after he'd read the piece.

'I've just read the piece,' he said, 'and I'm *very* angry about it.'

The 'piece' in question – an action replay for those who missed it – appeared in the 23/11/74 *NME* issue, written by myself and Mr Kent in direct response to our witnessing of the Floyd on the first two nights of their four-day residency at Wembley. I'm afraid we were a little rude about them.

Mr Kent wrote an extended review-cum-critique, and I, through the back door, managed to secure an audience with Gilmour in which I confronted him with the accusations to be aired in the piece. The overall intention, see, had been, in the words of the introductory blurb, 'to get the Floyd back into perspective', a sentiment which Gilmour himself says he thoroughly condones. It was the *approach* that riled him.

Ultimately the phone call resulted in myself inviting Gilmour for lunch – partly as a placatory gesture, partly to prove that Kent and myself could, and would, stand by what'd been written and mainly because a re-match might prove to be interesting.

The axis of the criticism in the piece lay upon the fact (self-confessed by Gilmour) that on two consecutive nights the Pink Floyd made music of such low quality that it cast rather anvil-like aspersions on (*a*) their motivations (*b*) their overall musicianship (*c*) the feeling engendered by them in their audiences (both short and long term) and admirers – one of whom, *Sunday Times* critic Derek Jewell, pulled out some florid prose in an appraisal of the début Thursday night gig (described subsequently by Gilmour as 'probably the worst we've done on the whole tour').

Jewell wrote: 'Richly they merit their place among the symphonic overlords of today's popular hierarchy ... they reeled off, apparently effortlessly, a performance with musical textures so ravishing and visual accompaniment so surprising that, for once, the thunderous standing ovation was completely justified.'

Such bland acceptance irritates the band, says Gilmour, equally, if not more so than its denigrators.

'I don't think anyone on our level feels deserving of that kind of superhuman adulation number,' he claims, hacking at a piece of steak. 'But then a lot of them probably dig it. Sure, I'm cynical of our position. I don't think we deserve it. But I'm no more cynical of our position than I am of anyone else's on our level. I mean ... to try and maintain your perspective on what you are is totally different.'

The lyrics of 'Gotta Be Crazy' – as Nick Kent pointed out – reveal a very great deal of cynicism, particularly the line 'Gotta keep people buying this shit', which is tantamount to a sneer at the audience.

'Mmm. Yeah. It is possibly a sneer ... but not at the audience as a whole, but at the type of adulation bands like us get. I mean I think there is something wrong with that ... people needing hero-figures like that, thinking that rock musicians have all the answers.'

But don't you think that while not really being responsible for that element, the fact that it hasn't been challenged means that bands like the Floyd, through neglect, are helping compound it?

'Yes. Probably. But I think we're less guilty than most. I mean, we've made conscious attempts at fighting it.'

Such as?

'In things we've said in interviews and things like that. We've always said that we don't believe in that whole number, but it's very hard to get away from the image people put on you.'

How large a proportion of record buyers and concert goers buy music papers though? A question I did in fact neglect to add. Still seems a bit lame, though, eh? One would've thought that a couple of really finely honed satires would at least help ... but then, really, how concerned are bands about these kind of things? Motives-schmotives. It helps sell records. And you don't gnaw the digits that feed you.

Anyway, we're messing around here. To the specifics. Gilmour is raking through the apposite issue as he eats. He's inclined towards the John Peel reaction (thinly disguised in his mildly self-congratulatory 'Diary of the Domestic' unfolded each week in *Sounds*) that the piece was 'hysterical', overly personal and laced with supposed inaccuracies.

The first eleven of Kent's opening paragraphs make Gilmour particularly mad. He claims that description of his personal appearance and that of a member of the audience (and his attitudes) is totally superfluous ...

'I don't see any of it being in any way relevant,' says Gilmour in that sullen/placid tone of voice that could be either. Or both. 'So there's a guy like that in the audience. So what? There were probably others like him, but you find people like that at *any* concert – but then Kent probably *set out* to find one and he did.'

I assure him that our approach was in no way premeditated. There was no question of a pre-planned axe-job on *anyone's* part.

'Well, I just don't believe it of Nick Kent. I really don't. He's still involved with Syd Barrett and the whole 1967 thing. I don't even know if he ever saw the Floyd with Syd.

'He goes on about Syd too much and yet, as far as I can see, there's no relevance in talking about Syd in reviewing one of our concerts.'

But one of the new songs is about him.

'Yes, but that's all. In the beginning the songs were all his and they were brilliant. No one disputes that. But I don't think the actual sound of the whole band stems from Syd. I think it stems just as much from Rick. I mean, Syd's thing was short songs.'

As for hair-washing. Well, the subject got short shrift. I think, though, that dressing especially for a gig is something that Gilmour subconsciously associates with 'showbusiness' – about which more later. Meanwhile, in subsequent conversation with Carlena Williams, one of The Blackberries, the two black back-up chicks they hired for the tour, Carlena expressed delight at the opening paras.

'Sheeut!' she observed daintily. 'When Ah saw that bit about Dave's hair, Ah jus' cracked up. Ah had t'read it y'know?'

Back to Syd.

'The band just before Syd departed had got into a totally impossible situation. No one wanted to book them. After the success of the summer of '67 the band sank like a stone; the gigs they were doing at the time were all empty because they were so bad. The only way out was to get rid of Syd, so they asked me to join and got rid of Syd . . .'

This, by the way, is also Gilmour's comeback to my assertion that: 'It's almost as if the Floyd, having loafed about half-seriously as the Architectural Abdabs [sic], garnered their persona from Barrett and, when he dropped out, for want of anything better to do, clung on to the momentum he provided.'

Says Gilmour: 'By the time Syd left the ball had definitely stopped rolling. We had to start it all over again. *Saucerful of Secrets*, the first album without him, was the start back on the road to some kind of return. It was the album we began building from. The whole conception of *Saucerful of Secrets* has nothing to do with what Syd believed in or liked. We continued playing some of his songs because none of us was getting good enough material fast enough to be able to do without them.

'Which also, therefore, meant that I had to fit in with his style to an extent because his songs were so rigidly structured around it.

'Oh, and by the way, the band, when I joined, never ever said, "Play like Syd Barrett." That was the very last thing they wanted!'

This had been part of a quote I'd happened across while writing up the original interview. It came courtesy of former Floyd manager Pete Jenner. It had appeared as part of M. Kent's epic Syd Barrett piece last March and, to my knowledge, hadn't been contested then. I presumed it to be accurate.

Another part of the same quote had claimed that Syd's guitar technique of using slide and echo boxes was of his own invention. My quote had been 'the familiar slide and echo boxes were purely of Syd's invention' which, in retrospect, was, perhaps, a bit strong. Gilmour, anyway, hotly denies this.

'Why didn't you ask me about things like that during the interview?' he asks, righteously indignant. 'The facts of the matter are that *I* was using an echo box *years* before Syd was. I also used slide. I *also taught* Syd quite a lot about guitar. I mean, people saying that I pinched his style, when our backgrounds are so similar . . . yet we spent a lot of time together as teenagers listening to the same music. Our influences are probably pretty much the same – *and* I was a couple of streets ahead of him at the time and was teaching him to play Stones riffs every lunchtime for a year at technical college. That kind of thing's bound to get my back up – especially if you don't check it.

'I don't want to go into print saying that I taught Syd Barrett everything he knows, 'cos it's patently untrue, but there are one or two things in Syd's style that I know came from me.'

In the original, I had prefaced these suggestions by intimating that as a guitarist Gilmour appears to lack any immediately identifiable personality. The word I used was 'malleable'. He says he actually feels that such a word applied to his style(s) is a compliment. Most guitarists, he claims, are pretty narrow minded, restricting their possible range of operations. In that case, he could be accused of spreading himself too thinly – i.e., capable of most things, but not particularly outstanding at any one thing. Or is that the way he's intended it?

'No. But I work within my limitations. But then, whether I'm a good or bad guitarist isn't really relevant. I mean, I try my damnedest to do my best, although certainly for the first half of that tour I was, well – rusty. I hadn't played for a long time and my fingers were really stiff. But also I would say that I got very good by the time we were halfway through.'

And the accusation that from where you all stand it's impossible for you to relate any more to the thoughts of the average punter?

'If you're referring to that bit which says something about our "desperately bourgeois existences"...

'Well. I mean, how do you or he know how we live our lives? Apart from you – marginally – about me? Do you? Does Nick? He hasn't been to any of our houses. He's got absolutely no idea of how I spend my life apart from what you might have told him – and *you* don't know how the others live. Do *you* think my life is so desperately bourgeois?

'My house is not particularly grand. Have you seen Roger's house? He lives in a five grand terraced house in Islington. So I really can't see how Kent can sit there and say things like that. He's no idea of what he's talking about.'

He does admit to a kind of laziness in the band, though. He's also realistic about their individual instrumental prowess.

'In terms of musical virtuosity we're not really anywhere I think; individual musicianship is well below par.'

And no, they're not 'bereft of ideas' – just resting. And worrying about a follow-up to *Dark Side* which has, he claims, 'trapped us creatively'. In passing, he says the lyrics are obvious *intentionally*.

'We tried to make them as simple and direct as possible and yet, as we were writing them, we knew they'd be misunderstood. We still get people coming up to us who think that "Money – it's a gas" is a direct and literal statement that "we like money".'

The point – a good one I thought – about the appeal of Floyd (and similar bands) being in some way associated with the rapid sophistication in stereo equipment is tossed out entirely.

'Six years ago,' says Gilmour impatiently, 'we still sold albums and yet hardly anyone in this country had a stereo. It was all Dansettes then . . .'

And yet, from casual random sampling of friends with Floyd albums, invariably the first thing said is, 'Oh, such and such track sounds great on my stereo.' Surely this is a case of packaging to some extent taking priority over contents?

'No. That's ridiculous. I suppose the same criticism would then apply to Stevie Wonder records?'

Well, as it happens . . .

To Kent's rather brilliant summing-up.

'Personally,' Gilmour states stoically, 'I don't believe any of that rubbish about *Nineteen Eighty-Four*.'

I really do.

'But I mean what difference is there between our sort of music and anyone else's, apart from the fact that maybe most of the other bands just play music for the body? And they're hardly progressive at all. Not that I think we're wildly progressive either.'

But at its worst, a stage show like the Floyd's only dulls an audience's sensibilities even to the extent of sending them to sleep. Nothing is left for them to project their imagination into – it's the difference between the holding power of a radio play and a TV play. And in any case, how does it feel to be part of a show where the audience doesn't even give you a ripple for a good solo, yet applauds a bucket of dry ice every time?

'Yeah. That's all part of the dramatic effect, isn't it?'

And *that's* a lame comeback.

'We went through a period where we blew out our entire light show for two years and there was no real difference. I personally know for a fact that it wouldn't make any difference if we did it again. We've never been hyped. There's been no great publicity campaign. It's built up purely on the strength of gigs.'

'I don't think we're remotely close to that thing about tapes, do you?'

On the strength of the Wembley things, yes. You looked bored and dispirited.

'Not bored. Definitely dispirited. It gets very depressing when you're fighting against odds like dud equipment. Energy soon flags. We weren't pleased to do an encore because we didn't deserve it.'

Why didn't they say so, then? You know, don the olde showbiz Batcape?

'I'm not interested in disguising my feelings on stage with showbiz devices. I've seen hundreds of bands do that. Does anybody respect them? From what he writes, Nick Kent seems to believe in it all – the old idea of The Show Must Go On, Never Let The Public See Your Feelings and things like that.'

Wouldn't the discipline of forcing *just a little* of that attitude on yourselves help in situations like that?

'No. When I'm standing there I'm conscious of trying to give the most I can,' sez Gilmour emphatically. 'And I don't need to have clean hair for that.'

John Rowntree

Wish You Were Here

Records and Recording, November 1975

Depending on your age and your head, the music of the Pink Floyd will probably be etched deep into your just-post-adolescent consciousness. After *Ummagumma* the band vacillated: *Atom Heart Mother* was too full of gratuitous effects to count for much; *Meddle* seemed full of 'Echoes'; and, despite their concerts, the odd soundtrack album seemed to confuse the band's direction. *Dark Side of the Moon* proved the major recovery point – at the risk of pulling their heads far out of conventional rock into classical muzak, the Floyd concentrated on what they could do best – arranging and the technical side of recording. On this album came 'Money', a no-holds-barred motherfuckers-to-the-wall rocker that turned many a cynical head.

By extension they came to *Wish You Were Here,* undoubtedly their best album since *Ummagumma,* crammed with beautiful and surprising things. As ever, form easily outstrips content: the kernel of 'Shine On You Crazy Diamond' is a neat little exhortation to a lost colleague (Syd Barrett), on most other albums a three-minute filler. Preface with a hugely atmospheric jam, eating up a spectrum anywhere from David Bedford to Savoy Brown, add a scary little laugh after the first line of the lyric and you have a concept that dominates the album – around a quarter of an hour to begin with and another ten minutes at the end.

Another such device, on paper painfully obvious, translates Roy Harper's guest vocal on 'Have A Cigar' via the effect of tuning across a radio waveband to a sinister acoustic rendition of the title track. The use of extended saxophone solo against a Moog backdrop and much simple exploitation of the lead electric guitar as pure sound confirm experiments attempted on *Dark Side of the Moon.*

Cracking up

Wish You Were Here gives no clues as to where rock is going in the future; but then it did take about two hundred years before they ran out of ideas for symphonies.

Andy Leslie

Origin of Species

The Amazing Pudding, January 1984

Many musicians feel the best way to discover the strengths and weaknesses of new material is to go out and play it live for a while. To some extent the Floyd have enacted this policy; there are notable exceptions, of course, but plenty of examples that fit the rule.

Generally, one tour was allowed, but occasionally it was longer. Two tracks from *Animals*, 'Dogs' and 'Sheep' – originally called 'You Gotta Be Crazy' and 'Raving and Drooling', respectively – were played live almost three years before release.

Such activities are open invitations to bootleggers, thus it is possible to trace the development of these tracks over the years, which is (hopefully) what this article does.

The songs received their first exposure in July and August of 1974 on a short French tour and later, in the winter of the same year, on a British tour. Another new song, 'Shine On You Crazy Diamond', was given its first airing at the same time; at this stage the intention was to make the new LP from these three tracks. I shan't mention 'Shine On' any further in order to leave some space in this fanzine for the other articles!

In order to trace the evolution of 'Raving and Drooling' and 'You Gotta Be Crazy', it is easiest to concentrate on the lyrics, as these give an insight into both the writing process and the final songs.

'Raving and Drooling', in its original form, has fewer words than in later versions and most are fairly unspecific. Two lines ('He will zigzag his way back through / Memories of boredom and pain') got axed later and re-written into 'Pigs on the Wing'; ironic, as Gilmour later said: 'Roger ... is also accusing himself of all those [animalistic] qualities ...'

The music, at this stage, is structurally similar to the LP but very different in arrangement. It lacks the keyboard introduction, and the first verse takes it to the instrumental break, which goes on far too long without anything happening. It does include a quiet passage which was later to become the "prayer" section, but it is without vocal. A short second verse comes in where you'd expect – where the LP says 'Bleating and babbling . . .'. The lyrics were to remain essentially the same throughout the pre-album period.

'You Gotta Be Crazy' was more removed from its final version, bearing only a slight musical or lyrical resemblance to 'Dogs'. Generally, on these tours, the track is unenjoyable to listen to: messy and rushed, with the vocal garbled to incomprehensibility. Some lyrics were to be dropped almost immediately . . .

They gotta get you started early
Processed by the time you're thirty
Work like fuck till you're sixty-five
And then your time's your own till you die

. . . and not a moment too soon. Gilmour handles the vocal for the bulk of the track and sounds frankly fuddled by the speed of it all. Annoyingly, after the lyric has been hurtled through as far as the penultimate verse, it then slows down and lumbers to the extended final passage at an excruciating pace; the last verse is agonizing.

Significant quotes from the group indicate a certain dissatisfaction with the song: Gilmour said the songs were 'hurriedly knocked into shape' for the tours. Never a truer word . . .

A few bootlegs have surfaced from this tour. *Circus Days*, listed as *Europe '74* in the discographies, contains nearly complete versions of both tracks, and enables the inexperienced listener to have a really bad time seeing just how hurriedly these tracks were knocked into shape. Another – probably the best-known Floyd bootleg – is taken from the concert at Stoke on 19 November: *British Winter Tour '74*, which originally came in a nice full colour sleeve. Both tracks are included and, while essentially the same, are slightly more together and coherent. 'They're tons better now than we had them on the French tour,' said Gilmour. Hmm ... I suppose they're listenable!

With the UK tour completed, the band were free of live dates until April '75. During this lull, they lined up studio time, at which point it was decided to abandon or at least postpone the recording of 'Raving and Drooling' and 'You Gotta Be Crazy'. This would enable the Floyd to devote the whole of the new LP to the themes already present in 'Shine On'.

However, a tour was lined up, and one has to have songs to play, so both of the tunes – luckily for this article – remained in the live set. To be fair, they were still viewed as an ongoing, if delayed, project; Waters, after the release of *Wish You Were Here*, said: 'I think we'll record those ... in the next few months.'

For now, the schedule for the band was solid right through to mid-July: two North American tours, ending on 28 June, split by a block of recording in May and early June. These sessions needn't concern us here – as far as I can tell, the whole emphasis was on what was to become *Wish You Were Here*.

Although 'Raving and Drooling' and 'You Gotta Be Crazy' no longer figured in recording plans, they had previously had a considerable amount of work done on them in the studio. Both songs had calmed down, played with a heavily phased guitar, yet bright and mellow. The lyrics to 'Raving and Drooling' were OK in '74 and were left largely unchanged. The structure too was little different, but changes in the arrangement were considerable and made for a big improvement.

'You Gotta Be Crazy' had been the subject of a lot more work – the lyrics were certainly in need of it. The music was equally lacking; previously it bludgeoned and raced through at a breakneck and fairly uniform pace. A considerable amount of rearranging had come up with a decent song: the drums now came in after the first verse, but more importantly the verses had been slowed down and the pace broken to inject some melody. The final passage was shortened and enlivened, the injection of pace giving the power and anger it should have, rather than the mournful quality of previous versions: it makes for a fitting and evocative end to the track.

Bootlegs to emerge from these tours include the double LPs *Pigs, Wishes and Moons* (Boston, 18 June) and *Ivor Wynne* (Ontario, 28 June), both of which include complete versions of both tracks and are excellent quality.

The Knebworth festival in July '75 saw 'Raving and Drooling' and 'You Gotta Be Crazy' dropped from even live performances as *Wish You Were Here* was now complete. The intention was still to record them, but not 'in the next few months'. In fact, 1976 was a year of less than feverish Floyd activity – no gigs at all, although at some stage *Animals* was recorded for release in January 1977.

But, as things stood in 1975/76, there was still no anthropomorphic concept . . .

Waters: 'It wasn't until we were recording those pieces it occurred to me that they could be cobbled together under the title *Animals*.'

Gilmour: '*Animals* started with those two numbers which we wrote, and Roger had another song, which had a different title, but was about pigs. And having written "Pigs", he then looked again at "Raving and Drooling" and "You Gotta Be Crazy", realized how close they were to an animal concept and then, having already recorded most of "Dogs" and "Raving and Drooling", changed the lyrics slightly here and there, and tailored it more. We then did some extra bits of effects and stuff to change it all into that concept . . .'

And that's really the end of the story . . .

The two songs were worked on some more in the studio, but under a better atmosphere than the gloom of '75. 'It was a joyful album to make,' said Gilmour.

An important addition to 'Raving and Drooling' was the Floyd's real go at religion: 'I have looked over Jordan and I have seen / Things are not what they seem.' I'm not sure of the original sources, but 'Swing Low, Sweet Chariot' says (roughly): 'I have looked over Jordan and I have seen / A host of angels coming for to carry me home.' Work that one out for yourselves! Add the 'prayer' section and the song blames religion for a large part in the pacifying of people, making them sheep. 'The Lord is my shepherd' is a neat choice!

I don't think anyone would disagree that it is a better LP for waiting and gaining a thread. I would rather have things as they are on the LP than 'Raving and Drooling', 'You Gotta Be Crazy' and 'Shine On You Crazy Diamond' *circa* '75.

A short story by Johnny the Fox

Animal yarn

Record Mirror, 29 January 1977

They have, we are led to believe, been working on this project for most of the past year. Speculation as to the content and eventual arrival date has been rife since the autumn.

Then last week the world's Press and his wife were invited to Battersea Power Station for a preview (Why Battersea? Well, friends, its tall chimneys, plus a large inflatable pig, will feature on the album's cover).

The playback started and the furtive scribes commenced note-taking. 'We can't have this,' sneered the man from Harvest. 'We don't want them to review it on just one listen. Go and tell everyone to desist at once.' The sheepish scribes obeyed the dog's order and the music played on.

After a chicken meal, the album was played again. 'No note-taking again if you don't mind, gentlemen,' grinned the big dog, now walking on two feet and sporting a string of medals across his chest. A raucous laugh from the rafters over-awed the music. The sheep looked up and at each other, mouths open; the dogs strutted about and showed their teeth.

All agreed it had been a pleasurable evening. The grazing had been particularly good and the assembled sheep were now bleating to one another. 'It's a Dave Gilmour album,' mused a woolly wonder from the Moors. 'OK – as the second album in a double set,' assured a bespectacled ram and the adoring ewes shook their fuzzy heads, bleated and went off into the night, telling themselves over and over that what the EXPERTS had said was right.

As I was leaving, a leather-clad dog caught me by the scruff of the neck. 'You want another listen? It can be arranged. Come up to HEADQUARTERS tomorrow afternoon.' 'Does this apply to the whole flock?' I retorted curiously. 'No. All sheep are equal, but some are more equal than others. YOU have been chosen.' I left at once for the funny farm and found myself humming the rural licks from *Animals*.

The following day I went to HEADQUARTERS as instructed. There, there are many sheep who sit obediently at typewriters and a handful of dogs who are allowed to put their feet on the desks and bark orders at the woolly ones.

I was handed the ULTIMATE ARTICLE – a white label of *Animals*. I played it over and over all afternoon and well into the evening. I also obtained a copy of the lyrics.

Animals has four tracks, is an allegorical LP and will inevitably be compared to *Dark Side of the Moon*. The words are strong, bitter and they ask questions. The instrumental interludes are at times powerful; Gilmour's guitar work does predominate. It asks questions, but never really gives the answers.

The words must come from Roger Waters. I don't know, they wouldn't tell me. In fact, the pigs just didn't seem to want to let us know much at all about the album. In the words of the opening track (vocals over acoustic guitar backing) ... 'If you didn't care what happened to me, and I didn't care for you ...'. Do the pigs care, or did they just produce this album to fulfil contractual agreements?

I think not. This is a powerful and thought-out album. It will be as big as *Dark Side*. For your information, the tracks are 'Pigs on the Wing (part one)', 'Dogs', 'Pigs', 'Sheep' and 'Pigs on the Wing (part two)'. Who are the pigs, who the sheep and who the dogs, you must decide for yourself. This album may disturb you. It did me, even though the ideals and thoughts behind the words have been raised before.

The sheep looked from dog to dog and they all looked the same. It was five-thirty. The ANIMALS left HEADQUARTERS two by two. The little dog laughed to see such fun and life went on just the same, day in, day out. Where were the pigs? Who were they? The questions were soon forgotten and never answered.

Wet Dream

Sounds, 4 November 1978

No, not a Max Romeo compilation: just a fanciful name for a fairly auspicious entry by Pink Floyd keyboard player Rick Wright into the world of solo composition and heavy duty royalties.

And essentially, the outcome is an unqualified success. Helped out by semi-legendary sax sessionist Mel Collins, ex-Cockney Rebel Snowy White on guitars (and a couple of other semi-names), Wright produces, directs and stars in this, his first and very own magnum opus.

Not surprisingly, the instrumentals have a very definite edge over the songs, only one of which, 'Pink's Song', written by Wright's wife Juliette, is worthy of inclusion here. The lyrics elsewhere – standard Floyd truisms – are mostly superfluous, enhanced and/or redeemed only by the superb soloing of Collins (check 'Waves') and White ('Summer Elegy' and 'Against The Odds').

'Mediterranean C' showcases the formula: slow, deliberate intro, 'Atom Heart Mother' refrain, almost laborious build-up suddenly exploding into full-bodied audio-pageantry. When the instrumentation finally takes shape, it is always worth the wait. Just like the Floyd.

Ironically, Wright's keyboards/synthesizer don't always come across as the premier instruments, but he is, after all, the orchestrator without whom none of this would have been possible. The complete sublimity of Wright's concept is fulfilled on 'Waves', a glorious five-minute instrumental, a *tour de force* in concentrated mellifluent excellence.

The overall upshot of Wright's vision could be heard to be an album of Floyd out-takes, but if *Wet Dream* were to be regarded in that way, it would be a compliment (rather than an insult) to its composer.

A big production number into the bargain, *Wet Dream* stands up in its own right, no trouble.

Sid Beret

Writing on the wall for Floyd?

NME, 11 November 1978

No release date has yet been set for Pink Floyd's next mega-statement, but already mystery surrounds the idea behind the long-player.

Thrills was told by a reliable source that the title of the new Floyd waxing is *Walls*, and that to present the piece the Floyd are planning to delve deep into the realms of 'environmental theatre' (*Beats lasers – Ed.*).

According to one source, the Floyd are intending to take *Walls* to the public by constructing a wall between the audience and the stage. As for the group themselves, they'll spend at least some of the show as part of the audience, and not – as is customary in these rituals – on the stage itself. They were never all that strong on stage presence, after all.

When asked to confirm this, Harvest Records, the Floyd's record company, commented that it was the first they'd heard of this rather outlandish scheme. They did however inform *Thrills* that the working title of the New Floyd Album is indeed *Walls*.

The Floyd office, EMKA, were even less forthcoming. No, it's not called *Walls*, they said, and anyway it's too early to divulge info about the record. Both Harvest and EMKA did say that the Floyd are about to commence recording any day now and that Roger Waters has completed writing the thing.

Thrills understands that the group, these days not renowned for their beaverlike work-rate, have booked their own studios, Britannia Row, for three days a week for the next six months. Who, we ask, do they think they are; The Clash?

Jay Cocks

Pinkies on the wing

Time, 25 February 1980

Almost a decade ago, Pink Floyd played a two and a half hour concert on the shores of the Crystal Palace pond in London. To enhance their trippy riffs and overweening crescendos, the Pinkies brought on a fifty-foot inflatable octopus and detonated a fireworks display. By the time of the first encore, all the fish in the lake had died, victims of the band's cosmic boom and crushing decibels.

In the intervening years, the body count has dwindled. Pink Floyd still machine-tools the kind of head-shop Muzak that they helped pioneer during the first shocks of the '60s psychedelic movement and that, with considerable refining and embellishment, they shaped into 1973's *Dark Side of the Moon*, one of the largest and longest sellers in rock history. *Dark Side of the Moon* has sold six and a half million copies in the US since its release, has been on the charts for two hundred and ninety-nine weeks and recently rose from the nether regions to occupy a respectable place in the middle ground.

This late burst of activity is directly traceable to the surprise success of the new Pink Floyd album, *The Wall*, which has become the country's No. 1 album and which shows few signs of giving way to the competition. This is all the more remarkable because the two Floyd albums between *The Moon* and *The Wall* achieved only modest success. There was every reason to believe that the Floyd had gone under, sunk beneath the collective weight of their cosmic speculations and primal ruminations. The resurgence represented by *The Wall* and by the Pinkies' current tour, which is touching down only in New York City and Los Angeles, is a reminder that the only commercial constant in pop music is unpredictability.

Cracking up

Bass player Roger Waters, who writes most of the band's music, has tempered his lyric tantrums somewhat for the new album and has worked up some melodies that are rather more lulling and insinuating than anything Floyd freaks are used to. Spacey and seductive and full of high-tech sound stunts, *The Wall* has a kind of smothering sonic energy that can be traced to *Dark Side of the Moon* and even past that, to the band's early days on the psychedelic front lines. To fans, this continuity must be just as reassuring as the trendiness Waters has grafted onto his lyrics, which are a kind of libretto for Me-decade narcissism. Says Tom Morrera, disc jockey at New York City's pace-setting WNEW-FM: 'The Floyd are not as spacey as they used to be. They're doing art for art's sake, and you don't have to be high to get it. They'll take you on a trip anyway.' Travellers who may not want to sign on for this particular voyage may find themselves more in agreement with a vice-president at a rival record label who speculated, not without wistfulness, that the Pinkies 'make perfect music for the age of the computer game'.

The Wall is a lavish, four-sided dredge on the angst of the successful rocker, his flirtations with suicide and losing bouts with self-pity, his assorted betrayals by parents, teachers and wives and his uneasy relationship with his audience, which is alternately exhorted, cajoled and mocked. None of the dynamic exaltation of The Who and their fans for the Pinkies. To Waters, the audience is just another barrier, another obstacle to his exquisitely indelicate communion with his inner being. 'So ya / Thought ya / Might like to go to the show,' he sneers at some hapless fan.

Is something eluding you, sunshine?
. . . If you'd like to find out what's behind these cold eyes
You'll just have to claw your way through this disguise.

Sunshine might just as well try tunnelling out of Sing Sing with a soup spoon. Every avenue of Waters' psyche ends up against a wall, a towering edifice whose bricks have been mixed from the clay of emotional trauma, vocational frustration and, apparently, brain damage. Absent fathers, smothering mothers, sadistic schoolmasters, insistent fans and faithless spouses: 'All in all you were all just bricks in the wall.'

Urging caution on 'the thin ice of modern life', Waters' lyrical ankles do a lot of wobbling before he is indicted, some seventy-five minutes into the record, on charges of fecklessness, savagery and numbness. The presiding magistrate, a worm, sentences the singer to 'be exposed before your peers / Tear down the wall'. Lysergic *Sturm und Drang* like this has a kind of kindergarten appeal, especially if it is orchestrated like a cross between a Broadway overture and a band concert on the starship *Enterprise*. It is likely, indeed, that *The Wall* is succeeding more for the sonic sauna of its melodies than the depth of its lyrics. It is a record being attended to rather than absorbed, listened to rather than heard.

And watched. The Pinkies on stage are as carefully rehearsed as the Rockettes. Says saxman Dick Parry, who has backed them up, 'They've got everything down exactly. On stage with Floyd there's no spontaneity at all. They've got little pieces of tape everywhere, and if you stand in the wrong place they go crazy.' The Pinkies' new stage show is an extravagantly literal representation of the album, including a smoking bomber with an eighteen-foot wingspan that buzzes the audience on a guy wire and huge floats representing the songs' major characters, among them a thirty-foot mom who inflates to apparently daunting proportions with the throw of a toggle switch. There is also, of course, a wall, soaring thirty feet above the stage, spanning two hundred and ten feet at the top. At the start of the show, roadies – rechristened 'wallies' for the occasion – start stacking three hundred and forty cardboard bricks until, at intermission, the wall stands completed. During the second half, a few strategic ruptures appear, through which Waters and his fellow Pinkies – keyboard player Rick Wright, drummer Nick Mason and guitarist Dave Gilmour – can be glimpsed doing their stuff.

The inevitable apocalypse occurs on cue. The wall crumbles, bending on its collapsible support columns and bringing a storm of harmless rubble down around the Floyd. 'Outside the wall,' Waters sings, 'the bleeding hearts and the artists make their stand.'

Cracking up

The Pinkies would presumably find such company untidy, in the first case, or unflattering, in the second. As Waters pipes band and back-up musicians off stage with his clarinet, one recalls with renewed interest the fate of *The Godfather*'s Luca Brasi, who was sent to sleep with the fishes.

Fred Dellar

Fictitious Sports

Hi-fi News & Record Review, August 1981

Moving on to less raucous happenings, *Spot the Player* would, on the face of things, appear to be a solo album from famous Floydian and Man of Le Mans Nick Mason, who leads a band called Fictitious Sports. But in reality it's Mike Mantler and Carla Bley taking the escalator over the hill once more and doing it in the company not only of Mason, but also of Robert Wyatt, Chris Spedding, trombonist Gary Valente, ace saxman Gary Windo, bassist Steve Swallow and others of similar talent.

The songs, all penned by keyboardist Bley, are generally angular and a trifle melody shy, but with Wyatt handling most of the vocals, it wouldn't matter overmuch if *Yellow Pages'* greatest hits stood on the music stands. For Wyatt I love in the way I love Astaire. His is a non-voice, a plaintive call from the back of the hall. Yet, as he's so often proved, he's able to imbue even the slightest material with a wonderful feeling of melancholy; something which he does here on 'Do Ya?', which casts him in the role of an inarticulate lover, seeking the words to keep a relationship together but miserably failing to communicate. Mantler adds some equally full-of-feel daybreak horn and the whole is enough to cause tear-stains down the shirt-front.

Elsewhere, the partners in sport blow enterprisingly and sometimes brilliantly, always maintaining interest. And if *Spot the Player* ultimately fails to make out as the most inspired use of vinyl in our time, it at least proves that Floyd spin-offs are not to be ignored and wipes the taste of Roger Taylor's recent soirée from the mouth.

Richard Cook

Over the wall and into the dumper

NME, 19 March 1983

Like the poor damned Tommies that haunt his mind, Roger Waters' writing has been blown to hell.

Although *The Final Cut* is 'performed by Pink Floyd', it is entirely Waters' statement. Roughly, it runs like this – a far-flung railing at a failed society, a harsh melting back into the blood and darkness of war, false memories of an unknown father cast like forged photographs, elliptical parallels with a rich recluse, the disgusting insanity of power politics versus the needs of the work ethic, a terrible failed romance and a last quiet apocalypse. Something like that.

Waters has conceived it as a single narrative. Aside from some unidentified mutterings and a female chorus on 'Not Now John', his is the only voice to be heard: it picks out the words like a barefoot terminal beachcomber, measuring out a cracked whisper or suddenly bracing itself for a colossal scream.

The story is pitched to that exhausting rise and fall: it regales with the obstinacy of an intoxicated, berserk commando.

Waters has that part down cold, and he inhabits the shells of a frightened cynic and a pilled-up, love-sick millionaire with the same gloomy relish. It is an enormous conceit but it is delivered from the vantage point of a man with a huge audience. Waters namechecks Thatcher, Reagan, Paisley and Haig like an armchair mafioso. If he's going to say *anything...*

Why not, indeed? Why not choose to lambast these leaders when you know you have exactly the audience that has to be kicked and jolted – the multitudinous conservatism that will assuredly buy the new Floyd album?

Pink Floyd

In Waters' 'requiem for the post-war dream' the traces of his psychedelic antecedents are kicked over for good and for all: there is no refuge here in 'Another Brick in the Wall'. No singalong anthems brighten *The Final Cut*. The one episode to resemble a rock song is 'Not Now John', a sick celebration of business ignorance executed with military efficiency.

So why not? Because the flat presence of the artefact denies the message its force. As he realizes only too well, Waters' walls have sealed him up permanently. Every diatribe he releases as a Pink Floyd album will be filed beside the others. That conveyor belt of protean-faced consumers which populated *The Wall* will rack each record next to the other, and what will bother them isn't how effective a catharsis each one summons; it won't be how much they can assimilate and learn from a personal, provocative vision. What will bother them is why there aren't any tunes as good as 'Money'. That's rock music.

No matter how much Waters may burn and struggle over the sad, sick world he finds himself in along with the rest of us, his diagnoses sit in a stasis of unresolved, unmoving bitterness. The prescriptive rock record is a hopelessly romantic notion, and the one strength of his work is its refusal to offer solutions – but the negativity is soft, self-consuming, weighted by indulgence.

Waters stopped with *The Wall*, and *The Final Cut* isolates and juggles the identical themes of that elephantine concept with no fresh momentum to drive them. The composer might protest that there is no alternative: I would in answer direct him to John Cale's *Songs for a New Society*. There, the most invigorating, testing exploration of sound faced songs that spoke candidly and unflinchingly about the way we live now – not in Waters' flabby, inconsolable rhetoric but in the allusive sketches of an astute observer. Waters cannot detach himself from his agony long enough to make sense of it.

That is why the worst stretches of a long haul suffer from the most sentimental lapses of judgement: 'And if I show you my dark side / Will you still hold me tonight? / And if I gave my heart to you / What would you do?' In between these tearful prayers, David

Cracking up

Gilmour turns his long legato guitar up and down and Nick Mason beats and rolls as is appropriate. Richard Wright has realised his redundancy and left.

'I never had the nerve to make the final cut' – will Roger Waters have the gumption to call it a day now? The concluding irony of *The Final Cut* is that it is the expression of a man who loathes the demands of the rock cycle, yet is unable to move beyond the same linear constraints of the form. Underneath the whimpering meditation and exasperated cries of rage, it is the old, familiar rock beast: a man who is unhappy in his work.

Janet Huck

Up against the wall

Previously unpublished, c. February 1980

Pink Floyd's concerts are legendary for making the most flamboyant gestures in the biggest stadiums – but this time they've transcended themselves. During the first half of their Los Angeles show, celebrating their new album *The Wall*, a massive, half-finished wall – stretching across the eleven thousand seat Sports Arena – was completed. Slowly, brick by brick, the black-clothed crew walled off the musicians, separating them totally from their audience. The Wall stands insurmountable throughout most of the second half. But, at the end, a chant from the Floyd rose up louder and louder: 'Tear down the wall, tear down the wall . . .' A few people in the audience picked up their call for freedom as a series of Nazi images flashed, faster and faster, on the wall. With a murky low rumbling, the top bricks started to teeter, tumbling backwards in a unit. Then, with a hypnotizing roar, the rest of the carefully built wall crumbled, tossing the large white cardboard bricks dangerously close to the feet of the audience.

Through the ominous, warlike devastation and billowing green smoke wove the newly cleansed musicians, dressed in street clothes, walking slowly in single file like medieval minstrels and playing on simple acoustic instruments, no longer 'banging against some mad bugger's wall'.

Last year, when rude young punks came of age and respectability, the veteran rock group released their seemingly out-of-date concept album, *The Wall*. Some hip, post-punk observers expected their sales to tumble faster than their own prop, but the old-wave group – which has remained together for twelve years – refused to surrender to the new wave. When the expensive two-album set was released the last week in November, the flash marker was the biggest-selling, most-played album in the country.

Cracking up

Now, after ten weeks on the charts, it is sitting securely in the number one slot, having bumped the Eagles' *Long Run* weeks ago. The soon-to-be-double-platinum album has sold almost two million copies, and it may have a longer run yet. Their most successful album, *Dark Side of the Moon*, which was released in 1973 and made the underground cult stars into over-the-hill superstars, has stayed on *Billboard's* charts for a total of two hundred and ninety-eight weeks, popping up at a respectable number 45 this week.

When their limited tour – one week in Los Angeles and five days in New York – was announced, 'the computers,' as one reporter said, 'were pushed to warp drive' to handle the demand. In New York, more than thirty-three thousand tickets were sold in a record-breaking five hours. In Los Angeles, more than seventy-seven thousand seats were sold. A few Massachusetts fans, who couldn't get tickets in New York, bought LA seats and came three thousand miles to see their heroes.

The wall as a prop actually came before *The Wall* as an album. The massive project was originally conceived in 1978 when the Floyd's harried lead vocalist/bassist Roger Waters, scared by unsettling confrontations with hysterical fans, decided he wanted to protect himself with an actual wall in future performances. Before he started to write the message-laden music and lyrics, the ex-architectural student asked his long-time special effects assistant Graham Fleming if it could be done. The special effects wizard shrugged: 'You don't ask a lot of questions why,' he sighed, 'you start working.'

What he came up with is a massive white wall which stretches two hundred and ten feet across the Sports Arena floor and rises thirty-five feet off the ground. Waters' symbol of psychological isolation is made up of approximately four hundred and fifty individual fire-proof cardboard bricks that measure five feet by two and a half feet and weigh a hefty nineteen pounds. A crew of six – called The Brit Row Brick Company – lay down three hundred and forty of the foldable bricks every night in about forty-five minutes. 'The show backstage is more exciting than the show out front,' declared Fleming.

There were plenty of problems. First, Fleming had to design a self-supporting wall which wouldn't accidentally crush the musicians on stage, yet would come down on cue: he came up with ten metal columns which were planted inside the bricks to keep them from tumbling down prematurely. A master control board monitors the up and down movement of the columns so they don't stick out the top of the wall and give the secret away. The columns are topped off with levers which can knock the individual bricks either back or forth: when the wall has to crumble, the operator drops the column supports row by row and flips the levers, sending the bricks crashing down. For safety, the top rows are knocked back on the stage, giant metal cages protecting the equipment and musicians. They have about a minute from the end of 'The Trial' to scamper out of the cages and off stage, but once Dave Gilmour didn't move fast enough and was caught in the cage as the nineteen-pound bricks crashed down. The lower rows, which are less likely to bounce into the audience, are knocked to the front of the stage. 'If we didn't control the collapse of the wall, we'd wipe out the first twenty rows,' said Fleming, 'then they couldn't come back for another show.'

The other basic problem is how to lay all the bricks in time to the music. Fleming sent an engineer to a fork-lift company in Seattle for two and a half months to design a new lift system; the result was five man-lifts which rise thirty feet to transport the crew up to the top of the wall. When they were first delivered in December, the pumps didn't work. 'At that point we didn't think we'd ever make it,' remembered Fleming.

To make sure they could get the wall up and down in time with the music, Fleming and his Brit Row Brick Company started rehearsal two months ago. They first set up the wall in the Culver City Studios in early December, assembly lasting two to three weeks. Then they rehearsed constructing the wall; the first time, it took two hours from the first to the last brick. 'Nobody would be left in the audience,' chuckled the dry Englishman. It took them three weeks of muscle-straining work to get their timing down, but the worst night was dress rehearsal with the band. In case there are any time problems with the wall, the band have written some expandable riffs to cover the delayed brick-laying; that night the band played on and on as the crew struggled with shiny, stiff new bricks which had replaced the well-worn ones they had been practising with for weeks. 'The band was asleep,' said Fleming.

The morning of the opening night, the crew were joking around the Tropicana pool before they were bussed to the arena. 'The show – maybe it'll go on,' sighed one. But, miraculously, every night they have finished laying the top row before they close the last cut-out where Waters is singing 'Goodbye Cruel World'.

But the spectacular Floyd didn't just build a wall and tear it down: they had a lot of other large-scale effects. In ninety minutes of rock opera, they pranced a twenty-five-foot-high crotchety schoolmaster across the stage by manipulating it like a giant marionette, inflated a grotesquely large mother figure that huffed and puffed disapprovingly and zoomed a near life-size World War One fighter plane across the entire arena. Banks of lights pulsated in time to the music, and huge portable lighting cabs, looking like giant insects, slunk around the edge of the stage, probing obscure areas with searching lights.

They surrounded the audience with three hundred and sixty degree sound which made some people jump at uncomfortably close heavy breathing or violent echoes that assaulted them first from the right, then from the left and then from the back. Alternatively, they transfixed them with scary animation, in comic-book colours, of flirtatious flowers that made love, then devoured each other, and red and grey hammers that marched across the wall, growing bigger and bigger, with Nazi-esque precision.

Next to the enormous technical problems of the wall, all these effects seemed like child's play. The gargantuan black pig was a hold-over from their last tour. Fleming's crew used to pull it back by hand, but sometimes the audience caught it: 'The band would never know when it would make it back,' said Fleming. So this time, they designed a special track so the pig emerges and returns on cue: 'We could make it sit up and beg if we wanted to. But the fun element is gone – a child could operate it ...' The inflatable mother puffs up with no problems, but the sparkling hair of the praying-mantis wife doesn't flash enough. 'We need a new hairdresser,' cracked Fleming.

The only spectacular glitch was an opening night fire. As the band marched on stage, they let off a glittering array of fireworks, which accidentally set fire to an overhead drape. Most of the audience thought the pyrotechnics were just part of the show, but after dodging pieces of burning curtain for a few minutes, Waters finally stopped the performance entirely to let the stage crew extinguish the flames. Despite changing the drapes to a less flammable material, the Fire Department wouldn't let them try the fireworks again. 'That was the biggest disappointment,' said Fleming, 'there's a definite gap.'

Amidst all the gee-whiz effects, Pink Floyd don't act like normal egotistical rock stars on stage. Primarily musicians, they come to play. They wear regular street clothes: T-shirts, worn Chino pants with the knees bulging out, and button-down, wash-and-wear shirts that look like they came out of the drier a few minutes before. They don't jump around or use flamboyant, Jaggeresque gestures – they tune up carefully and start playing almost exactly on time. One night they apologized for a fifteen-minute delay because of a massive traffic jam that kept hundreds of fans outside the arena at show time. At times they act as if it's just another job that has to be done; consequently, some of the audience think they are cold and impersonal. 'It's like they don't know the audience is out there,' said one record company executive, Columbia A&R man Peter Philbin.

In fact, they pace the show without reckoning on any participation from the audience. The performance is speeded up or slowed down according to problems with the special effects and, like an opera, one song is rolled into the next without any time or space for applause. And Waters almost never addresses the audience – once he yelled 'Is there anybody out there?' but those lines are actually part of the script. However, one night he did say, 'Here's the man you've been waiting for – Gilmour!' and then anxiously asked if anybody liked his pig.

Of course, the wall robbed the audience of any intimacy; toward the end of the first half, you could only see the band through five-foot cutouts, almost as if you were watching them on a television set. During the second half, the audience got only occasional glimpses of the band: Gilmour gave a searing solo on top of the wall and Waters sang one song in a motel room mock-up that folded out from the wall. But at other times he just sang with his back to the audience.

In 1977, Pink Floyd did a nationwide tour of large baseball stadiums, that veered out of control. The gigantic audiences of fifty thousand were too far away to see or hear much and started to make their own show. Stoned and drunk, they set off fireworks and beat each other with bottles. 'It was hell,' said Floyd leader Waters, 'it made me very angry.' The increasingly depressing experience culminated in their last show, in Montreal, which had festival seating for eighty thousand people. Hundreds were crushed up against the wire beneath the stage and throughout even the quiet acoustic numbers, they yelled, 'Get down!'

'I had had it,' remembered Waters. 'Halfway through, I found myself spitting on one particular guy who wouldn't stop yelling. He wasn't interested in the show. None of the audience was really responding in any genuine way to what was going on on stage; they were all interested in their own performances. There was a real war going on between the musicians on stage and the audience.'

Bitter and angry, Waters withdrew to the quiet English country-side with his new family to develop a project which would keep him out of the rock and roll battleground. Intending that the concept be strong enough to make into a good movie, the pragmatic Waters knew he had to develop it as a musical project first, in order to get it off the ground. So he wrote it as a live show that could be done in just a few cities, in order to iron out the bumps and make it work as a theatrical piece, before turning it into a shooting script that a studio would be interested in.

The central idea was to construct an actual wall across the stage to protect and separate him from the aggressive audience, a concept that was expanded to become a metaphor for the psychological isolation that a person develops in his life. 'The wall was a foundation. Everybody puts bricks in their own wall at different times in their life,' he explained.

The first half of the project is strictly autobiographical. His father was killed when he was three months old, and his mother smothered him to compensate for the loss; his grammar school teachers humiliated him. 'But they didn't succeed in smothering me,' he said proudly. 'I escaped into the narcotic but self-expressive world of rock 'n' roll. Like the character in the programme, I toured around the world madly; finally discovering it's not as good as I thought it would be. It wears a bit thin. In the meantime, I left his [*Pink's*] old lady at home and she goes off with somebody else. That's very personal: my wife left me for another man. I was crushed and withdrew to a hotel room. The character goes loopy and incarcerates himself in a hotel as he has already become psychologically isolated. The conceptual theme is that that kind of isolation breeds psychic and moral decay.'

The second half of the album and show comments on how other rock stars are destroyed by their experiences: 'Different people get crushed in different ways. Some become babies. They break things. They exert their power because they are famous rock 'n' roll stars, indulging infantile whims.' Asked whether he had a particular rock star in mind, Waters said curtly, 'I don't want to go into it.'

But he was willing to discuss some of the pressures which turned adults into infantile rock stars: 'The problem is the money. You are a vehicle for a lot of people to make a lot of money; their lives and fortunes depend on you continuing to perform. They will do anything to keep you working – give you anything, indulge you. That's why so many start behaving like babies. It's comfy to have people baby you. They think it's clever when you throw a TV out of a hotel window.'

However, part of the second half is autobiographical – or at least represents his fantasies of what was going on: 'He is forced to go back and perform because nobody else makes money if the show doesn't go on. He's forced back on stage by a cynical doctor who injects him with an enlivening substance, and from the time he leaves the hotel room and arrives on stage, he turns from Dr Jekyll to Mr Hyde. He is the whole band; like Pink is the whole group in the programme. He turns into Mr Hyde and the band become fascists. It's still us, but in a different frame of mind. We have turned into fascist pigs like I turned into a fascist, spitting in Montreal; the surrogate band represents me spitting on people.

'The character starts talking about putting all the Jews and "coons" up against a wall and sending them back where they came from. That's when we start showing the slides of the hammers marching across the screen – it's supposed to turn into a great rally. The audience love all that kind of stuff. They are happy to fall into a fascist rally; they can be led into doing anything the group tells them to do.

'The rally is supposed to reach a crescendo,' continued Waters, in a low, unemotional monotone. 'But he rebels. We rebel. That's when he sings, "I want to go home and take off the uniform." But they don't let him. He is dragged off to the bunker where he waits for the worms, waits to be put on trial. The verdict is to be judged by his peers.'

Waters wanted to be judged by his peers because most of the people around him thought the project was ridiculous, doomed to failure. 'So many people thought it was insane. Robbie Williams, our lighting guy for years and years, told me that up until the first night, he thought it was completely insane. He, like others, thought the audience would insist on hearing old material. I have been under enormous pressure to do encores; so many people have said the audience will tear you to pieces – they will destroy the stage. They put the audience in the same position. But I couldn't care less what they thought; I only wanted to express how I felt. It was a big gamble which is paying off – the audience, the crew and the musicians are all enjoying it.'

*

Roger Waters has clearly emerged as the leader of the band. 'I make the decisions,' he declared without a trace of humility. 'We pretended it was a democracy for a long time, but this album was the era of the big own-up. It was a mildly painful experience for some of us because we have been pretending we are all jolly good chaps together. It's a load of rubbish. Ten years ago it was true, but not for the last six or seven years.'

Indeed, Waters decides what the whole group will do. In July 1978, he called a meeting of the band to present both his tapes and script for *The Wall* and another project. In effect, he gave them an ultimatum: the band would have to do one or the other – it didn't matter which because Waters would do the other as a solo project. The band voted for *The Wall*, then started working on it in their own peculiar way. They don't communicate directly or verbally at all: 'They communicate through technology,' explained Michael Kamen, who arranged all the orchestral back-ups for the album. 'Roger will make a demo in his studio and send it to Gilmour, who will add some tracks or overdub and send the tape on. All the members of the band have acquired separate identities.'

But after exchanging tapes for two months, Waters decided he needed help from an outside producer, and hired heavy metal heavy Bob Ezrin, who shepherded Kiss to the platinum circle. 'I couldn't do it all myself,' said Waters. 'Dave and I have produced all our albums together, but I had to provide all the motivation and direction.' Ezrin reworked Waters' original script, which the author himself described as 'childish notes'. 'Some parts were thought to be too personal, some didn't fit musically, and some songs just weren't good enough,' he explained.

Under Ezrin's urging, Waters dropped a silly, hackneyed song entitled 'The Death of Sisco', in which a DJ harangued the audience, and cut out personal references – especially early dates in Waters' life which are meaningless to their fans who were born after World War Two (for instance, Waters had written a line about 1944 when his father died). Despite these changes, Waters admitted that it's impossible to follow the convoluted plot line, particularly the garbled phone calls from Mr Floyd to Mrs Floyd.

Ezrin wasn't the only one to help Waters polish up his rock epic. Dave Gilmour, the lead guitarist who is a genius with technology, wrote the catchy music to 'Young Lust' and 'Run Like Hell'. The other two members didn't contribute anything. 'They just played on the album,' said Waters curtly, dropping the subject very quickly (when asked directly about Rick Wright, whom he constantly humiliates, Waters bristled: 'I'm not going to go into Wright').

The rock opera, which came out of the strained collaboration between the Floyd, is very gratifying to its originator. 'It's wonderful,' said the softly spoken Waters, finally allowing a spark of emotion into his voice. He admitted that the lyrics were somewhat aloof, but only because they told a story. 'On *Dark Side of the Moon*, there was an awful lot of wishy-washy claptrap.' After reciting one long, trite passage very rapidly, he took a breath and added, 'That's an awfully long way to say it doesn't approve of organized Christianity. Besides, people take rock lyrics too seriously. Some rock poets like Dylan and Neil Young have something to say, but most rock lyrics are second-rate.'

And he insisted that *The Wall* is a lot better than their last album, *Animals*. '*Animals* was only released because we succumbed to material greed. However, I thought *Wish You Were Here* was a fairly cohesive piece of work. I built on it to make *The Wall*.' But he readily admitted that the lyrics were bitter: 'It was largely drawn from the dark period in my life when my marriage was breaking up because of touring. Then the tours weren't going well. It was a tough period of my life, but writing about it helped me externalize some of those bad, bitter feelings. Now I feel ten times better. I'm on the up.'

Although he feels better about his life as a rich rock and roll star, he did say that he has some ambivalence about the money, the fame and the power that goes along with it. 'I always thought, as a child, that having a lot of money was wrong. I was brought up on *Daily Worker* bazaars. When my mother couldn't get someone to sit with me, she took me along to the meetings of the British–Chinese Friendship Organizations to watch movies of the heroic struggles of the People's Republic. One never loses that stuff. On the surface, I have no strong inclination to go into politics or to buy a B-52 and fill it up with supplies for the starving millions, but those feelings of guilt can't ever be totally exorcized. Having a family changed my perspective immeasurably. I want things for them – but the money still makes me uneasy.'

Waters' guilty feelings made him shy away from any publicity or move to make him into another Jaggeresque personality: 'After not talking to the Press for so long, I discovered there was a mystique which had grown up around us. We started enjoying the mystery. It's very nice; nobody knows who we are. I can walk around backstage and nobody recognizes me. I can even walk out into the audience: I could walk around the buildings in the last tour and check it out without anybody coming up to me. It's great. I don't like strangers coming up, like they know me – I don't want to talk to strangers. When they do come up, my vibes say, "I don't want you around," so they don't over-stay their welcome.'

Indeed, Waters is unapproachable, wary of strangers. His voice is very soft-spoken, rarely rising above a low monotone – but it's a demanding voice. He's almost like the president of a multi-million company who is so feared that he doesn't have to scream to get people to do exactly what he says – immediately. Right before the show, he makes a tour around to the different crews – special effects, sound and so on – to check whether they had any problems or whether they had fixed some minor faults from the previous performance. As soon as he showed up, the crew heads ran over and started nervously reporting what progress had been made. Only once did I hear Waters raise his voice. One stage crew hadn't turned on the TV set for the motel room scene the night before, and he was complaining, 'It's the only fucking thing they have to do. Make sure it's done.'

Waters expects the same rapt attention from his audience. When asked what was the role of a rock audience, he quickly snapped 'Passive,' throwing his head forward as if he were spitting once again on that odious fan. 'Like they're in a theatre. You bloody well sit there. I hate audience participation. I hate it when they want you to sing along: it makes my flesh creep. Yelling and screaming and singing is great in church, but not at our shows, thank you very much.'

This time, Waters is overjoyed that the audience is simply sitting there and taking it all in. But he went off on a tirade about one over-excited fan: 'I missed a great opportunity last night [*the final night of the LA gig*]. In the first half, some asshole was shining a battery-operated pocket laser on the screen. There he was playing with his little red dot on our screen. I didn't do anything because there was so little of that kind of mischief going on; I just thought they'll find him and [*at this point, his voice grew nasty*] take his little toy away and break it. It's such a drag for ten thousand people if one person is screwing it up by having his piece of fun.

'Anyway, I realized afterwards that I should have changed the words in "Hey You" from "Breaking bottles in the hall" to "Playing laser on the wall" – like that's what the song is about: playing with a laser on a wall. If they can't understand what I'm trying to do ... to fiddle with toys while I'm doing serious work, they should stay home. Some people say that's a pompous attitude. But that's how I feel. If he wants to play with his laser, let him bloody well play with it in his garage and do his own laser shows there.'

However, when Pink Floyd make a film about *The Wall*, Waters is going to use the audience a great deal. He wouldn't talk about it, but probably the controlled audience will be instructed to turn into a crazed mob, led on by the fascist surrogate band. They have to make a movie about the project in order to recoup the money they are losing on the two-city tour. Every night they put the elaborate show on, each member of the band loses $15,000 apiece; over the twelve nights, the show cost the band $800,000. Waters calculated that they would have to charge $30 a ticket instead of $12 and $15 to break even. 'The audience is really getting more than they paid for,' he remarked, but added: 'The album is selling like hot cakes, so the enormous gamble is paying off.'

But will the band which doesn't talk to each other any more stay together for the film and more albums? 'We're too lazy to split up,' remarked Waters.

Trevor Dann

Faded Pink

Sunday Telegraph, May 1984

Pink Floyd ceased to be a band in the real sense of the word some years ago. Its four wealthy members lived thousands of miles apart and met only briefly to record individual contributions to albums like *Wish You Were Here* and *The Wall*, under the increasingly dominant direction of Roger Waters.

Their epic album, show and film *The Wall*, and the appropriately named *The Final Cut*, were massive achievements, both financially and artistically, but pushed the inexorable process of disintegration even further.

And now with the release of three solo projects, Floyd fans must finally face up to the fact that their heroes are no more. As so often during the untidy break-up of a once great band, its constituent parts are falling over themselves to expose their limitations as solo artists.

First in the lead was guitarist David Gilmour, whose *About Face* is a competent though thoroughly unmemorable set which too often sounds like a pastiche of Floyd's heavier pieces. At its best the playing is robust and confident; at its worst it is smug and unadventurous.

The big surprise came from Richard Wright, who teamed up with Dave Harris, the former singer with electro-disco band Fashion, in a promising collaboration called Zee. Unfortunately, *Identity* has none, being merely a bland and derivative exercise in metronomic synthesizer playing, dominated by Harris' lugubrious vocals.

But the biggest blow to Floyd's reputation comes this week from the man who formed the band in Cambridge in the mid-'60s and grew to be the answer to his own ironic question, 'Which one's Pink?'

Cracking up

Roger Waters has spent a year and a considerable part of his fortune on an album and forthcoming stage show called *The Pros and Cons of Hitch Hiking*, which must rank as one of the all-time rock follies.

From Gerald Scarfe's graphics on the sleeve to the everything-including-the-kitchen-sink production, it is an outrageous caricature of later Floyd. The theme, explored through the hackneyed device of a dream sequence, appears to be Waters' bizarre, even aberrant sexual hang-ups. But the lyrics are so obtuse and the melodies and arrangements so tired and cliché-ridden that the work dissolves into self-parody on an epic scale.

Even the presence of celebrated musicians like Andy Newmark, David Sanborn and Eric Clapton – hopelessly miscast in Gilmour's traditional role – cannot save a project which seems destined to become a yardstick by which monumental flops will have to be judged.

Roger Holland

Profiles

Sounds, 21 September 1985

There was once an amusingly successful corporation known as Pink Floyd. And even as their drummer and junior partner, Nick Mason managed to make so much money that he could afford to indulge his every whim.

One of these whims was to make a short film about his past and another of his whims, fast cars. Drafting in a number of faceless, soulless musos, he makes a diabolically bland soundtrack album. I hate fast cars, I hated Pink Floyd and I hate this record. And I bet the film is a pile of shit too.

Return of the
living dead

Douglass MacDonald

Now that's what I call music!

The Amazing Pudding, November 1987

Was it dear old Sigmund Floyd who viewed the whole of life as man's striving to return to infancy? Perhaps he was right. Perhaps that's why I feel we should sing the praises of the new album. Because it is, I believe, a return to the true spirit of Pink Floyd, a triumphant reassertion of the values that made this the greatest of all rock groups.

Specifically, *A Momentary Lapse of Reason* is a musical and sonic triumph. Right from the start, the Floyd placed tremendous emphasis on the *sound*; on the building and furnishing of huge musical structures, clothed in spectacular audio techniques. Syd Barrett's wild excursions on the guitar, the wordless powerhouse of 'Interstellar Overdrive', the special effects of the azimuth coordinator and the success of *Dark Side of the Moon* in its quadraphonic form are just some of the examples that attest to Pink Floyd's interest in the sheer sound of their music. The band has built much of its character and much of its success on sonic extravagance, from the multi-track ingenuity of *Dark Side* and the choir and orchestra effects of *Atom Heart Mother* to the velvet-black luxuriance of the introduction to *Wish You Were Here.*

Roger Waters' intensely personal visions, that led to the savage individual tragedy of *The Wall* and the plangent universality of *The Final Cut,* actually steered the group away from what I believe is its true character into a curiously alien and rather barren territory. *The Wall* was a stunning live experience – apart from anything else, the PA was the most magnificent piece of sound engineering I've ever heard – and the film was, dramatically, very powerful. Simply as music, however, it wasn't that marvellous by Pink Floyd standards.

The Final Cut is a wonderful blind alley of a masterpiece: perfect, but essentially sterile because there seems nowhere to go on to from there. *The Pros and Cons of Hitch Hiking* might have the ingredients of a good novel or film, but apart from Collins and Clapton and the occasional burst of orchestral spectacle from Kamen, it's musically wholly unmemorable. The concept has taken over from the actual work, and it doesn't seem to be a very interesting concept anyway.

Radio KAOS doesn't do anything for me at all, except irritate with its musical impoverishment, best exemplified by those mindless disco sounds that seem to be the only 'songs' in the whole piece. Waters' apparent obsession with 'concepts' has resulted in a string of albums that diverge further and further from the roots of Floydianism – but now, at last, we have this magnificent new album that resoundingly restates Floyd's dedication to music, *music*, MUSIC!

Instead of Waters' pared-down, anguished – almost recitative – simplicity, with the words asserting supremacy, we have sonic exuberance, with music firmly back in the driving seat. The sound is rich, multi-layered; fascinating in its excitement and depth and colour and variety. The words are inconsequential, simply a peg to hang the music on. And on side two, they're virtually dispensed with altogether: it's a huge, glorious exploration of superb and richly rewarding sound – the most sheerly beautiful music Pink Floyd has created since *Wish You Were Here.*

And to forestall the critics: no, I do not agree that they're simply rehashing old ideas that were worn out ten years ago, and which Waters had been trying to replace and renew with his dramatic concepts. (And just in case anyone thinks that I'm simply having a go at Waters, can I ask you please to read again my comment on *The Final Cut?* Waters is a man of huge talent, but it happens that his present-day preoccupations simply aren't mine.) No, without Waters, the Floyd has picked up its true self again and started off on the road of musical progression once more.

Whoever the musicians are, *A Momentary Lapse of Reason* sounds like a genuine Pink Floyd album – and that's a good start. The newness shows, for example, in the churning vigour of 'The Dogs of War', possessed of a kind of raw, pounding energy more characteristic of AC/DC than traditional Floyd, and wholly unlike the bitter savagery of 'Another Brick in the Wall'.

The drumming throughout is a refreshing development in Floydery – whether it's the influence of Appice, or Mason having a rush of blood to the fingertips, there are lots of inventive sounds to enliven the textures and drive the music along in a way that's quite a departure from the timeless quality of much Floyd music. This has pace and exuberant enthusiasm.

And how magnificent it is to hear a guitar solo break away and not feel that it's going to be brutally cut off just when it's getting going, in the interests of some wretched dramatic twist in a concept.

A Momentary Lapse of Reason is a superb new beginning. Most of side one is excellent, and what isn't excellent is magnificent. Side two is just wonderful. Forget the personalities. Don't worry what the words say. Just turn up the volume, open your ears and revel in the sound of Pink Floyd that you always loved. Welcome back!

Roger Waters - new album, single, tour and two films!

Press release, 6 April 1987

Former Pink Floyd leader Roger Waters has confirmed plans for a new album and tour later this year . . .

Based around a fictitious Southern California radio station, KAOS, the album explores the relationship between Jim, a renegade disc jockey fighting a lone rear-guard action against format radio, and Billy, a phone-in listener. Billy and Jim share a concern for the increasing domination of the market forces over everyday life: the station jockey fears the total depersonalization of radio, while Billy fears that the misuse of satellite communications, far from bringing people closer together, has brought the earth to the edge of destruction.

Legendary disc jockey Jim Ladd features on the album as the KAOS jock. Coincidentally, his real home station, KMET in Los Angeles, is currently the centre of national interest in the USA following its close-down after a hard-fought battle by staff against a changeover from an eighteen-year policy of broadcasting rock and roll to disco in search of profits.

'The whole issue of the increasing takeover of broadcasting by market research-based programming is a subject of great concern in the States,' says Waters. 'Its effect is to dramatically change the face of radio for the worse, and the effect does not apply only to radio. If you are governed by the lowest commercial denominator, you end up with no KMET, only disco stations; no theatre, only soap opera; and no *Ordinary People*, only *Rambo*.'

Waters' storyline for the album is also in the process of being developed into a screenplay which he aims to have in production next year. This follows the completion of a screen treatment of his previous album, *The Pros and Cons of Hitch Hiking*, which is also expected to go into production in the near future.

Unusually for Waters, *Radio KAOS* will be launched with a single, 'Radio Waves', on line for release 11 May.

James Galway

A night to remember

Sunday Telegraph, 3 March 1991

The night that Roger Waters staged Pink Floyd's *The Wall* at the Berlin Wall last July was the most amazing thing I have ever seen. There were so many famous musicians taking part, and the crowd stretched as far as you could see. As I stood there, I thought the last time this square had so many people in it was when Adolf Hitler addressed a crowd here. And I felt tremendous relief about how greatly the world has moved on since then.

I was in Berlin playing in a concert, and I had decided to go and see the show anyway. I thought I'd take three of my kids and my two godchildren from Berlin. Then I was asked to play in it.

The scene was indescribable. I've never seen so many people at a concert in my life. There were four cranes, mounted with lights and TV cameras, and during the rock-opera they built up this wall, about twice the size of Covent Garden. They got the crowd screaming, 'Tear down the wall, tear down the wall.' Then from behind the wall up came the stage, with all the artists on it. I was very impressed with Roger Waters' speed in putting this on so soon after the Berlin Wall's collapse, because it was rather like doing Wagner's *Ring* with only one rehearsal.

I played a number with Joni Mitchell. You get a fantastic warmth from being in a group with great musicians, but it was the reason for the event that really pulled at my heart-strings. Roger Waters said he'd never put on *The Wall* again until the Berlin Wall itself was pulled down, and the plan with this was to raise £5 for every person killed in war this century.

I lived in Berlin for six years when I played in the Berlin Philharmonic, and the Wall was a horrible-looking thing. Wherever there's a wall there's a problem – suddenly people talk different languages.

Return of the living dead

Every musician should know *The Wall*: if they don't, they should be ashamed of themselves. It's one of the greatest things written in the history of rock.

Roger Waters returns

Ice, May 1992

Ex-Pink Floyd bassist and founding member Roger Waters has a new album due later this year, *Amused to Death*, that already has Columbia executives salivating in anticipation. The album is presently planned for the end of June, but delays in shooting the first video could push it to as late as September.

One has only to listen to Columbia's East Coast Marketing Director, Mason Munoz, talk about the album to have his curiosity piqued. 'It's the best stuff that Roger Waters has ever written, and he's written some great stuff,' Munoz tells *ICE*. 'If we could call this Pink Floyd instead of Roger Waters, I'd be willing to bet – and I'm not a betting man – that it would sell ten million in this country alone. It's really incredible. You'll understand when you hear the first thirty seconds of the first track.'

Munoz speculates that the right chemistry with producer Pat Leonard was one of the key ingredients in Waters producing such striking results at this point in his career. A concept album like Waters' Pink Floyd masterwork *The Wall*, we asked Munoz what the subject matter of the new record was. 'All I can tell you is Roger has been watching a lot of TV,' he says, 'and it's some very biting commentary on new technology and satellite dishes and how they've changed the world for ever.' Something like label-mate Bruce Springsteen's new song '57 Channels (and Nothin' On)'? 'Nowhere near as polite,' Munoz replied without missing a beat.

'The first single is so spectacular that we've been given the assignment of making the best video that's ever been made – *and* the budget to do it. So I've got to somehow produce a video that is every bit as spectacular as the song is, and that's not easy.' Not anticipating a negative answer, we asked Munoz if Waters would tour to support the album. 'I hope so,' he said. 'If he tours, it'll be such a spectacle. All I can say is, for anybody who was ever struck by anything that Pink Floyd did, this will really blow their mind.'

Tom Hibbert

Who the hell does Roger Waters think he is?

Q, November 1992

'So how's Syd these days?' If one happened to bump up against an existing member of the legendary rock combo Pink Floyd in some 'social situation' (cocktails at Brands Hatch, probably), that's the only thing one would be inclined to say. 'How's Syd?' one would go, and the existing member of Pink Floyd – whether Dave Gilmour or Nick Mason or the other one – would, no doubt, blink briefly, pop a cheese 'n' pineapple-savoury-on-a-toothpick into his mouth, bray, 'What? Cor! Frightfully good, these canapés!' and wander off to hob-nob with Nigel Mansell or somebody really interesting.

'Syd' is, of course, Syd Barrett, original member of Pink Floyd, beautiful boy who wrote extraordinary things like 'Apples and Oranges' and 'Astronomy Domine' and flipped his cork and disappeared. But there is another original member, no longer in the legendary rock experience that was 'Floyd', who appears to be a degree off beam: Roger Waters. He's the one who invented giant inflatable pigs, the one who tortured schoolyards of children by making them sing his catchphrase ('We dahn nee nur edercayshun, we dahn nee nur fort corntrawel') all out of tune, the one who once recorded a 'song' called 'Several Species of Small Furry Animals Gathered Together in a Cave and Grooving With a Pict', the one whose doomy sound 'anthems' about 'alienation' and how awful everything is have worried listeners all over the world for several years.

In the guest lounge of a genteel hotel in the picturesque town of Stockbridge, Hampshire – where Waters has a home because the fishing is excellent down here, apparently – the lofty rock icon sits gazing at the cover of an ancient *Country Life*, a pint glass of local ale before him. He's got jeans on. He's got long hair. And he's wearing exactly the same T-shirt (well, it's a different shade – pink not black – but of identical cut) that he was sporting on the cover of Pink Floyd's 1969 LP *Ummagumma*. One has to ask. 'How's Syd?'

'I don't know. I haven't seen him for ten years ... more than ten years, probably. I don't know what went wrong with Syd because I'm not an expert in whatever it is, what they call schizophrenia. I don't know a lot about it. Syd was extraordinarily charming and attractive and alive and talented but ... whatever happened to him, happened to him.'

Roger Waters is thought by many to be the gloomiest man in rock. *The Wall* was gloomy and his solo LPs, *The Pros and Cons of Hitch Hiking* and *Radio KAOS*, were gloomy, and his latest work, *Amused to Death*, is frightfully gloomy. Waters' voice drones along to warn us that: a) there's a squaggly Jeff Beck guitar solo coming up any minute; b) everything is horrible, especially television, war, the entire universe and Andrew Lloyd Webber.

In recording *Amused to Death*, Waters has utilized a snazzy new scientific recording concept that's called 'Q Sound' (nothing to do, I hasten to add, with this magazine, which should immediately sue) and with this natty new technique, if the listener sticks his/her head in the correct place betwixt the speakers, all sorts of amazing things happen! Isn't technology fab? I tried this at home. It didn't work that well because I have a minor deafness problem, but standing and forking my neck at an uncomfortable angle, I could clearly detect (I think) the sound of a peacock rattling pencils inside an old electric kettle (or something). Marvellous! More discernible still was the gloomy groan of some bloke who was saying how ghastly everything is ...

Roger Waters folds his arms and defies his beer as I compose a second question. Which is: 'Are you or are you not the gloomiest man in rock?'

'You can't expect me to take a question like that seriously,' he says, in his posh, soft voice. 'I refuse to answer that question on the grounds that it is stupid.'

Immediately I warm to the man. He has such a chip on his shoulder it's a wonder his arm doesn't drop off.

'I've been reading the nonsense that's been written about *Amused to Death*. Adam Sweeting [music journalist who said, in the *Guardian*, that the LP wasn't much cop], well, he's a complete prat. Always was, always will be.'

I protest. Adam Sweeting is not a prat; he's entitled to his opinion and a very nice man to boot, I say. Waters will have none of this.

'Sweeting is not a nice man. I don't know him but I know him. He says I write twaddle. He's wrong! He's one taco short of a Mexican meal. Sweeting is not the only arsehole; there's other cunts like Andy Gill and Charles Shaar Murray.'

Andy Gill and Charles Shaar Murray. They write for Q.

'Do they? Who gives a fuck who they write for when they can't fucking write?' This man is argumentative. This man is, er, several bass guitar notes short of a decent tune.

'It is extraordinary that Andy Gill and Adam Sweeting and Charles Shaar Murray didn't notice *The Wall*. They are supposed to be music journalists; how could they not have noticed this extraordinarily well constructed, deep and meaningful and moving and important piece of work? What the fuck's the matter with these arseholes? And now, with *Amused to Death*, they've missed another one. Those journalists, Adam Sweeting and Andy Gill and the other fucker and all the rest, they should be in hospital. I am confident that I am really clever and that I am really good at what I do so I'm not going to have prats like Sweeting and Andy Gill and Shaar bloody Murray telling me that I'm no good because they're wrong. *Amused to Death* is fucking, fucking good. Isn't it?'

He fixes me with a steely eye and I say that *Amused to Death* is probably magnificent but I can't really tell because, due to my 'technical problems', I cannot appreciate the superb and magnificent benefits of 'Q Sound'. He accepts this weedy excuse. He says:

Return of the living dead

'Well, anyway, I am one of the best five writers to come out of English music since the war.'

Let us turn the clock back. Let us go a-whizzing away to the 1960s when the world was young and Pink Floyd were wearing preposterous neckerchiefs and singing about Arnold Layne, a character given to stealing women's underwear, on drugs in clubs like UFO. What grand times those must have been.

'No, they weren't,' says Mr Gloomy. 'I don't want to go back to those times at all. There wasn't anything "grand" about it. We were laughable. We were useless. We couldn't play at all so we had to do something stupid and "experimental".'

This is too much. Pink Floyd's first LP, *Piper at the Gates of Dawn*, is an absolute monument of, er, a record that's quite good.

'Well, that was Syd. Syd was a genius. But I wouldn't want to go back to playing "Interstellar Overdrive" for hours and hours.'

Waters doesn't seem to like being in pop groups very much at all. In 1973, his group recorded *Dark Side of the Moon* and billions of people bought it (even though it was useless) and, naturally, this commercial success cheesed off Roger enormously.

'We'd cracked it. We'd won the pools. What are you supposed to do after that? *Dark Side of the Moon* was the last willing collaboration; after that, everything with the band was like drawing teeth; ten years of hanging on to the married name and not having the courage to get divorced; ten years of bloody hell. It was all just terrible. Awful. Terrible.'

Yes, Waters, the Mr Glum who refuses even to sniff at his brimming beaker of beer, is the gloomiest man in rock. He's enough to depress a gadfly. Perhaps I should jolly up the proceedings by telling you, soaraway-twingo-Bingo-*Sun*-style ... Twenty Things (Trimmed Down To A Handy, Fun-Packed Eight) You Didn't Know About Roger Waters, probably:

● **He doesn't much care for Radio One!**

'Radio One won't play my fucking single ('What God Wants')

147

because they know it's no good. They know it's not as good as Erasure or Janet fucking Jackson. They know that the British public shouldn't be listening to it. It makes my blood boil! If you're not seventeen with a baseball hat on back to front, they don't want to know.'

● **He's crackers!**

'It is very important, in our current predicament, that we try to give each other the chance to confront our feelings about things. There's some branches of the medical profession that now agree with me, saying that it's vital to hang on to what you felt when you were sixteen or seventeen or four, retaining a grasp on that stuff we had when we were children, when we saw the picture of the world in bright colours and strong sensations before it was all turned into a grey, uncaring mush by Adam Sweeting and Andrew Lloyd Webber.'

● **He doesn't (unlike other people) much care for war!**

'What irritates Adam Sweeting and Charles Shaar Murray and Andy Gill and all you journalists is that I gloomily and boringly enough find that my concern with war as big business doesn't diminish as the years go by. I feel just as gloomy about it at the age of forty-nine as I did when I was seventeen. I'm sure that my hatred of war was spurred on by the death of my father. I find myself compelled to feel for everyone's father or son who is killed in a war – and for what?'

● **He's crackers!**

'It's important for people to grasp sensations, like the kind of feeling I get when I am fishing. Some of us are gatherers and some of us are hunters. I'm a hunter. I need the mud of a river oozing between my toes. It's like Proust.'

● **He doesn't much care for Sinead O'Connor!**

(Ms O'Connor appeared at Waters' 1990 performance of *The Wall* in Berlin, in aid of Leonard Cheshire's Memorial Fund for Disaster Relief.)

'It was very, very hard work organizing that *Wall* concert but everyone was fabulous to work with – Bryan Adams, Van Morrison, Cyndi Lauper, bloody brilliant. All brilliant. Except for Sinead

O'Connor. Oh, God! I have never met anybody who is so self-involved and unprofessional and big-headed and unpleasant. She is so far up her own bum it's scary. With *The Wall*, she was so worried about her image, she was so worried that there weren't any other [adopts Irish "brogue"] "young people on the show". I and everybody else were old farts in her opinion so she was worried that she was doing something that wasn't "street" enough. And because it wasn't "street" enough, she came up with this brilliant idea: she said that I should employ Ice-T or one of those people to re-work one of my songs as a rap number! I am not joking! And neither was she fucking joking! That's the sad thing – she was serious! And then a couple of months after the show, when the record was out, she did an interview on American television, millions of viewers, and she rubbished the whole thing, said the *Wall* concert was a load of wank. I don't give a fuck what she thought about it but she should have kept her fucking mouth shut because it could only hurt the charity, the memorial fund and everything that Leonard [Cheshire] had done. She doesn't understand anything. She's just a silly little girl. You can't just lie in the corner and shave your bloody head and stick it up your arse and occasionally pull it out to go ["brogue"], "Oh, I tink this is wrong and dat is wrong" and burst into tears.'

● **He doesn't much care for 'stadium rock'!**

'Rock 'n' roll in stadiums is genuinely awful. These concerts are just like Tupperware parties – held in honour of the Great God Tupper – with fifty thousand people, only they don't buy Tupperware, they buy hot dogs and T-shirts and occasionally look up to watch those disgusting video screens that are all out of sync and make you feel sick and torture you. It's funny how people try to work their way around the greed of it all. Like U2 whose rationale is [feigned Irish accent] "Ooh, we have to play in stadiums 'cos all our fans want to come and see us." Well, fine: give your fans a really shitty show in a stadium – but for fuck's sake don't charge them twenty-five quid for it!'

● **He's a wag!**

'Michael Jackson performs in stadiums, too – but he's not doing it for himself, he's doing it to save all the little children in the world.'

● **He's crackers! But not** *that* **crackers because he doesn't much care for Andrew Lloyd Webber!**

(There's a lyric on *Amused to Death* which runs thus: 'Lloyd Webber's awful stuff / Runs for years and years / An earthquake hits the theatre / But the operetta lingers / Then the piano lid comes down / And breaks his fucking fingers.')

'Andrew Lloyd Webber sickens me. He's in your face all the time and what he does is nonsense. It has no value. It is shallow, derivative rubbish, all of it, and it makes me very gloomy. Actually, I've never been to one of his shows but having put that slightly savage joke on the record, I thought I'd better listen to some Andrew Lloyd Webber and I was staying in a rented house in America this summer and the people who owned the house had a whole bunch of his rubbish so I thought I'd listen to *Phantom of the Opera* and I put the record on and I was slightly apprehensive. I thought, Christ, I hope this isn't good – or even mediocre. I was not disappointed. *Phantom of the Opera* is absolutely fucking horrible from start to finish.'

Waters has spent many years of late in a suing situation. This is because what he does not much care for most of all is the new so-called Pink Floyd. In 1983, after the *Final Cut* LP, Waters flounced from the band. Four years later, the others, Gilmour, Mason and Wright, assembled, called themselves Pink Floyd, played lots of Waters songs on stages before huge and enthusiastic audiences, and made pots of money. Meanwhile, Waters toured to promote *Radio KAOS* but he wasn't called Pink Floyd so nobody gave a hoot. This made Roger gloomy. Lengthy litigation ensued. The animosity lingers.

'When those people went out calling themselves Pink Floyd, it made me very, very gloomy. And it made them very happy. Well, I don't know if it did make them happy. I don't think they are happy, actually. You should ask them. Ask them: "Are you happy? You sold out. You sold out everything. Did it make you happy?" I mean, how can they find it within themselves to go on stage and do my songs – songs from *The Wall*? I wrote *The Wall* as an attack on stadium rock – and there's "Pink Floyd" making money out of it by playing it in stadiums! Oh well, that's for them to live with. They have to bear the cross of that betrayal. They have to live with the denial of what the work was about. But when all that nonsense started, it made me fucking gloomy. I stood by a river and stared at myself in the water. Pathetic, I said. They despoiled my creations and there was nothing I could do about it.

'My one pathetic victory was that they had to put testicles on the pig [i.e. the blow-up pig he designed for the cover of the *Animals* LP, the pig that broke loose from its moorings at Battersea Power Station and ran amok through the Home Counties' skies]. If the pig had been exactly the same as the pig that I designed, I could have stopped them using it in their shows. So they put balls on my pig. Fuck them. Gilmour and Mason now own the name "Pink Floyd". They keep it in a box.'

Waters chuckles a chuckle born of loathing and self-pity. If only I had a shiny sixpence, I might press it into the old man's palm.

Earlier in this conversation, Waters 'pointed out' that he was one of the five best writers of music since the war. So who could possibly rank above him, I wonder? With furrowed brow he ponders the question. 'John Lennon,' he says. 'I'm trying to think,' he says. 'Er, I can't think of anybody else. You see, I don't much like listening to records. I'm a bit isolationist and insular. I'd rather be fishing. The list of great writers is very, very short but I am definitely in it. Er, who else is there that's better than me? I really don't know. Freddie Mercury, maybe . . .'

Roger Waters stares into his untouched pint pot. Then he picks it up, apparently toying with the idea of putting it to his lips. He smiles to himself and then he grins at me. He does not take a drink. Careful, as they say, with that axe, Eugene . . .

Mark Paytress

Shine On

Record Collector, January 1993

With the acrimonious parting of the ways between ideas man Roger Waters and the remaining trio, it's a wonder that the band members ever agreed on this partial history of Pink Floyd at all. Commercial considerations weren't entirely to the fore – neither the Floyd's first (*Atom Heart Mother*) nor last (*The Final Cut*) chart-toppers are included here. But ignoring the seemingly arbitrary choice of 1968's *A Saucerful of Secrets* and the post-Waters *A Momentary Lapse of Reason* from 1987, *Shine On* basically celebrates the Floyd in the '70s. A full-blown *Floyd in the '70s* box would have made far more sense, as would splitting the group's career down the middle and proceeding from *The Piper at the Gates of Dawn* to, say, *Obscured by Clouds*, followed by a second volume containing everything from *Dark Side* onwards.

I can't believe that *Shine On* truly represents the band's own selective guide to the best of Pink Floyd; rather, it's an idiosyncratic variation on their most popular work, and the inclusion of *Saucerful* and *Lapse* is tantamount to sheer bloody-mindedness. Perhaps it was the band's way of showing some self-assertion, particularly in the light of their refusal to so much as even entertain gentle suggestions from *The Amazing Pudding*, the respected and eminently knowledgeable Floyd-zine. Calling in the experts has been good enough for Bob Dylan, Jethro Tull and Jefferson Airplane, but not, it seems, for Pink Floyd.

Sergey Mikhlick

The post-war dream

The Amazing Pudding, April 1992

Moscow, 6 June 1989: Bykovo Airport; nearly three o'clock; raining. We managed the two thousand kilometre flight from Kerch; now we were in the capital of the USSR, four hours before the Pink Floyd concert. We had no tickets, but were confident that we'd see the famous musicians anyway. Our huge desire, heightened by the length of our journey, was now a ball which rushed along, flying to the mark: the concert.

Our haste was connected with the place where, for two nights already, a MYSTERY had occurred and thousands of people had come into contact with a dream. The traffic jam interrupted our reflections. The bus driver turned the wheel to find the way out – unsuccessfully. He decided to change the route, through the new Moscow regions. It was drizzling . . .

We watched, tired and cheerlessly, for the capital blocks. Despite the length of our route to the centre of town, we didn't see any billboard or advertisement about the Pink Floyd gigs. It seemed that the favourite stars often visit this city and the Russian publicity services were too tired to offer these amusements for the people.

At last we arrived at Olympic Stadium, where the concerts took place. We were surprised at the lack of fuss about the concert: the arches of Olympic inspired only indifference and calm. A few people stood near the box offices and gazed at their closed windows. Nearby was a plywood board on which it was written that the Barruchehi firm is the organizer of the Moscow shows. The words were written without any inspiration and the billboard looked like a film publicity placard in some country club, not in the city.

There was more sorrow with a rumour that the concert might not take place, because the previous concert, on 5 June, had been cancelled after a local tragedy. There was no source of objective information.

An hour and a half before the gig, I saw the first ticket tout. He wanted fifteen roubles for one eight-rouble ticket. I asked to see his goods and saw the standard tickets, without any symbols or the name Pink Floyd.

Suddenly, many people appeared on the square in front of the stadium, all looking for tickets. The only question they asked was, 'Have you got a spare ticket?' My friend queued for the box offices but they were closed. Later I bought two tickets: the touts sold them for fifteen roubles and twenty-five roubles.

The crowd grew. Tickets now cost thirty to fifty roubles each. It was about half an hour to the show and we had time for ice-cream. We found our seats on a big plan of Olympic and went to enter the stadium. A group of foreigners, apparently Bulgarians, bought tickets for one hundred roubles. We saw people saying, 'I'll buy a ticket for *any* money!' When I entered the stadium it was already dark. It was seven o'clock.

The audience stood still, waiting. I made my way through the rows and took a seat (I'm still not sure I took *my* seat!) as 'Shine On You Crazy Diamond' started. The show had begun!

My first impression was that I was seeing a DREAM. It was a real staging of my long-standing dream – when I heard about them, listened to their music. Now I could really see them, though without Waters! The dream was a reality. Sometimes I felt scared. Also, I felt a regret of the past, of wasted years. It was a very long way to meet the Pinks!

It was a wonderful dream! The audience met every song with great enthusiasm; it was quite clear they knew the band's work. Even Gilmour's addresses in English to the audience were received animatedly – it was amazing, because not many people in Russia know English. I think it was the warm and friendly atmosphere created by the musicians.

The concert was one whole show: they didn't switch on the general light between songs. Nobody bowed before the audience as they do at Russian bands' concerts. It was some witchcraft game.

Return of the living dead

Gilmour prepared each song in the dark as the audience waited quietly: then two or three sounds or chords revealed his songs and the whole hall exploded!

I watched the musicians through my binoculars: their instruments, their emotions. Gilmour's face radiated pleasure. I saw irritation only once – when he sang 'Money'. The sound of money on the tape woke some strange wish of the audience to make this sound LIVE and they began to throw money on the stage. This avalanche of silver and copper made many unpleasant minutes for the band. Their expressions were perplexed and irritated. I don't know what Gilmour thought about it, but I'm sure he remembered all sorts of unprintable English words!

I knew about Floyd's light effects beforehand, but it's better to see them once than just to know. I was really in shock! The flying pig and bed were absolutely terrific too! It was also very interesting to look at the round video screen; in 'The Dogs of War', I had the impression that the dogs, with their luminous eyes, were running onto the stage and out into the hall. Music, lights and video were so correlated that you felt on the border of reality and fantasy.

The musicians worked as gods. Gilmour and Page struck the audience with guitar and saxophone solos. Page's long hair flew behind him all over the stage. The vocalists worked as amazing machines.

There were many Russian servicemen among the crowd. They began to throw their caps onto the stage. Page caught one and then all the Floyd had them! It was unusual to see Gilmour with a Russian military cap on his well-known head. His eyes shone! People cried. One old man cried so much, the tears rolled down his face. He'd never seen *such* a concert.

After the show, the audience didn't want to leave the stadium. We didn't want to go away. But, finally, the concert was over. Thanks, Pinks! I had the magnificent dream!

David Bennun

The Division Bell

Melody Maker, 16 April 1994

At a secret moonlight ceremony in a small rural churchyard, the reviews editor threw back his cowl and presented to me, on a hempen cushion emblazoned with prisms, the new Pink Floyd album. 'Take this, Brother,' he intoned, 'may it serve you well.'

I raised my right hand and gave him the ritual response.

'Will Thursday be OK?'

Onto the coven stereo it went and, bliss of bliss, the rumours were true. A return to the elegant melancholia of *Wish You Were Here*. Hanging in the air like far-off thunderclouds, a track to rank with the most fragrant of modern ambient. A dignified, descending piano phrase curlicued with the distilled anguish of David Gilmour's guitar. 'Cluster One.' Magnificent.

Unfortunate, then, that the remaining hour should bring all the joy of chewing on a bucket of gravel.

This is the frustrating thing. Unlike his contemporaries, most of whom seem to have no clue as to what made their music good in the first place, Gilmour must have a clear idea why people who were but a twinkle in free love's eye when the Floyd were founded cherish those early '70s soundscapes. The delicacy of the instrumental, 'Marooned', which paraphrases *Dark Side of the Moon* to just the right degree, is a dead giveaway. It's as if he's dropping hints, amid the drear and desolate stodge that makes up most of the album, that he can still work magic.

It's only fair to point out, reading through the lyrics, that *The Division Bell* is a work of genuine gloom. Nobody could accuse Gilmour of being self-satisfied. Bitter, morose and disillusioned, more like it. I say 'reading through the lyrics' because you will quite possibly perish from boredom if you attempt to find this out by listening to the songs themselves. Next to *The Division Bell*,

Return of the living dead

1987's monumentally turgid Floyd comeback, *A Momentary Lapse of Reason*, sparkles in the memory as a refreshing fountain of light-headed verve.

Stupid, I know, to expect any better. And infuriating that the album should bait us with the prospect of it. I can, it teases, but I won't. Sit down and eat your suet.

No, thanks.

Jim Greer

A year in the life of rock 'n' roll

Spin, October 1994

Idly flipping the channels on the large-screen TV in my four-star hotel room (I make so much money writing this column that I mostly just roam the country looking for the best room service nowadays), sipping a mini-bottle of champagne from the mini-bar and fluffing, from time to time, my gigantic pillows, I happened to come upon something of nearly cosmic sociological significance that I am not sure anyone else caught, or at least I have yet to see the reports: the selling of Pink Floyd on QVC.

Did anyone else see this? QVC had a Pink Floyd sellathon, or a Pink Floyd-athon; it sold bits and pieces of the band like it was hawking housewares or hardware or cubic-zirconium all-terrain vehicles or something. I can't believe no other rock band ever thought of this before, but it stands to reason that the Floyd, a corporate rock band before there was such a thing, would be the first to summon the requisite entrepreneurial gusto. After all, in the bright new dawn of corporate sponsorship, QVC is simply a larger medium through which to disseminate the band's underlying message of awe-inspiring consumerism.

Here is what Pink Floyd is saying to you. You no longer need to earn your rock epiphanies. You no longer need even attend the concert at which these epiphanies will be carefully programmed for you. You can *buy* a piece of the rock, and you can do it from the comfort of your own home, as they say, or, as luck might have it, from the Hugh Hefner suite at the Four Seasons. Hell, I was gonna go down to Lounge Ax tonight to catch Palace Songs and Barbara Manning, but this is much easier, and much less smelly. Comfortably numb, indeed.

The QVC host, who I'm pretty sure was the guy on whom Chris Elliot based his 'Get A Life' character, is remarkable – even for home-shopping television – in both his unctuous charm and his all-consuming vapidity. '*Atom Heart Mother*,' he purrs to his rapt audience. 'One of my favourite album covers. It just *really* says a lot about rock music to me.' The cover to *Atom Heart Mother* is a picture of a cow. You know that, right? *A picture of a cow.* If that says a lot about rock music to this guy, I wonder what he'd make of a dressing room full of penis drawings? He goes on to flog Pink Floyd tour T-shirts featuring album covers from twenty years ago, which is about when anyone with a semblance of rock taste stopped listening to Pink Floyd, so I guess this makes some kind of sense.

The T-shirts are modelled by a young woman called Shannon, who does her best Eddie Vedder impression, eyes squeezed shut in an approximation of musical bliss, rocking gently on her heels. Rocking gently, after all, is about the most you can do to Pink Floyd. The band's music plays incessantly in the background. I enjoy the show, periodically yelling 'Rock, Shannon, rock!' at the TV screen, but Shannon is not being paid to rock, and everyone knows that these days you must be paid to rock.

A saucerful of dollars

Evening Standard, 4 August 1988

Sheila and I looked at each other. As if the artichokes had not been enough, what were we supposed to do with the sea of melted cheese bubbling in the pot that had been placed in the middle of the table? It was 1970, and in the home of the Pink Floyd's Nick Mason the Peels were trying to come to terms with their first fondue.

People often assume that if you have a job like mine – Radio One disc jockey, latecomers – you spend much of your time cavorting with the rich and famous. What are, say, Bros really like, people want to know – and I know they do not believe me when I say I have never met the blighters. And what about the woman who thought I shared a flat with Lou Reed and Stevie Wonder? How we hated it when it was Stevie's turn to cook breakfast.

But I did know a Pink Floyd. Still do, I suppose, although the last time I saw Nick at a charity stock-car event at Wimbledon earlier this year, he asked me how the family was with that far-away look, directed at a point half a league beyond my left shoulder, that tells you that even if you announce in a sepulchral voice that the whole lot of them were wiped out in an avalanche, all you are going to get is a nod and a murmured, 'Great!'

But come back in time with me to 1968 and the bottom of a boat drifting on the Serpentine. Lying in the bottom of the boat is Marc Bolan – endure this name-dropping for a moment, will you? There's not much more of it – and a hundred yards away the Pink Floyd are playing 'Saucerful of Secrets'. Looking back on it, this was probably the high point of the flower-power summer. The Floyd were the perfect band for this perfect day, their muscular evocations of time and space – whatever that may mean. One of my three appearances in 'Pseud's Corner' came when I compared the Pink Floyd sound to the sound of dying galaxies.

Return of the living dead

Tugging at the oars, bronzed muscles rippling in the bright sunshine – oh, all right – I brought the boat closer to the shore. Would they play 'Set the Controls for the Heart of the Sun'?

Peering myopically back, I do not, to be disarmingly frank, remember when I first heard the Pink Floyd. This, I assure you, is nothing to do with drug abuse. I smoked dope, of course. In some of the, er ... pads at which I was welcome it was virtually obligatory to do so. I never cared for it that much, though. Smoking anything usually made me feel sick, and no one thought it especially cool if you had to remove yourself from the chortling circle on all fours and head for a retching session beneath the highly coloured pictures of multi-armed Indian deities in the loo.

Did I see the band first on some children's television programme? The one on which they played 'Astronomy Domine'? Or had I heard and seen them as I lolled with affecting and fraudulent casualness against the wall of UFO in Tottenham Court Road?

It was not until the Pink Floyd came to Mother's club in Erdington, Birmingham, where I played the records only inches below a black ceiling permanently dripping with condensation, that I met any members of the band. Just about everyone – Fleetwood Mac, Family, Fairport Convention, to trawl the F's – played at Mother's and to experience the Pink Floyd bringing 'Interstellar Overdrive' to some sort of thunderous resolution in this confined space bordered on the transcendental.

Syd Barrett had long since moved on and the recruitment of Dave Gilmour, on initially somewhat tentative guitar, had ensured that we avid consumers no longer heard live any of Syd's rum little songs. Songs which had the claustrophobic effect of being locked in an old-fashioned nursery overnight. Also, Ron Geesin, a regular contributor to the programme which I was presenting for Radio One, was working with Roger Waters; the result or results of their labours to be offered up to the nation on the *In Concert* programme – or, as it was more commonly known, *The Sunday Repeated On Wednesday Show.*

Pink Floyd

A few hours before the recording of the new work in the BBC's Paris Studios in London's Lower Regent Street – an extended composition which involved a twelve-piece brass section and a twenty-piece choir – it still had no title. So, having suggested to the band that we should choose a newspaper headline at random as a title, I strode to Piccadilly Circus, bought an *Evening Standard* and returned to the Paris. Having rejected the traditional TOP FOOTBALLER IN TUG OF LOVE SHOCK, the attention of the Floyd was drawn to a story about a woman who had been equipped with some sort of nuclear pacemaker. ATOM HEART MOTHER ran the *Standard*'s caption and 'Atom Heart Mother' the work became.

That evening's recording went just fine and has been comprehensively bootlegged since, usually with my trite introduction intact. But 'Atom Heart Mother' never made as much sense in the studio or on record as it did at the Bath Festival later that year, when Sheila and I dozed in our Land-Rover beneath the stage after a grim day of being menaced by security personnel apparently in the grip of some near-medieval mass psychosis.

Hearing the band, the brass and the choir storming away over our heads as we drifted in and out of sleep was an experience eclipsed only by such moments as the births of our children and Alan Kennedy's goal in the Parc des Princes in Paris.

From this point on, the Floyd's march to mega-being status became a stampede, although I always took some sort of obscure pleasure in the certainty that they could have joined the audience at one of their own gigs without being recognized. Quite an achievement, that.

By the time that *Meddle, Dark Side of the Moon* (nineteen million and still selling), *Wish You Were Here* and *Animals* had come and gone, what little human contact I had had with the band was over. The most recent communication to come my way regarding the combo was what I regard as a slightly vulgar – if typical of the age – Press release announcing that Dave Gilmour and Nick Mason were to be the first Brits to help themselves to some new sort of Ferrari. A car costing, if memory serves, £163,000 a time.

Return of the living dead

Jealous? Of course I am. But as what *Q* magazine has rather prettily called 'the guardians of a unique legacy', perhaps they deserve the pleasures such an exotic purchase must bring.

Gerald Scarfe

Outside the wall

Scarfe by Scarfe, 1986

The helicopter takes off from beside the Hudson River, wheels right and flies dangerously under the bridge. 'I do that once in a while,' says the pilot, 'to liven things up.' We bump our way over the silver and grey evening map of New York to Nassau Coliseum. The band and I jump out, duck under the rotor blades and into the black limos.

The big blue silhouette of the arena stands out against the yellow and orange sky and we drive up the ramp and into the mouth of the monster building. The huge steel shutter slides down behind us. We are backstage at the Coliseum, a vast dry dusty cavern of concrete pillars, giant travelling boxes, a mass of electronic equipment, cables, wires, ropes, a giant circular cinema screen, guitars, keyboards and empty beer cans.

Roadies with ID badges step back as their bread and butter whispers by. Steel barriers and heavy heavies guard the band's area. We get out in an area of pretend civilization, a large Astroturfed square, sided by four trailer caravans, café chairs and café parasols over the café tables – very tasteful – very nice. To amuse the band there are pinball machines. Each caravan is loaded with drink and food. Here the band rests.

Outside, thousands press against the turnstiles, patiently filing to the seats. Excitement mounts. Stalls sell T-shirts, programmes, souvenirs, badges, sweatshirts, posters, postcards, buttons, hamburgers, frankfurters, soft drinks, beer, sandwiches – anything. The area fills and the noise increases.

The show starts. There is nothing like the roar of a crowd, ten thousand strong, giving its appreciation in these vast arenas. It's the most exhilarating sound. It's no wonder that rock stars go slightly mad with self-importance.

Return of the living dead

As the band plays, a huge alienating wall is built across the front of the stage spanning the whole arena, cutting the audience from the band. My giant puppets stalk the stage like great ghosts and three of my animated films are projected onto the huge wall simultaneously and synchronized with the live band. It all works like a dream. It's a success.

It always amazes me to see the end result of what started as a few scribbles on a piece of paper. Roger and I had sat for hours planning and designing the show in detail, and here it was, a giant Roman circus.

After the show the band come back onto their safe green Astroturf looking tense but relieved. The sidewalk café tables are peopled now with grinning hangers-on.

Going home – the long black limo.

We drive back to New York, the bottles of drink clinking gently as we speed over the concrete slabs. The rock star, a hunched figure in a racoon coat, sits in the middle of the black leather seat clutching a beer can.

Although we are doing sixty miles an hour, a lunatic bearded figure stares in at the window. 'Hey, Roger! Will you sign my album?' He leans further out of his driving seat causing his car to bounce and sway. It feels like disaster to me. Our driver knows what to do. He accelerates – so does the lunatic. We are joined now by another bouncing lunatic on the other side of the limo. The three cars speed down the motorway neck and neck. Oh, I've had enough of Rock and Roll.

Forthcoming attractions

Alan Jenkins (ed.)

Floyd on film

Spot the Bear, February 1992

It is well known that Pink Floyd have provided atmospheric and moody yet fascinating and not boring at all soundtrack music for films such as *More* and *Obscured by Clouds,* but some of their other film soundtrack work remains unknown because it has never been released on record. EMI have at least two soundtrack LPs recorded by Floyd during their most creative period in the late '60s lying around on a shelf somewhere, and have repeatedly refused to release them in spite of the dozens of letters from fans which besiege their offices every three or four years. What's the matter with you, EMI? Isn't it about time you put out these lost treasures?

The first of these is the soundtrack to *Lesbian Nuns On Big Motorbikes* which was released in 1969 but only shown for a limited period in a disreputable pornographic cinema round the back of a betting shop in Stockholm before it was withdrawn and forgotten about. It was released on video in 1983, but Floyd's soundtrack had been replaced with a cocktail-lounge jazz quintet playing selections from *The King And I.*

The Pink Floyd soundtrack includes material which was originally intended for a scathing and bitter concept album about the Methodist Church, plus one Syd Barrett number called 'Flossy the Pig'. We don't know what any of it sounds like though; probably 'Careful With That Axe, Eugene' but with worse lyrics.

The other film soundtrack, recorded the same year, was for a film called *How To Do Woodwork.* This short film, presented by television's 'Mr Handyman' Bill Godfrey, explains the best way to make your own shelves and put them up, either in the kitchen or living room.

Floyd's unreleased music for the film includes many songs about wood, including the fabled eighteen-minute soundscape 'Sawdustland'. In an interview for *Melody Maker* in 1970, Nick Mason said: '"Sawdustland" is our best track so far. It's so evocative. All you have to do is lie back and close your eyes, and there you are – in a shed with some tools.'

We think it's high time for proper video releases for these films complete with their original soundtracks. How about it EMI?

More

The Record Song Book, 1 August 1969

Pink Floyd were commissioned to compose the musical score for the film *More*, shown at the Cannes Film Festival recently. The film was directed by Barbet Schroeder and stars Mimsi Farmer and Klaus Grunberg.

All thirteen titles on the original soundtrack recording were composed and played by the group. The music is sometimes purely instrumental, sometimes both instrumental and vocal, *always* extremely interesting and arresting. Quite weird in parts too. Try the 'Main Theme' on side two, for an example.

But it's not all like this. There's a super little Spanish bit that sounds almost traditional, and there are other equally contrasting tracks. They did a great job!

Bernard Rose

Wind of change

Sounds, 7 February 1987

For those who persistently knock the British film industry, *When the Wind Blows* would appear to be the superlative antidote. This is only the fifth British animated feature film ever to be seen in the cinema, but as it employs a unique new animation process, I trust it will herald many more.

Past films about nuclear war have been very serious affairs, but this adaptation of Raymond Briggs' novel tackles the daunting subject in an entertaining and enlightening way.

Jim and Hilda Bloggs, a retired, easy-going couple, are caught up in their own world of nostalgia, and it takes a nuclear bomb hurtling towards them at several thousand miles an hour before Jim is at all ruffled.

Brought to life by brilliant vocal performances from Peggy Ashcroft and John Mills, this conforming, optimistic and very English couple look back to the last war for hope and inspiration. They can't quite get to grips with the fact that Germany, our old arch-enemy, is now our ally, and that Russia 'with that nice Mr Stalin', our old ally, is now our arch-enemy.

They reminisce about the Anderson shelters at the bottom of the garden and fondly remember the posters they used to stick on the walls. Like many of their generation, they had rather a good time in the last war.

This time, however, it will not be the same. Briggs is able to show just how unprepared we all are for nuclear conflict, and makes a complete mockery of the government leaflets like *Protect and Survive* that were available until comparatively recently. The Bloggs can't really understand this new technological age, and comically refer to computers as 'commuters'.

Cut off from the outside world, our hero and heroine try to

make sense out of it all in a typically British way, when there is so little sense to be made, and it's very refreshing to see life after the bomb treated in such a human way. The consequences of a nuclear winter have become a taboo subject, but are depicted here with sensitivity and subtlety.

The film promotes our awareness in a comical way made all the more effective by a harrowing, yet marvellously underplayed film score from Roger Waters. It is perhaps too British to achieve success in the USA, but if it raises our awareness of the dangers of conformism in Britain, then it deserves to be called successful.

Peter Whitehead

Tonite Let's All Make Love in London

Press release, 1994

I lived in Cambridge for one year painting, after graduating in crystallography. Syd Barrett was having an affair with the daughter of the house – Juliet Mitchell – and one of his early bands practised in the house. It sounded awful to me, like listening to Schoenberg!

His friend was Anthony Stern, with whom he had a double exhibition of paintings in Cambridge. When I moved to London and started filming, Anthony became my assistant and sound man and worked with me on all my films of the next few years. We always went to see his friend Syd playing with various bands.

I fell in love with Syd's girlfriend – on a frequent bounce – Jenny Spires, and, during a tempestuous fling, still loyal to Syd, she suggested I film the Floyd and use their music in my new film *Tonite Let's All Make Love in London*. I recorded two songs – one of which now (1994) sees the light of day for the first time – and filmed the recording studio session.

None of us had any idea they were going to be that big. Jenny was so high on acid all the time she wasn't able to see my good qualities and went back to Syd. I was very jealous and upset, but still decided to use the music!

Karl Dallas

Floyd's soundtrack becomes new album

Melody Maker, August 1982

Pink Floyd's Roger Waters flew out to the States for the US launch of the film of *The Wall* this week, leaving behind him a half-finished soundtrack album which has blossomed into a fully fledged new project for the Floyd.

'We were contracted to make a soundtrack album,' he said just before he left, 'but there really wasn't enough new material in the movie to make a record that I thought was interesting.

'The project then became called *Spare Bricks*, and was meant to include some of the film music, like "When the Tigers Broke Free" and the much less ironic version of "Outside the Wall" which finishes the movie; the sequence with the kids playing with the milk bottles, plus some music written for the movie but left on the cutting-room floor.

'I decided not to include the new version of "Mother" from the movie because it really is film music and it doesn't stand up. It's a very long song and, besides, I'm bored with all that now.

'I've become more interested in the remembrance and requiem aspects of the thing, if that doesn't sound too pretentious.

'Anyway, it all seemed a bit bitty, when I came up with a new title for the album: *The Final Cut.*'

Did this mean that it would be the Floyd's final album?

'I would doubt that very much,' said Waters.

'From that title, the whole thing started developing a different flavour, and I finally wrote the requiem I've been trying to write for so long, *Requiem for the Post-War Dream*, which became the subtitle of the album.'

A track of the new music for the album, 'The Fletcher Memorial

Home' – Waters' father was called Eric Fletcher Waters – seemed to indicate that the new album will complete the movement from the personal hang-ups of the rock-star hero of the *Wall* album to the more explicitly political stance of the movie.

The song, which contains a great guitar solo, points the finger at named politicians like Reagan and Haig, Thatcher, Brezhnev, as well as unnamed 'South American glitterati', presumably our junta allies and enemies in Chile, Argentina and the rest.

'It's become obvious that we were attempting the impossible in trying to finish the album before I go to the States, so we have got to the stage of a rough throw-together of all the work we've done so far.

'After about a week's work on the American launch, I'm going to take a holiday, and when we get back in September we'll finish the album.'

Brian Mulligan

Waters' view – just too black to be credible

Record Business, 19 July 1982

The Wall is a truly nasty film, relentless in its pursuit of depicting the worst excesses of human behaviour, a study of madness and the corrupting effects of violence and alienation. Roger Waters' view of mankind is totally and morbidly hopeless. He offers no solutions, no hope for the future. Love, even that of a mother for her fatherless son, is depicted as being unhealthy. The bleakness of Waters' vision is dramatically underlined at the end of the film when the wall is symbolically blown apart to reveal a scene on the other side no less desolate, with a young boy casually using a Molotov cocktail as a plaything.

Confusing, overlong, always disturbing and frequently frightening in the way the camera explicitly dwells on blood, rape, war and rotting humanity, *The Wall* is obviously painfully autobiographical. Waters' message seems to be that violence may be the only antidote to the claustrophobic way in which people's lifestyles are determined.

It catches up with Pink, a burned-out rock star, in his hotel room in Los Angeles, living in his own private hell, a hair's breadth away from madness and suicide. Lacking dialogue in the conventional sense, it leaps from present to past, to nightmarish visions of the future, sequences regularly enhanced by Gerald Scarfe's monstrous animation. Bob Geldof, who plays Pink, is uninhibited and hugely impressive. His destruction of the hotel room and subsequent self-mutilation are two of the film's more chilling moments.

Such is the awful fascination of what's happening on the screen that it is not always easy to give proper concentration to Pink

Floyd's music, but there are certainly occasions when the juxtaposition of visual and sound images, both equally violent, make a stunning impact on the senses.

Brilliant though director Alan Parker's film is, it was good afterwards to get back into the street and find that there were still ordinary human beings walking around. Hopefully its message will not be taken to heart by impressionable youth.

Tim Healey

Obscured by Clouds

The World's Worst Movies, 1986

A personal reminiscence: many years ago I went to see a double bill of 'youth' films at a crowded cinema in Islington, North London. The first movie was Jimmy Cliff's raw reggae triumph *The Harder They Come* (1972) – arguably the most powerful rock film ever made – which kept the audience enthralled throughout. The second movie, which boasted a soundtrack by Pink Floyd, perhaps suffered by comparison with the Jamaican classic. Nevertheless, I still think of it as positively the *least* powerful rock film ever made: a flaccid farrago of pretentious poop about a bunch of boulevard hippies seeking Shangri-La in the jungles of New Guinea. It was called *La Vallée* (1972); in translation, *The Valley* or, more preciously, *The Valley (Obscured by Clouds)*.

The film was made by Barbet Schroeder, a director already notorious at the time for an opportunist documentary he made about Idi Amin. The plot introduces beautiful Bulle Ogier as Viviane, wife of a French diplomat, who is on the look-out for exotic native artefacts to stock a chic boutique in Paris. Her particular desire is for some rare bird-of-paradise feathers and, in the company of a young Englishman called Olivier (Michael Gothard) and his wealthy friend Gaetan (Jean-Pierre Kalfon), she embarks on an expedition to the remote interior of New Guinea, heading for an uncharted declivity referred to on the maps as a valley 'obscured by clouds'.

During this portentous quest we are treated to much lushly scenic photography by the distinguished Nestor Almendros, a certain amount of erotic loveplay in the jungle and to druggy experiences among primitive villagers, all backed by what has kindly been referred to elsewhere as the 'appropriately trancelike' droning of the Floyd. *Wow*, veteran longhairs may find themselves breathing, *far out*. But what no brief review can possibly communicate is the tedium of the movie's soulful stares and meaningful conversations about life, nature and civilization presented by our band of boulevardiers.

The finale comes somewhat abruptly as, weary and depleted, the adventurers stagger to the misty and barren brow of a hill beyond which lies the valley of the quest. Will they reach it? What will they find there if they do? We are left with many tormenting questions; chief of which is, did the film-makers run out of money? It is all very well to end with an enigma, but after the rich cinematography of the earlier sequences, the finale looks suspiciously as if it may have been filmed on the embankment of some French municipal reservoir.

Back to that Islington cinema: I watched through to the end in the company of two friends, all of us hypnotized by the movie's awfulness. And when the lights came on and we rose to leave, we found ourselves in an almost empty cinema: the packed crowd of the earlier movie had simply melted away.

A collection of
great dance songs

Introduction

'Money'. 'Another Brick in the Wall'. And, of course, 'Beset By Creatures of the Deep'. Not to mention 'A Rooftop in a Thunderstorm Row Missing the Point'. The list of classics in the Pink Floyd canon is simply, er, listable. And here's the whole grisly story, from A to Z.

Taste and relevance are the criteria for inclusion. Among the absentees are Ron Geesin's tracks from *The Body* and the material that David Gilmour has recorded with other artists but not had a hand in writing (which would constitute a small book in itself). All bar the most outlandish bootleggers' inventions have also been omitted.

For all the myriad cover versions of Floyd's songs, the post-Barrett band rarely permitted other writers' compositions to contaminate their sphere. Nick Mason instructed the *NME* that Floyd had 'no musical policy whatsoever ... apart from the age-old thing of not doing other people's material. Obviously, our own interests us more.' The few that have slipped through the net – at soundchecks and club gigs – include Little Feat's 'Lafayette Railroad', Ace's 'How Long', Bill Withers' 'Ain't No Sunshine', Stevie Wonder's 'Living For the City', and other rock 'n' soul classics. That they have thus far resisted the temptation to commit these to tape can only be counted as a blessing.

The A to Z song format has been adopted because an album-by-album examination would doubtless have rendered both compiler and reader comatose; here, you never know which era is coming next. Moreover, it's not inappropriate for a band who favoured ruthlessly prosaic titles like 'Time', 'Money' and 'The Womb Bit'. It's also fitting that one of the few 'progressive' bands to have bothered writing songs (as opposed to triple-album suites) should have their work examined track by track. And, of course, it's a good opportunity to fillet the illuminating bits from lots of features whose inclusion in full would doubtless render even the most ardent Floydhead (even more) zoned out.

Few of the soundbites here are likely to be eagerly seized upon by the *Oxford Dictionary of Quotations*. But they do add up to give some insight into Floyd's songwriting; if only to expose it as a less cosmically orientated process than over-enthusiastic fans have imagined. 'Are we to presume from *Atom Heart Mother*,' enquired *NME*, 'that the Floyd are concerning themselves with man's eternal conflict with machines, and with the contrasts and gulfs between the extremes of the two, or is it just that it makes a funky title?'

Here's the answer.

A

Absolutely Curtains *Obscured By Clouds*
Gilmour – The majority of people who like to listen to music do
want to hear singing. They want to hear a voice telling them
something. The fact that that voice is babbling inanities doesn't
seem to matter terribly much. I would rather have someone playing
something beautifully on a guitar or sax or synthesizer than have a
voice babbling inanely.

Against the Odds *Wet Dream*
Wright – There's a lot of things in the songs ... questioning
where my roots are, where I want to live, whether I should be in
England. It's all about this place in Greece. 'Against the Odds' is
about this village where I originally went on holiday and now it's
my second home.

Alan's Psychedelic Breakfast *Atom Heart Mother*
Mason – I still consider us to be the last of the gifted amateurs. I
always thought our technical ability was quite limited ... We were
using cheap electric keyboards played backwards through a foot
pedal, yet we were perceived as music intellectuals.

All Lovers Are Deranged *About Face*
Gilmour – I call it my heavy metal track ... Mick Ralphs likes
that one. I just fancied a bit of headbanging before I got too old
for it.

Amazing Pudding, The
The inexplicable banner under which 'Atom Heart Mother' was first
unveiled. The title was subsequently appropriated by a Pink Floyd
fanzine, established by Ivor Trueman in order to finance his Syd
Barrett magazine, *Opel.*

Pink Floyd

American Bomber, The *When the Wind Blows*
An instrumental snippet, reprised on 'The Russian Missile' and 'The British Submarine'.

Amused to Death *Amused to Death*
Waters – I had at one point this rather depressing image of some alien culture seeing the death of this planet – coming down in their spaceships and sniffing around; finding all our skeletons sitting around our TV sets and trying to work out why our end came before its time – and they come to the conclusion that we amused ourselves to death.

And the Address *Profiles*
Mason – I'd like to be a writer, but I don't feel that I've got a lot of stuff burning inside me that I've got to get out, so in a way it's not a burden because it means at least I'm not a frustrated Floyd composer.

Anderson Shelter, The *When the Wind Blows*
Waters – What's interesting about the Civil Defence and County Council leaflets, about what to do in the event of a nuclear attack, is that they're a very good reference point for us all in the face of governmental directives. Now, in 1987 – although I'm sure these things still exist, and maybe haven't changed much over the last fifteen or twenty years – it's very easy to look at them, and to ridicule them, which this film does.

But there's a lesson to be learned: that if you read stuff now that is more contemporary, the possibility exists that it's just as ludicrous. Something that's been put out by the Government, or by an elected body of some kind, may be worth nothing to anybody.

Another Brick in the Wall pt. I *The Wall*
Waters – It is personal for me, but it's also meant to be about any family where either parent goes away for whatever reason; whether it's to go and fight someone or to go and work somewhere. In a way, it's about stars leaving home for a long time to go on tour . . . and maybe coming home dead, or more dead than alive.

A collection of great dance songs

Another Brick in the Wall pt. 2 *The Wall*
Julie Burchill, *The Virgin Rock Yearbook,* 1980

Undoubtedly the worst thing to happen to popular music since, say, Pink Floyd formed was the occupation of the Number One single position by Pink Floyd during this country's crossover into the '80s. Superstitious or not, there's something really sickening about going into something new when something so old and dead is doing so well.

(Ironic, too, that punk – *so* important – was caught in the middle; the middle of anything being just where it shouldn't be – the start of something or the end, yes. It wasn't for nothing that the adolescent Rotten embellished a Pink Floyd T-shirt with the sacred, scathing 'I HATE' – Pink Floyd represent everything that is sloppy and inferior about this country.)

'Another Brick in the Wall' really was another nail in my heart (a beautiful, underrated single by the ugly, overrated Squeeze) – imagine people buying like sheep a record telling them not to let themselves be rounded up by collies.

The way spineless libertarians flocked to the pap as being 'anti-establishment' was great fun to see; the incredible brainlessness of liking anything 'anti-establishment', no matter how hack! Talking of hacks, the *New Musical Express,* in a moment of sublime shallow stupidity (it wasn't irony or sarcasm; the *NME* hasn't had a sense of humour for, oh, a good two years now) called it 'the most anti-establishment Number One since "God Save the Queen"'. As if 'anti-establishment' was synonymous with 'glamour' or 'rebellion' or 'excitement'! Just the opposite!

Another Brick in the Wall pt. 3 *The Wall*

Waters – That's the moment of catharsis. (*Gleefully*) Isn't that where we break the TV sets?

The original lyrics boasted 'I don't need your drugs to bring me down, down, down'; a line which was but one victim of producer Bob Ezrin's 'editorial insistence'...

Ezrin – The record used to be Roger's life story and there were dates in the lyrics that put him at thirty-six years old. Kids don't want to know about old rock stars.

Any Colour You Like *Dark Side of the Moon*
Gilmour – We used to do very long, extended jamming on stage – interminable, many people would say, and probably rightly ... and that's what that one came out of.

4.30 AM (Apparently They Were Travelling Abroad)
The Pros and Cons of Hitch Hiking
Waters – I've written an explanation of what *Pros and Cons* is about, although it was quite clear to me what was going on. The narrative is by no means linear, however.

Apples and Oranges *single*
Barrett – It's unlike anything we've ever done before. It's a new sound. Got a lot of guitar in it. It's a happy song, and it's got a touch of Christmas. It's about a girl who I saw just walking round town, in Richmond. The 'apples and oranges' bit is the refrain in the middle.

Peter Jenner – You can't walk around the kitchen humming to The Pink Floyd. I mean, if you had the sort of sound they're making in the clubs coming over the radio while you're doing the washing up, you'd probably scream.

4.37 AM (Arabs With Knives and West German Skies)
The Pros and Cons of Hitch Hiking
Waters – (The album is) forty minutes of waking and dreaming, based initially on a dream that I had some time before: a specific dream about travelling in Europe where the spectre of the resurrection of Nazism came to me and all kinds of things like that ... but basically it was just a record about sex.

Arnold Layne *single*
Mason – We were asked to record six numbers, pick out the best two, then find a record company that would accept them. We recorded the first two, and they were snatched away and we were told, 'That's it!' All the record companies wanted the disc, so it was

Syd, age 3, and Rosemary Barrett, age 4$\frac{1}{2}$, enjoy a day at the beach (*Peter Anderson*).

The young Syd Barrett (*Peter Anderson*).

Syd Barrett, age 14, at home in Cambridge (*Peter Anderson*).

Syd at Butlins
in the early '60s
(*Peter Anderson*).

Syd at girlfriend Libby Gausden's home in the early '60s (*Peter Anderson*).

Syd in his back garden on his 17th birthday (*Peter Anderson*).

Pink Anderson (above) and Floyd Council (below), from whom the band took its name (*Kip Lornell/Blues Archive*).

Pink Floyd in its first incarnation (*Peter Anderson*).

An early performance (*Peter Anderson*).

Syd Barrett and Roger Waters performing, 1964 (*Peter Anderson*).

David Gilmour (*Peter Anderson*).

At the Camden Arts Festival, 1969 (*Brain Damage*).

Somewhere in Europe, 1969 (*Brain Damage*).

At the Hyde Park Free Concert in July 1970 (*Brain Damage*).

Performing *The Wall* in concert at Nassau Coliseum, 1980 (*Elliot Tayman*).

A rare shot of David Gilmour and Kate Bush performing at Amnesty International's Third Secret Policeman's Ball in March 1987 (*Julie Angel*).

In concert at Barcelona, 1988 (*Marc Malagelada*).

Live in Chicago, 1994 (*Brain Damage*).

Live in Chicago, 1994 (*Brain Damage*).

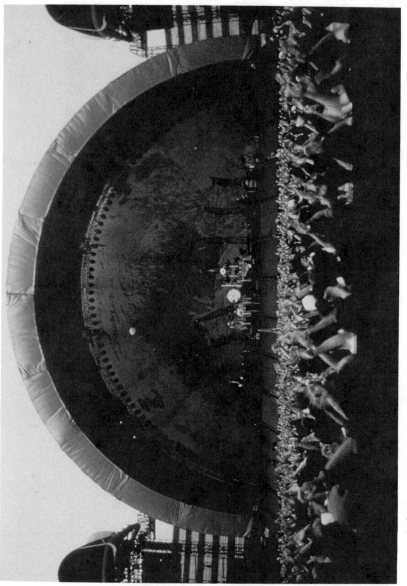

A daytime concert, a very rare event for Pink Floyd, in Oslo, Norway in August 1994 (*Brain Damage*).

Rick Wright, Billy Corgan of The Smashing Pumpkins, and David Gilmour performing at the Rock 'n' Roll Hall of Fame Induction Dinner in 1996 (*Elliot Tayman*).

At the time of the release of *Pulse* in 1996 (*Brain Damage*).

just a case of holding out for the biggest offer. But by the time
'Arnold Layne' was released, we had already progressed and changed
our ideas about what a good hit record should be. We tried to stop
it being released, but we couldn't. Still, it doesn't matter now.

Barrett – 'Arnold Layne' is nothing but a pop record. It wasn't
intended to represent anything in particular. It's just us.

Phil Collins – The Floyd I've never loved, apart from 'Arnold
Layne'. It was different, it was interesting, but I don't remember
going away very musically impressed.

Astronomy Domine *Piper at the Gates of Dawn*

Barrett – It all comes straight out of our heads, and it's not too
far out to understand.

Mason – It doesn't really have a meaning or a story. It's a very
typical Syd Barrett song.

Waters – Syd had one song that had anything to do with space:
'Astronomy Domine'. That's all. That's the sum total of all Syd's
writing about space and yet there's this whole fucking mystique
about how he was the father of it all.

At the End of the Day *Profiles*

Mason – There is one track where we actually ended up using an
old eight-track. I think it's 'At the End of the Day'; we used some
really old tape, a sort of original demo of it, because we couldn't
quite recreate the feel on later attempts.

Atom Heart Mother *Atom Heart Mother*

Mason – As a starter to it, Roger and I put down the whole
thing, just bass and drums, which was a crazy thing to do. We used
parts of that but basically it all got chopped up anyway, so it was a
totally unnecessary, amazing feat of brilliance. Totally useless.

Ron Geesin – 'Cos I was their mate, at the time (*sniffs*), they
proposed this thing that they wanted brass and choir for ... They
provided me with really what I would call the backing tracks. They
did have some of the 'astral slide guitar' on them in places – but I
really formed all the top, all the ... I don't know, the icing on the
cake or something ...

Working most of the time on my own but part of the choir section was done with Rick ... it was really just him and I discussing where the 'float' should go, where the wisps of smoke or lines ought to go.

Wright – It just doesn't flow very well. There's lots and lots of edits in it. I wasn't happy. I was at the time, but, thinking back, I'm not happy.

Gilmour – All I've ever tried to do is play music that I like listening to. Some of it now, like 'Atom Heart Mother', strikes me as absolute crap, but I no longer want or have to play stuff I don't enjoy.

Ron Geesin – I still like 'Atom Heart Mother' because it sends me a few grand a year in royalties and it was fun to do.

Waters – I wouldn't dream of performing anything that embarrassed me. If somebody said to me now: 'Right, here's a million pounds, go out and play "Atom Heart Mother", I'd say, "You must be fucking joking. I'm not playing that rubbish."'

John Peel – Particularly in America, people would spend weeks in debate about what the title meant. People are quite capable of starting religions (*laughs*) based on 'Atom Heart Mother'. You know, some attractive blonde woman would be called Atom Heart Mother and the rest of them would call themselves Red Indian names and worship her ...

Attack, The *When The Wind Blows*

Waters – I thought *When the Wind Blows* was brilliantly written and filled a hitherto empty slot in English literature.

B

Baby Blue Shuffle in D Major
An early title for 'The Narrow Way pt 1'.

Baby Lemonade *Barrett*
The name 'Baby Lemonade' was subsequently adopted by a group described in *NME* as a 'Glasgow buzzsaw guitar outfit'.

Ballad of Bill Hubbard, The *Amused to Death*
Waters – *Amused to Death* deals with the argument of whether TV is good or bad – and I set out to show that it can be both. A great inspiration to me was a television documentary in which World War One veterans talked about their experiences. It was from this programme that I sampled dialogue . . .
There was always a question mark in the back of my mind as to how relevant it was to include Alfred Razzell's dialogue. I found it very moving but I didn't know whether anyone else would. So far, the reaction has been favourable; they're making the connection. That original programme confronted the horrors of war and told the real story. It was an example of television taking its responsibilities seriously.

Biding My Time *Relics*
Gilmour – How do I relax? Well, getting drunk, falling about and being a bastard. Yeah, all that stuff.

Big Theme *La Carrera Panamericana*
Mason – I suppose there's a moment of irritation when people assume a rock star can't be serious about other things. You just hope that, sooner or later, people will start to understand you're serious. But I don't have any plans to leave the band. I'm a musician. Motor racing is a passion for me . . . it might be a bad thing to turn that passion into a job.

Bike *Piper at the Gates of Dawn*

Norman Smith – It was a pretty difficult job, actually, with Syd, because I think Syd used music with sort of lyrical phrasing or, if you like, he used lyrics with musical phrasing.

It was a statement being made at a given time, that meant that if you came back five minutes later to do another take, you probably wouldn't get the same performance. You probably wouldn't get the same tune (*laughs*) or musical composition . . .

It made editing virtually impossible . . . I think, if I remember rightly, we went through quite a few of Syd's songs and he played me a few, and it was very difficult to figure out which I liked and which I didn't like, so we'd come back to them and maybe try those songs again (*laughs*). Which made it even more difficult . . . It was a very slow, unwinding process.

Waters – I listened to *Piper* again the other day. Dated isn't quite the word. I just don't think much of it'll last, that's all.

Bike Song, The

The working title for 'Bike', edited just in time for the final master of *Piper at the Gates of Dawn*.

Birdie Hop *Opel*

A Barrett title rumoured to refer to UFO co-founder John 'Hoppy' Hopkins.

Black Ice *Profiles*

Mason – I made *Fictitious Sports* more as an exercise. There's more longevity in *Profiles* . . . it's strong enough to be accepted as a 'proper' record.

Blue Light *About Face*

Gilmour – 'Blue Light' is in fact two separate tracks recorded at the same tempo. Afterwards, neither was interesting enough individually, so we just hacked them up with scissors, made up a new drum part and got the bass player to redo his part. It was hundreds of pieces of two-inch tape just stuck together. Bob Ezrin suggested putting the brass parts on them.

There wasn't going to be a solo; it was just going to be a fade-out. I was finishing the vocals on the last day of recording before we mixed. For the amusement of Bob Ezrin and the engineer in the other room, I made a silly speech, and they left the tape running after the vocals ended. So that's mixed in there slightly. Bob said, 'Now that you've got that silly speech on there, maybe we should stick a little guitar solo on the end.' So I said OK.

'Blue Light' is not the lyric I'm proudest of on this record. It's a signal for danger: on top of police cars there's a blue light ... I can't really illuminate on the song. It's a double meaning really: everything in the song pertains to either a girlfriend or to our illustrious leader, Margaret Thatcher ... but only in a vague way. Not particularly deep and meaningful, that one.

Gilmour's 'silly speech' runs thus: 'I'm not awfully good at this funky sort of thing but sometimes, when the inspiration strikes, I can get down with the best of them.' The song now languishes in Floyd's Hall of Shame.

Blues
A title appended, by more prosaic bootleggers, to the blues instrumental performed at shows in 1971. More daring compilers have opted for 'Blues Improvisation', 'Blues Jam' and 'Pink's Blues'.

Bob Dylan Blues
An unreleased Barrett song recorded in 1970. The lyrics boast: 'I've got the Bob Dylan Blues / I've got the Bob Dylan Blues / My hair and my hat's in a mess / but I don't give a damn about that.' The tape is believed to be in the possession of one D. Gilmour.

Body Transport *The Body*
Geesin – The film people just couldn't find the right people to do the score for a film completely about the human body. As a last resort, and I mean a last resort, the producer Tony Gardner phoned John Peel and John recommended me, because I had dabbled in documentaries and a few commercials in my time.

Boo To You Too *Fictitious Sports*
Mason – What I obviously hope is that people who are interested

193

in the Floyd might give it a listen, simply on the grounds that it's relevant to the band.

Boom Tune

Joe Boyd – I was looking for a follow-up to the Purple Gang's 'Granny Takes a Trip' single and so I asked Syd to give me a tape of his songs. He had some really cheerful, melodic, wonderful tunes; one of which was 'Boom Tune', which the Purple Gang were definitely going to do. But somehow it never happened, and I lost the tape.

This may be an alternative title for 'Here I Go', in view of the latter's line, 'What a boom this tune'.

Boppin' Sound, The

A title logged at Abbey Road in February 1968 during the *Saucerful Of Secrets* sessions. This may be either an unreleased piece or a working title for an album track.

Brain Damage *Dark Side of the Moon*

Waters – The line 'I'll see you on the dark side of the moon' is me speaking to the listener, saying 'I know you have these bad feelings and impulses, because I do too; and one of the ways I can make direct contact with you is to share the fact that I feel bad sometimes.'

Mason – The human race doesn't move backwards, so there's obviously going to be a lot more unpleasantness and general ghastliness.

Bravery of Being Out of Range, The *Amused to Death*

Waters – The first two verses were written in the mid-'80s and are an evocation of Ronald Reagan. But the third verse used to be about Berlin – 'Berlin babies sing this song' – and that's gone. So this is the only bit specifically to do with Desert Storm ... the theatre of the people in the bar watching television and enjoying *us* winning is what that third verse is about.

Breathe *The Body*

Waters – I take myself more seriously than they think somebody in rock 'n' roll ought to be allowed to. In rock 'n' roll we are not allowed the breadth of expression that you are if you write books, for instance. If you write books, you can be Enid Blyton or Harold Robbins or Kurt Vonnegut or Thomas Mann or anyone you like, and that's OK because it's accepted that these things can be very disparate . . . But a lot of journalists, particularly, get very possessive about rock 'n' roll: 'It's gotta be like this . . . If it's not Bruce Springsteen, it's no good . . .'

I don't know. Maybe it is just so much neurotic wailing. It's fun, anyway.

Breathe *Dark Side of the Moon*

Waters – As succeeding generations of young executives at film companies think, 'Christ, we can make a lot of money off this,' I get offers. Luckily, I can stop it because I wrote so much of the music that I'm in control. There will never be a film of *Dark Side of the Moon*. It would be madness.

Bring the Boys Back Home *The Wall*

Waters – For me, (this) is the central song of the whole album. It's about not letting anything become more important than friends, wives, children, other people . . .

The song, added Waters, 'took on a whole new life' at the 1990 performance of *The Wall* in Berlin.

Leonard Cheshire – To be honest, I am more of a big band man. Glenn Miller, that type of thing. I quite like the Inkspots, too.

Burning Bridges *Obscured by Clouds*

Waters – Given what we put on it, I don't find it bad.

Mason – I thought it was a sensational LP, actually.

By Töüching *Identity*

Wright – I know the criticism of computers is that they take the soul out of music, but I don't see it. Music is an expression of something inside of you. It doesn't matter whether you play it on a piano or program it into a computer as long as the result – the song – is the way you want it to be.

C

Candy And A Currant Bun *Arnold Layne b-side*

Waters – I used to smoke a little dope from time to time, but there was nothing strange about the way we lived. Certainly, some of the music was a little bit strange within the context of the times as they were then . . .

Can't Get My Motor to Start *Fictitious Sports*

Mason – Carla (Bley) knows that I've got a particular weakness for cars – an obsession shared with Mike Mantler, her husband. We spent an awful lot of time, when we should have been recording or engineering, talking about cars, so I think she felt that was extremely well suited!

Careful With That Axe, Eugene *Ummagumma*

Gilmour – 'Careful With That Axe, Eugene' is basically one chord. We were just creating textures and moods over the top of it – taking it up and down. Not very subtle stuff. There was a sort of rule book of our own that we were trying to play to – and it was largely about dynamics.

Wright – It's not a huge message to the world, you know. We often pick titles that have nothing really to do with the songs.

Ron Geesin – The Floyd have never incited anyone to violence, so from that point of view they have made a contribution to the world. They were always quite a peaceful orchestra, even with Roger screaming his head off, as he still tends to do.

Waters – There was a famous occasion in the Cobo Hall in Detroit. It was fantastic. We used to have these bins specially made, that were made of mild steel to put the charges in. In a number called 'Careful With That Axe, Eugene', there's a particular point where I scream loudly and these bangs go off behind us. We'd ordered these bins to have half-inch steel bottoms and quarter-inch steel sides; they came back and they had quarter-inch steel bottoms, so we said, 'No, that's not enough,' and sent them back. Instead of taking them apart and rebuilding them with half-inch steel bottoms, they put another quarter-inch steel plate on top of the first one. And it superheated. I've no idea of the physics involved. Inside this bin, holding it down, is a stage weight. A big fourteen-pound stage weight, and it exploded. Went off like a bomb. There was nothing left of this bin; it disappeared. The top of the bass cabinet it was standing on, which was made of three-quarter-inch marine ply, just . . . it just wasn't there any more. How nobody was killed we will never know. A guy sitting thirty rows back in the audience copped a piece of this marine ply – hit him in the stomach. All the speakers – every single speaker in the gear – blew immediately. I just remember feeling this hot blast on the top of my head and seeing the back of the Hammond organ go spiralling up into the air in slow motion.

Of course, the audience thought it was fantastic. They were on their feet for . . . seemed like hours.

Carrera Slow Blues *La Carrera Panamericana*
Valentine Lindsay, Mason's co-driver in the Panamericana race, told the *Mail on Sunday*: 'If we'd cheated like some of the others, we could have done better, but Nick was too honest!'

Cat Cruise *Wet Dream*
Wright – I do have acoustic guitars at home, but the only reason I have them is either as a social thing, strumming away and singing with friends, or for writing on sometimes . . . I know all the chords but I'm not any more interested in it than that.

Chain Of Life *The Body*
Geesin – I was getting on well with Roger as a human, you know; we played golf together. It's a pity more people don't play golf together . . .

Chapter 24 *Piper at the Gates of Dawn*
Barrett – That was from the *I Ching*. There was someone around who was very into that. Most of the words came straight off that.

Childhood's End *Obscured By Clouds*
Bernard Butler (ex-Suede) – People used to say, 'Oh, you can't listen to that prog rock nonsense,' but I don't care. Some of their stuff is amazing. It takes my breath away. I wasn't around then so I have to backtrack. Now I've discovered Pink Floyd, I can't understand why people listen to The Orb.

Chooka-chooka-chug-chug
A working title from Barrett's abortive 1974 sessions. The tape boxes also list other description-cum-titles, including 'If You Go, Don't Be Slow', 'Echo Stuff' and 'John Lee Hooker'.

Cirrus Minor *More*
Waters – We did sixteen tracks for *More* in five sessions; which for us is silly – and we suffered from it. Actually, I quite like it, though we'd like to play that one down.

Clowns and Jugglers *Opel*
Malcolm Jones – He called it 'Clowns and Jugglers' and decided to call it 'Octopus' later. I'd have preferred it to be called 'Clowns and Jugglers', actually; I think it's a much nicer title.

Cluster One *The Division Bell*
Gilmour – We stopped trying to make overtly 'spacey' music and trip people out in that way in the '60s. But that image hangs on and we can't seem to get shot of it.

Come In Number 51, Your Time Is Up *Zabriskie Point*
Gilmour – We spent three or four weeks in Rome doing *Zabriskie Point*. It seemed like an age, and Antonioni didn't like anything for his film, really, that we did. I mean, he only used three pieces in the film. One was a kind of remake of 'Careful With That Axe, Eugene', which is probably what he got us for in the first place.

Come On Big Bum
Title spotted on a 1984 Dave Gilmour set-list, alluding to . . .

Comfortably Numb *The Wall*
Gilmour – I actually recorded a demo of 'Comfortably Numb' at

A collection of great dance songs

Bear Les Alps studio while I was there doing my first solo album, but it was only a basic little chord pattern which was really not much else. It was too late in the day; it was after the drummer and bass player had gone home and I was on my own, working away. I had a lyric for that song but it was of no value in that circumstance, so we put lyrics of Roger's on it instead.

Waters – I was in Philadelphia; I had terrible stomach pains. I can't remember exactly when it was, but this idiot said, 'Oh, I can deal with that,' and gave me an injection of some kind. God knows what it was, but I went (*sound of hitting floor*).

That's not really what it's about, though. The song is actually about the kind of living death condition that a lot of people find themselves in when life seems unreal to them and they can't work out why.

Gilmour – We argued over 'Comfortably Numb' like mad. Really had a big fight; went on for ages ... These things that seemed so important at the time, I can hardly remember why one thought they were (*laughs*). We recorded two versions: I doubt if I could even tell the difference these days. They were exactly the same tempo. One was just a little looser – I'd call it a sloppier version myself and I liked it slightly tighter ...

Waters – ... So when Ezrin and I went off to do vocal parts, Dave spent a week re-recording the track ... It came over on the twenty-four-track tape and Ezrin and I were both really expecting it to be great ... and we put it on and looked at each other and (*yawns*) ... because it was just awful – it was stilted and stiff and it lost all the passion and life the original had.

Ezrin – I fought for the introduction of the orchestra on *The Wall*: the expansion of the Floyd's sound to something that was more ... 'filmic' is the word. This became a big issue on 'Comfortably Numb', which Dave saw as a more bare-bones track, with just bass, drums and guitar. Roger sided with me. So it's a true collaboration: David's music, Roger's lyric and my orchestral chart.

Gilmour – Roger and I had a real shouting match at this Italian restaurant in north Hollywood. We'd gone there with Bob Ezrin to have it out over something – probably 'Comfortably Numb', because the only thing I'd really argue with Roger over was my own music. With his music, I wouldn't bother . . .

Slash – David Gilmour is a great player . . . All the Pink Floyd albums are really great. But I think my favourite playing of his is on 'Comfortably Numb'. It sounds so good; it's got this weird tone to it.

Coming Back to Life *The Division Bell*

Gilmour – 'This strange but irresistible pastime'? Oh, it's sex, obviously. Sex and procreation.

Committee, The

Music written for *The Committee* (1968), consisting of eleven minutes' worth of instrumental segments, plus an early version of 'Careful With That Axe, Eugene'. Bootlegs of this material – which was never officially released – are lifted from the film soundtrack and thus also include dialogue.

Mason – The music had been made in a single morning and, as it was not very convincing, there was no point in releasing it.

Cönfüsiön *Identity*

A resounding lack of ringing cash tills greeted the release of 'Confusion' as a single. A planned video for the song was promptly scrapped.

Corporal Clegg *A Saucerful of Secrets*

Waters – I was demoted from lead guitar to rhythm guitar and finally bass. There was always this frightful fear that I could land up as the drummer.

Country Song

Another mysterious entry in the Floyd recording log. It may be a working title for a piece such as *Zabriskie Point*'s 'Rain in the Country'.

Gilmour – There isn't really a wealth of unreleased material. If we all got killed in a plane crash and they wanted to delve through the archives in order to release thirty-four other Pink Floyd things, they'd have a very hard time.

A collection of great dance songs

Country Theme *La Carrera Panamericana*
Mason – It's all a terrible mistake. We thought we were going to Torremolinos! We were given a drivers' briefing that was clearly calculated to put the fear of God into all of us. We were basically told the road has been destroyed by rain, the bridges are washed away and the Mexican police are going to arrest us for the slightest infraction and throw us into gaol. Apart from that, everything's looking absolutely terrific!

Cruise *About Face*
Gilmour – I can't feel it in me to commit myself to nuclear disarmament, but there are specific aspects of the campaign I'd agree with. One is not having cruise missiles in our country and particularly not near where I live! But it would be immoral to expect America to retain nuclear weapons in order to protect us when we don't keep them to protect ourselves. It's a difficult question.

Crumbling Land *Zabriskie Point*
Gilmour – A country and western tune which he could have got done ten times better by numerous American groups, but he used ours. Very strange . . .

Cry From The Street *David Gilmour*
Gilmour – I do want to make another solo record sometime or another, but that's sometime in the future. That's strictly as a sideline to Pink Floyd. That doesn't mean that there is any discontent within Pink Floyd . . .

Crying Song *More*
Waters – The argument we are constantly coming up against is that you can't have the luxury of socialist principles and compassionate feelings about people who are less well off than you are; you can't sincerely have feelings for them; and you can't sincerely feel the system's wrong, and wish there was some kind of a socialist system, here and elsewhere – and still have five grand in the bank, or whatever. Which is an argument we're constantly having.

201

Pink Floyd

Cüts Like Ä Diämönd *Identity*
Gilmour – I haven't listened to much of the Zee album. I've listened to a couple of tracks. It doesn't stun me particularly.

Cymbaline *More*
Waters – I think we, and a hell of a lot of other groups, are in a position now to start raising standards a bit, but we don't ... The reason that they haven't is that the money's there, and people are prepared to spend it on them doing what they're doing now, so they go on schlepping around the country ... and maybe they get a new and wonderful buzz out of it, communicating with the audience every night, but I don't believe it. It's a job, a fucking well-paid job, with all the ego-boosting and stuff and everything, and I think it becomes very mechanical.

D

Dark Globe *The Madcap Laughs*
Peter Jenner – I think Syd was in good shape when he made *Madcap*. He was still writing good songs, probably in the same state as he was during 'Jugband Blues'.
Malcolm Jones – I always liked this one, actually.

Dark Side of the Moon
A Waters song written during the *Meddle* sessions. It failed to make the album but evidently seemed like a good idea.

Deafinitely *David Gilmour*
Gilmour – The basic writing is, I think, quite good (on the album). I'm very happy with all the stuff. I could have spent a lot more time honing the ideas down and making it a bit more compact ... but I really wanted to get in and do it fast. I was only three weeks recording it and it does show a little bit.

Death of Sisco, The
A song referred to only in the Janet Huck piece reprinted in this book. 'Sisco' may have been a typographical error, as 'Disco' would seem more plausible.

Do Ya? *Fictitious Sports*
Robert Wyatt – Musicians don't say what we think of each other, it's uncool!
Mason – I'm president of the Robert Wyatt fan club, or I would be if there was one. I really like his style very much.
Robert Wyatt – I was just a session singer and a very honoured one too.

Doctor, The
A working title ('Comfortably Numb'?) or unreleased track from *The Wall*. Similarly vague titles from those sessions include 'Education',

'Prophet', 'Synth Theme' and the more helpfully monickered 'Overture for Comfortably Numb'.

Dogs *Animals*

Gilmour – I did one or two very nice, slightly different guitar solos on it that I was quite pleased with ... It's two-part in the melody sections, but the last line of the first solo, I believe, is a three-part descending augmented chord. Which is quite nice and I was very proud of it; I thought it was very clever. Then Roger went and wiped it out, by mistake, and I had to recreate it.

Wright – Roger's preoccupation with things such as madness and the business is something that I didn't feel nearly so strongly about, at the time anyway. So that made it very difficult for us to communicate about it.

Dogs of War, The *A Momentary Lapse of Reason*

Gilmour – I had the idea and explained it to Anthony (Moore). He came up with the first draft of words; we chopped and changed it over quite a long time until it wound up as it is. The music was done, fairly much, when we had a computer accident that took a sample of someone laughing and accidentally played it. In the background, this laughter actually sounded like dogs yapping and the way I'd sung the demo also had elements of that long before we had that lyric. It's about physical and political mercenaries, really.

Mason – I like 'Dogs of War' because it's a great R&B track to play live.

'The Dogs of War' twice topped the 'Worst Floyd Song' section of *The Amazing Pudding*'s readers' poll. Conspiracy theorists may wish to note that former *numero uno* 'Seamus' also has a doggy theme. Were the famously cat-loving Floyd attempting to usurp man's best friend?

Dolly Rocker *Opel*

Gilmour – He's not a happy person ... He's just completely on another level.

Dominoes *Barrett*

Gilmour – The song just ended after Syd had finished singing and I wanted a gradual fade so I added that (final) section myself. I played drums on that, by the way.

Don't Leave Me Now *The Wall*

Waters – A lot of men and women do get involved with each other for lots of wrong reasons and they do get aggressive towards each other and do each other a lot of damage. This is obviously an extremely cynical song ... (*laughs*) Yes, it is very depressing – I love it, I really like it.

Doreen's Dream

The distinctly unexotic working title for 'Julia Dream'.

Dramatic Theme *More*

Wright – Doing the music for films is very challenging – it means that we have to express facts and scenes in music. And financially it pays off, and so leaves us more time on our own to develop our individual ideas.

Drop In From The Top *Wet Dream*

Wright – Doing this album has helped me get back my creative energies for the next Floyd thing.

4.58 AM (Dunroamin, Duncarin, Dunlivin)
The Pros and Cons of Hitch Hiking

Waters – When we were recording *The Wall*, I needed a melody suddenly because it was developing as a theatrical idea. I thought: Hang on a minute, there's one in *The Pros and Cons*; you could take it out of its quiet self and treat it very monolithically and bombastically and it would sound completely different and it might work. So I tried it and it did work in its new context, but for me it never lost its identity as this quiet, dreamy tune that was the beginning of *Pros and Cons*.

Actually, I make the reference later on, in the middle of side two, at the end of 'Dunroamin, Duncarin, Dunlivin', when the truck driver is throwing the hero out of his cab. I get the orchestra to play it and it resolves to E minor, so we actually do play it once like 'In the Flesh', which is just ... a joke ... for people who remember *The Wall*.

E

Echoes *Meddle*

Gilmour – Have you ever heard that musical thing where they get a tone that seems to go on; you know, like those Escher paintings where the staircases go up and up and up, never getting anywhere? Well, there's a tone and it keeps going 'ding ding ding ding', and up and up and the same time they are surreptitiously taking out high frequencies, so that it never gets anywhere. That's what the choir on the end does right on the very end of 'Echoes'.

Waters – Up until then, I think I was still stuck with all the airy-fairy mystical bollocks from the '60s.

Gilmour – I don't remember exactly when I began to be proud of my playing. I would imagine it was in the early '70s. At the end of 'Echoes' is this kind of guitar orchestra going on, about four different parts all joining together to create a sound. I still think that is wonderful.

Mason – Why did we drop 'Echoes' in '87? Because it wasn't much fun to play. It was a bit dull. It's very repetitive. It can be quite nice but we just found there wasn't enough 'meat' in it to make it interesting . . .

Eclipse *Dark Side of the Moon*

A forty-five-minute piece toured around the world during 1972. Premièred at the Brighton Dome in January of that year – a performance that collapsed midway owing to 'severe technical horror' – it was laid to rest in September in Canada, only to re-appear the following month in London under what was apparently its original monicker, *Dark Side of the Moon*. The 'Eclipse' title was resurrected when Waters decided that the piece needed a more climactic finale.

Waters – It is more theatrical than anything we've done before;

more into the whole theatre/circus thing. And in concept it's more literal, not as abstract as the things we've done before. It's more mental – we've gone mental.

Wright – *Eclipse* is a better title for it.

Waters – The album uses the sun and the moon as symbols; the light and the dark, the good and the bad, the life force as opposed to the death force. I think it's a very simple statement saying that all the good things life can offer are there for us to grasp, but that the influence of some dark force in our natures prevents us from seeing them.

Chris Thomas – One of the questions was, what is the dark side of the moon? That's when Jerry (*Abbey Road doorman*) said, 'There's no dark side of the moon, really – as a matter of fact, it's all dark.' We just said, 'Wow, we've got to finish the album with that.'

Alan Parsons – The bit you don't hear is that after that he said, 'The only thing that makes it look alight is the sun.' The band were too overjoyed with his first line, and it would have been an anticlimax to continue.

Effervescent Elephant
A working title for . . .

Effervescing Elephant *Barrett*
Apparently one of the first songs Syd wrote, this remained sufficiently high in his estimation to be played live for the BBC and at a one-off London gig in 1970.

Barrett – I used to enjoy playing live; it was a gas. But so's doing nothing. It's art-school laziness, really.

Embryo
A live staple in the early '70s, originally recorded for the studio half of *Ummagumma*. Released on the Harvest sampler *Picnic*, it can now be found on the spiffing US compilation *Works*.

Gilmour – We all went off it for some reason. We never actually finished the recording of it . . . and EMI got Norman Smith to mix it, and they released it without our OK.

Empty Spaces *The Wall*

Waters – Everything that happens to (Pink) isolates him even more. His difficulty is constantly compounded because at no point is he able to take a side-take on himself ... It's very difficult for any of us to slide sideways and say, 'Hold on, what's really happening here is ...' Like most of us, Pink is on his particular set of tracks and can't get off because he doesn't even know he's on them.

5.06 AM (Every Stranger's Eyes)
The Pros and Cons of Hitch Hiking

Mason – He played the demo tracks for us and we thought it best he record it as a solo album. I suppose if we'd said, 'Oh, please, please, Roger, can we record it?' we probably would have, but it was something he had to get off his chest and I'm glad he did, even if (the LP) hasn't been commercially successful.

Waters – There's something to be said for disastrous business miscalculation and failure in the marketplace.

Cherry Vanilla, the song's 'waitress' (and the hitch-hiker on 'Apparently They Were Travelling Abroad') is a self-styled 'rock chick' who has worked with Andy Warhol, David Bowie and Vangelis, releasing two LPs of her own in the late '70s.

Eyës Of A Gÿpsy *Identity*

Wright – Musically, Floyd and Fashion (*Dave Harris' former band*) were at opposite ends of the spectrum and I suppose it was a bit odd at first when Dave said he could remember going to Mother's in Birmingham to see us perform when he was fourteen; but from the moment we actually started working together, we realized just how close we were.

F

Fallen Angel
The prototype for *Amused to Death*'s 'What God Wants'.

Fallout, The *When the Wind Blows*
Waters – I think it's quite depressing, but Raymond Briggs' humour is very compelling and consistently lifts the film out of the possible troughs of morbidity that it could have sunk to ... It makes a desperate story palatable ... just (*laughs*).

Fat Old Sun *Atom Heart Mother*
Wright – It's very hard for us to play in the daytime. They wanted us to play at three o'clock on a Sunday afternoon at Wembley in 1974 but none of us could face the idea of getting up on stage at that time of day.

Fearless *Meddle*
Gilmour – There are songs on that album that are more significant than 'Echoes' – the one with 'You'll Never Walk Alone' on the end of it ...
Wright – We featured the Liverpool supporters because they're the best football crowd in the country for what we wanted.
Waters – What's interesting about it, for me, is that it's interesting musically: (*sings riff*). Funnily enough, that was a tuning that Syd showed me. It's a really beautiful open G tuning, for anybody who wants to tune their guitar: G-G-D-G-B-B.
Among those for whom such advice came in handy was former Marillion singer Fish, who covered 'Fearless' on his *Songs From the Mirror* album in 1992.
Fish – I missed the significance of pop in the early '70s because I was too busy getting deep and meaningful with my Genesis, Floyd and Van Der Graaf Generator albums.

Pink Floyd

Feel *The Madcap Laughs*
Gilmour – It was like one side of the album was six months' work and we did the other tracks in two and a half days. The potential of some of those songs ... they could have really been fantastic.

Final Cut, The *The Final Cut*
Gilmour – 'The final cut' in film terminology is the finished article. When you stick all the rushes together basically in the right order, you call it the 'rough cut'. And when you've cleaned it up and got it perfect, you call it 'the final cut'. It's also an expression for a stab in the back, which I think is rather the way Roger sees the film industry.

Quizzed on their favourite films in 1974, the Floyd selected *Beyond the Valley of the Dolls* (Gilmour), *The Seventh Seal* (Mason), *Cool Hand Luke* (Wright) and *El Topo* (Waters).

Fingal's Cave
A guitar-crazed instrumental out-take from the *Zabriskie Point* sessions.

Flaming *Piper at the Gates of Dawn*
John Peel – I'd like to be able to convince you that I was into Pink Floyd years before anyone else, but I was probably into the Floyd about a year after everybody else. That first LP obviously came as a bit of a revelation.

Flapdoodle Dealing
An unreleased, early live number.
Mason – We probably realized there wasn't any future in recycling R&B.
Gilmour – You mean you realized you were never going to be any good at playing it. They used to do a lot of Bo Diddley covers. It was great (*laughs*).

Fletcher Memorial Home, The *The Final Cut*
Gilmour – I think there are three great tracks on that album:

'Fletcher', 'The Gunner's Dream' and 'The Final Cut'. A lot of the rest of it and the general feel to the album is not to my taste, really.

Flight From Reality

In late '75, Waters told *Rock Et Folk*, 'I'm working on another piece, "Flight From Reality", which is very strange.' It is not referred to anywhere else, but may have been doodlings for *The Wall* or *The Pros and Cons of Hitch Hiking*.

Folded Flags *When the Wind Blows*

Waters – One of the problems with the whole of the political structure – and particularly that of North America, borne out very much by Reagan – is that people enter politics because they want to be rock stars or, in Reagan's case, film stars. He never managed it so he became the President of the United States instead . . .

He'll do anything for a pat on the back from the electorate and, by God, it works. They love him. An extraordinary thing is that surveys conducted in the States now show that they go: 'Oh, no, I don't agree with his policies; the guy's obviously an idiot . . . but I like him and I'm gonna vote for him.' Which is what I call the soap opera of state. I don't know Reagan personally; he may very well be a nice chap . . . but he's senile.

4.56 AM (For the First Time Today pts 2 and 1)
The Pros and Cons of Hitch Hiking

The more fastidious Floyd fan may care to note that the two halves appear on the b-side of the 'Every Stranger's Eyes' single in correct numerical order.

Waters – *The Pros and Cons of Hitch Hiking* is a fairly complicated piece of work which people will take as they will – or not take it at all, in most cases.

Four Minutes *Radio KAOS*

Waters – I don't know if you've ever been on an aeroplane that you think is going to crash . . . I have. You just go to jelly . . . but you do get off it thinking, God, that's the last time I'm ever getting on a bloody aeroplane.

Pink Floyd

Free Four *Obscured by Clouds*

Gilmour – On *Obscured by Clouds* there are one or two significant things. 'Free Four', for example, has got all the stuff about Roger's father being killed, and 'buried like a mole in a foxhole' or something, and 'Everyone's still on the run' – which is where all this *Wall* and *Final Cut* stuff came from.

Funky Deux *Wet Dream*

Wright – I'm no Keith Emerson, for sure. Besides, my hero is Miles Davis.

G

Games For May
An early title for 'See Emily Play'.

Get Back to Radio *The Tide is Turning b-side*
Waters – It wasn't like I had an idea: 'Oh, I know, I'll write this piece about this spastic Welsh kid who gets moved halfway across the globe by the market forces.' I decided the time had come to start writing some new material and the first one was 'Get Back to Radio'. It just popped out and it went: 'Like an ember glowing in the dark, I had almost grown cold; frozen like a soldier standing at the flag-pole; like a player they all said was too old; I had been tempted to hand in my key'... that was the first verse. 'But I am not alone; I feel that you are with me; I'll not be a packet of crap on MTV; I am a man; I will not be a number; Get back to radio.'

It's not on the record although it's central to the theme ... and *KAOS* all developed out of that.

Get Your Filthy Hands Off My Desert *The Final Cut*
Waters – Don't get me wrong: I'm not a pacifist. I think there are wars that have to be fought, unfortunately. I just don't happen to think the Falklands was one of them.

Gigolo Aunt *Barrett*
Gilmour – We had basically three alternatives at that point, working with Syd. One, we could actually work with him in the studio, playing along as he put down his tracks – which was almost impossible, though we succeeded on 'Gigolo Aunt'. The second was laying down some kind of track before and then having him play over it. The third was him putting his basic ideas down with just guitar and vocals and then we'd try and make something out of it all.

It was mostly a case of me saying, 'Well, what have you got then, Syd?' and he'd search around and eventually work something out.

John Peel – I actually recorded 'Gigolo Aunt' myself for a projected album of spoken word stuff that was quickly aborted. I had three tunes ready when they pulled it, one of which was 'Effervescing Elephant', also on the *Barrett* album.

Give Birth to a Smile *The Body*
Geesin – I think I've encouraged Roger to leave the Floyd ever since I first met him – not that my encouragement would have had any weight at all! I saw him as one of those individuals, one of those creators who would carry on through. Although he obviously found that from his point of view the Floyd was a convenient vehicle to carry his ideas.

Gnome, The *Piper at the Gates of Dawn*
Alan Parsons – I must say that when I first heard their music, I wasn't terribly impressed. I was working at Hayes (*for EMI*) and the *Piper at the Gates of Dawn* album came to me for duplication, and I was thinking if this was to be the music of the future, I wasn't looking forward to it. But, like a lot of stuff, you get to like bits of it over a long period.

4.50 AM (Go Fishing) *The Pros and Cons of Hitch Hiking*
Waters – Andy Fairweather-Low and I played through some of the songs from the *Pros and Cons* album and I was struck by how good they sounded. Looking back, that record dragged a little but, individually, some of the material was excellent.

Going to Live in LA *Radio Waves b-side*
Waters – I don't want them to sit and think about (*KAOS*) deeply, unless they want to ... If people care to read the lyrics and look at the map and follow the story and work it out, then all well and good.

It can mean lots of different things to different people, but when I make a record, what I'm interested in doing is moving people in the way I've been moved by other people's records – and it doesn't have to be because there's some significant political or sociological comment in it.

A collection of great dance songs

Gold it's in the . . ., The *Obscured by Clouds*
Mason – We didn't aim *Obscured by Clouds* to be a Pink Floyd album, but just a collection of songs. There were various styles on the album with plenty of rhythm and different tempos. I agree that it hasn't got the same impact as, say, *Dark Side of the Moon* or *Meddle*, but it was an enormous success and has become, in France especially, a classic album.

Golden Hair *The Madcap Laughs*
Barrett – I've got books lying around at home: Shakespeare and Chaucer, you know. But I don't really read a lot. Maybe I should.

Goodbye Blue Sky *The Wall*
Waters – The best way to describe this is as a recap of side one. It's remembering one's childhood and then getting ready to set off into the rest of one's life.

Goodbye Cruel World *The Wall*
Waters – That's (Pink) going catatonic, if you like. He's going back, he's curling up and he's not going to move. That's it. He's had enough. That's the end.

Bob Geldof – A lot of what happens to Pink is his own fault. I think he brings it upon himself. People who try to achieve something – and then, once they've achieved it, can't handle it – are essentially weak people. You shouldn't strive for something if you don't know what you want it for.

Sam Brown – I thought Bob Geldof was brilliant in *The Wall*. It was nice to see him keep his mouth shut for that length of time!

Waters – There was never any pussyfooting about what he thought about Pink Floyd or the music . . . 'cos he was extremely scathing about the whole thing and I never tried to persuade him differently. You know, these bog-Irish: you can't tell them anything. They wouldn't understand. I'm not going to waste my time on Geldof, trying to explain *The Wall* to him. He understands; he just doesn't realize he understands. If there's one man in the world who understands, it's got to be Geldof . . . bless him.

Pink Floyd

Gotta Be Crazy
The unwieldy and frequently unlistenable template from which 'Dogs' was wrought.

John Peel – Er ... liked hearing all their oldies ... wasn't too sure about their new stuff. Much of this latter served to highlight that the Floyd, as they have observed often enough themselves, are a bit pushed for a vocalist.

Grand Vizier's Garden Party, The *Ummagumma*
The Grand Vizier was the title given to the Prime Minister of the former Ottoman Empire. History has chosen not to record his thoughts on tedious drum solos.

Mason – My musical background prior to Pink Floyd could be described as sparse. I did have some violin lessons for a period of some weeks from a woman called Mrs Tchaikovsky (*giggles*), but I don't think they've had a big impact on my approach to the drums.

Grantchester Meadows *Ummagumma*
Waters – I must say that *The Final Cut* means a hell of a lot more to me than *Ummagumma* ever did.

Wright – 'Ummagumma' is a Cambridge expression for 'fuck'.

Waters – *Ummagumma*, yeah. What a disaster.

Great Day For Freedom, A *The Division Bell*
Gilmour – There was a wonderful moment of optimism when the Wall came down – the release of Eastern Europe from the non-democratic side of the socialist system. But what they have now doesn't seem to be much better.

I'm fairly pessimistic about it all. I sort of wish and live in hope, but I tend to think that history moves at a much slower pace than we think it does. I feel that real change takes a long, long time.

Great Gig in the Sky, The *Dark Side of the Moon*
Wright – I think the 'mortality section', or 'Great Gig in the Sky' as it's called now, is a really nice piece of music. One of the pressures for me – and I'm sure all the others – is this constant fear of dying, because of all the travelling we're doing on the motorways of America and Europe, and the planes. That for me is

a very real fear. Trouble is, it doesn't come across like that on the record, so that's a weakness of it.

Alan Parsons – They simply said, 'Who shall we get to sing this?' And I said, 'Well, I know a great singer . . .' There was a bit of direction given: they said, 'Sorry, we've got no words, no melody line, just a chord sequence – just see what you can do with it.' She was only there for a couple of hours.

Clare Torry – They didn't know what they wanted – just said it was a birth and death concept. I looked suitably baffled and just sang something off the top of my head. I got such a shock when the album came out and became a massive hit.

Alan Parsons – As I remember she did two or three tracks, from which we assembled the best bits for a master version. But somewhere in the archives there are the bits we didn't use, and I'm sure it would make for an interesting remix version one day.

Clare Torry – I thought myself very daring to invoice EMI for twice the going rate of £15!

A 1990 poll of Australian radio listeners awarded this the title 'Best Song To Make Love To', ahead of a list that boasted the more overtly romantic sounds of Prince, Madonna and The Cure.

Green is the Colour *More*

Gilmour – *More* had rather a bad reception; probably because of the dialogue – they were saying things like 'Groovy, man, let's get high.' Schroeder was a foreign director and, though he spoke English, he didn't know the subtle difference between what slang was acceptable and hip and what wasn't.

Gunner's Dream, The *The Final Cut*

Waters – 'The Gunner's Dream' is about powerlessness. The door opens suddenly and you find you're face to face with a bloke in jackboots in a country like South America or Algeria or France during the occupation. You cry, 'No you can't do that to me – I'll call the police,' and they reply, 'We are the police.' Your life slips into a nightmare. The most precious thing in this world is that your life is not controlled by someone else.

H

Happiest Days of Our Lives, The *The Wall*

Waters – We actually, at this school I was at, had one guy . . . I would fantasize that his wife would beat him. Certainly she treated him like shit and he was a really crushed person. He handed as much of that pain on to us as he could and he did quite a good job of it.

It's funny how when you get those guys at school they will always pick on the weakest kid. So the same kids who are susceptible to bullying by other kids are also susceptible to bullying by the teachers. It's like smelling blood. They home in on it – the fear – and start hacking away, particularly with younger children.

Have A Cigar *Wish You Were Here*

Gilmour – Roy (Harper) had never sung anyone else's lyrics before, I don't think, and I guess he finds it a little strange to work within the confines of someone else's material, really. I think he found that difficult. But, like a trouper, he got it together.

Harper – He can write songs, but Roger's never going to be in the Top 100 as a rock singer. He tries hard, he's a good lad. Anyway, neither of them could get up there. I just stood at the back, leaning against a machine and laughing. I said, 'I'll sing for you . . . for a price.' Roger said, 'What's the price?' I said, 'A season ticket to Lords for life.' He said all right, so I went and did it. It took me till the next day to do it. I had to go away for the night and learn it but I never got the season ticket to Lords!

Waters – I think it was a bad idea, now. I think I should have done it . . . Not that I think Roy did it badly – I think he did it very well; it just isn't *us* any more.

Gilmour – We met some people in the record industry . . . we couldn't believe how they could possibly have jobs. And we still do.

A collection of great dance songs

Have You Got It Yet?
A manic track designed by Barrett to confuse his bandmates.

Heart Beat, Pig Meat *Zabriskie Point*
Gilmour – Awful, rubbishy echoed stuff . . .

Here I Go *The Madcap Laughs*
Malcolm Jones – He wrote it, I seem to recall, in a matter of minutes. The whole recording was done absolutely live, with no overdubs at all. Syd changed from playing rhythm to lead guitar at the very end and the change is noticeable. Syd, however, would change like that often . . . That accounts for the 'drop' during the solo, as Syd's rhythm guitar is no longer there!

Hero's Return, The *The Final Cut*
Mason – Roger's very good about criticism. I mean, he hardly ever kills anyone. Quite often people are let off with just a broken leg!

Hero's Return pt. 2, The *Not Now John b-side*
Karl Dallas – The previously unreleased verse and chorus (it's hardly significant enough to be described as part two) underpins the post-war relevance of the hero's experiences over fire-bombed Dresden. This is *Slaughterhouse-5* from the air; a war in which the killers are just as much the victims as the killed.

Hey You *The Wall*
Waters – Bob Ezrin called me up and said, 'I've just listened to side three and it doesn't work.' I realized that 'Hey You', conceptually, could go anywhere and it would be a much better side if we put it at the front. So that is why those lyrics are printed in the wrong places because that decision was made very late.
Pink's behind the wall *a)* symbolically and *b)* he's locked in a hotel room with a broken window that looks out on to a freeway. It's a cry to the rest of the world, saying 'Hey!', you know, 'This isn't how it should be.'
Dave sings the first two verses, then there's an instrumental passage, and then there's 'But it was only fantasy', which I sing –

which is a narration of the thing. 'The wall was too high as you can see / No matter how he tried he could not break free / and the worms ate into his brain' – that's the first reference to the worms. Worms have a lot less to do with the piece than they did. They were my symbolic representation of decay, because the basic idea behind the *Wall* thing really is that if you isolate yourself, you decay.

High Hopes *The Division Bell*

Gilmour – The song originated from a phrase that my girlfriend suggested, about how time brings you down. Oddly, the line that she gave me wasn't really important. There was just something in it that sparked me into thinking about my childhood and my life in Cambridge. So, if you like, the first thing that got written for the album was much more personal than I've tended to be. And I suppose it set the scene for what was to follow.

Highway Song

An unreleased track from 1969.

Hilda's Dream *When the Wind Blows*

An instrumental using Ye Olde Birdsong Sound Effects tape.

Hilda's Hair *When the Wind Blows*

Waters – The one that is the most successful is the scene at the end of the film, where they die; which was the thing I had most trouble with ... in terms of the score. In fact, I should credit one of the keyboard players, Matt Irving, who, when I was starting to think about it, said to me – a very penetrating remark – 'Remember *Spinal Tap*?' I tried to remember *Spinal Tap*, where the guy is sitting by the piano and saying, 'This is a little tune ... and it's a sad song, and it's in D-minor, the saddest of all keys.' That was our starting point, that D-minor ... it's a strange piece.

Holiday *Wet Dream*

Wright – I think city life is closer to reality than living in the country, in modern life. All our problems stem from living in cities

220

... so the lifestyle people have out there is the answer to the problems.

Home *Radio KAOS*

Waters – Ian Ritchie, who produced the record, is quite distressed that I didn't call it *Home*, which for a long time was the working title, because one of the things that the record is about is what home is. Is home keeping out of the weather? Being reasonably well fed? Being safe? Is home doing those things in the context of the family? We all think we understand what we mean by the idea of home. But is home the most important thing to a human being in the sense of belonging to a certain thing or person? Having that sense of security and the feeling you are not going to be moved on or blown to pieces? The feeling that you have the right to a continuous existence within the context of the society to which you belong from the moment you are born to the moment you die in order to arrange yourself into a good shape to die in?

I don't know ...

Hope

From Roy Harper's *Whatever Happened to Jugula*. The music is based on a song co-written by Pete Townshend and Gilmour for *About Face*, which was eventually released as the title track of Pete's *White City*.

Hot River *Fictitious Sports*

Mason – Apart from being a fairly nonsensical song, it's really a Pink Floyd pastiche – as you might guess, if you listen closely. It has all my favourite clichés of the last fourteen years as far as the drum track's concerned; Chris (Spedding) doing a slightly Dave Gilmour-style guitar; and a vocal track lifted straight off *Dark Side of the Moon* – apart from where it disappears underwater.

Household Objects

Unreleased recordings using, as can be divined from the title, domestic implements. A section using wineglasses can be heard at the beginning of 'Shine On You Crazy Diamond'.

Alan Parsons – We spent something like four weeks in the studio on it and came away with no more than one and a half minutes of music.

Höw Dö Yöü Dö It *Identity*
   Wright – I'll never forget Pete Murray saying on *Juke Box Jury* that we were just a cult and would last for six months.

How Do You Feel?
An unrecorded song about the Floyd's endorsement of Gini in 1974. The waggish Waters also referred to it as 'Bitter Love' – Gini being a lemon drink.
   Gilmour – They wanted to pay us a lot of money to go and do a commercial. When we were down there in the desert, we posed in front of sand-dunes with Evian spray water all over our sweaty bodies and stuff. It all felt a little funny ... It was uncomfortable. We'd never tasted the fucking drink anyway.

I

I Can't Breathe Anymore *David Gilmour*

Waters – Dave was a male model and van driver who'd worked in bands, and he had no pretensions to expressing any of these ideas. He may have now, but he didn't then, either through the band or putting on shows, the theatre of it . . . Dave was a fucking good guitar player and a very good singer.

I Get Stoned

An unreleased track from the Floyd's first recording session.

Andrew King – 'I Get Stoned' was probably the first song that Syd ever wrote. 'Sitting here all alone – I get stoned . . .' A very simple little song.

I Was Wrong *Fictitious Sports*

Mason – Originally, I had arranged to go to America and make an album using all sorts of material, but then Carla sent me a cassette with some of her ideas. It was very different from what she had done before and absolutely in line with what I like. So I thought it would be much better to do that than to struggle desperately to find things that work together.

Ibiza Bar *More*

Mason – We have to do the soundtrack in a week, which is very cool, because otherwise we'd spend three months doing it, going back and changing things all the time.

If *Atom Heart Mother*

Gilmour – I find it hard to write stuff that is overtly cheerful. Roger obviously does too (*laughs*). Certainly with Roger, one would get the impression, from what the public sees of him, that he's a permanently miserable character, but that's far from the truth.

If It's In You *The Madcap Laughs*
Gilmour – Roger and I sat down with him, after listening to all his songs at home, and said: 'Syd, play this one – Syd, play that one.' We sat him on a chair with a couple of mikes in front of him and got him to sing the song.

I'm a Mineralist *Fictitious Sports*
Carla Bley – 'I'm a Mineralist' wasn't just a joke at the mineralists' expense. Steve (Swallow) and I are obsessed with nature – it was about us too! I just love rocks and trees: our religion is nature.

In the Beechwoods
An unreleased track from May '68.

In the Flesh *The Wall*
Waters – The idea is that these fascist feelings develop from isolation. This is really him having a go at the audience, or the minorities in the audience. So the obnoxiousness of 'In the Flesh' – and it is meant to be obnoxious – is the end result of that isolation and decay.

In the Flesh? *The Wall*
Waters – At the end of 'In the Flesh?' you hear somebody shouting 'Roll the sound effects', et cetera, and the sound of bombers. It gives you some indication of what's happening. So it's a flashback.

The Scorpions cite their performance at the 1990 Berlin *Wall* show as one of the highlights of their career.

Klaus Meine – Playing *The Wall* is very exciting, not only from a musician's point of view, but as a human being. It's very emotional.

Rudy Schenker – Some people in Germany said, 'What is Roger Waters doing here?' But there are walls in our minds, there was a wall in Berlin, so to make this opera happen in Berlin was a good idea.

Interstellar Overdrive *Piper at the Gates of Dawn*
Andrew King – Syd had a unique way of mixing. He would throw the levers on the board up and down apparently at random,

making pretty patterns with his hands . . . He wouldn't do anything unless he thought he was doing it in an artistic way.

Waters – I wasn't thinking about musical policy in those days – not that I think much about it now. Most of the stuff on the first album was Syd's. The only thing that was much like what the group was going to do later was the thing that we all did together, 'Interstellar Overdrive', which we don't like playing much now.

Pete Banks (Yes) – I remember Pink Floyd playing to twenty people and things like that. They used to support, and everyone used to leave because it was all very free-form. There weren't any tunes, and a number would last maybe twenty minutes, which, for then, was quite outrageous.

Barrett – We play for people to dance to. They don't seem to dance much now . . . but that was the initial idea, so we play loudly and we're playing with electric guitars. So I mean we're utilizing all the volume and effects you can get.

You hardly ever get the sort of dancing right from the beginning that you get just as a response to the rhythm. Usually people stand there and they sort of work themselves into some sort of hysteria (*laughs*) while they're there . . . Which I think, you know, is an excellent thing 'cos this is what dancing is.

A live version, recorded for *Ummagumma*, was instead pressed on to acetates and given to band members and friends. John Peel had one, which he loved until it was stolen.

Intro
The unimaginative but undeniably apposite title bestowed on *Live at Pompeii*'s opening piece – which is, intriguingly, different to that on the video re-releases. Neither version has an official title but both are clearly from the *Dark Side of the Moon* sessions.

Mason – It's quite fun, *Pompeii*, but it is now fantastically dated, which is really the reason why we did *Delicate Sound of Thunder* as a video – so that at least there's something that is contemporary.

Is There Anybody Out There? *The Wall*
The dialogue on this track is from an episode of the western *Gunsmoke*, entitled 'Fandango' . . .

Pink Floyd

MARSHAL DILLON: Well, we've only got about an hour of daylight left; better get started.

MISS TYSON: Isn't it unsafe to travel at night?

DILLON: It'll be a lot less safe to stay here. Your father's gonna pick up our trail before long.

TYSON: Can Lorka ride?

DILLON: He'll hafta ride. Lorka! Time to go! Shangra, thank you for everything. Let's go . . .

Israel *Profiles*

Rick Fenn – There was a time when we were considering it as an entirely instrumental album, but we had 'Lie For a Lie', which we wanted to go on, so we felt it needed another song to balance it out.

It Is Obvious *Barrett*

Gilmour – We always felt that there was a talent there; it was just a matter of trying to get it out onto record so that people would hear it and, of course, Syd didn't make it any easier for us . . . It was very, very difficult; not really very rewarding.

It Would Be So Nice *Single*

Mason – Fucking awful, that record, wasn't it? Singles are a funny scene. Some people are prepared to be persuaded into anything. I suppose it all depends on if you want to be a mammoth star or not.

It's A Miracle *Amused to Death*

Waters – We did a very up-tempo version, and Flea (*from the Red Hot Chili Peppers*) played a great bass line, but it wasn't right. Then Pat (Leonard) started playing it in half-time, and I started singing it in the tempo it now exists in. I put the cassette in the car and got that buzz; I was blown away.

I played it six times on the way back to the house and then sat outside and played it three times more just because I adored it. And two days later I got Jeff Porcaro in and he played those drums, which were amazing. And that was that.

J

Jews Harp and Windchimes
An unreleased track from 1969.

John Latham
An unreleased track from 1968.

Journey, The
A phantasmagorical suite cobbled together for a handful of 1969 gigs, comprising 'The Beginning' ('Green is the Colour'), 'Beset By Creatures of the Deep' ('Careful With That Axe, Eugene'), 'The Narrow Way', 'The Pink Jungle' ('Pow R Toc H'), 'The Labyrinths of Auximenes' (an unreleased instrumental, closing with the 'footsteps' sequence with which Floyd would show off their quadraphonic PA), 'Behold the Temple of Light' (another unique instrumental) and 'The End of the Beginning' ('Celestial Voices', from the end of 'Saucerful of Secrets').

Jugband Blues *A Saucerful of Secrets*
Peter Jenner – 'Jugband Blues' is the ultimate self-diagnosis on a state of schizophrenia ... 'I'm most obliged to you for making it clear I'm not here – and I'm wondering who could be writing this song.'

Julia Dream *Relics*
Wright – When Syd left the band, we got much, much better; not only 'cos we were playing with a maniac who, in his own weird way, was trying to make it as difficult for us to play as possible. Since he left, it forced the three of us and Dave into thinking: Well, what can we do now?

Just Another 12 Bar
A blues recorded in 1970 for the aborted *Live in Montreux* LP. The latter also boasted 'Astronomy Domine', 'More Blues', 'The Embryo' and the doubtless scintillating 'David Gilmour talks'.

K

Keep Smiling People
A live piece débuted in 1968. It enjoyed a spell as 'Murderistic Woman' before evolving, to the enduring benefit of subeditors, into 'Careful With That Axe, Eugene'.

Keep Talking *The Division Bell*
Gilmour – I have moments of huge frustration because of my inability to express myself linguistically as clearly as I would like to. A lot of people think that I express myself most clearly through the guitar playing.

King Bee
A Stones-endorsed Slim Harpo composition, which appears on a 'Floyd' acetate of hotly contested authenticity.

Barrett – We worked up to 'See Emily Play' and so on quite naturally from the Rolling Stones numbers we used to play. None of us advocated doing anything more eccentric.

L

Lanky pt. I *Opel*

Gilmour – I've listened to *Opel* and there's nothing on there that really illuminates very much or gives very much to anyone. I didn't approve of it, personally, but it's not my choice.

Lanky pt. 2

A thankfully unreleased seven-minute drum track.

Late Home Tonight *Amused to Death*

Waters – The pilot, it seems to me, is a victim as much as the woman ... Well, not so much (but) the pilot loses his personality. It's as if he's suborned by the arms industry and the politicians ... who turn them into heroes and make them fight in an unjust fight. It's because of the seductive, almost erotic character of their hardware.

Late Night *The Madcap Laughs*

Barrett – I always write with guitar. I've got this big room and I just go in and do the work. I like to do the words and music simultaneously, so when I go into the studio I've got the words on one side and my music on the other. I suppose I could do with some practice.

Learning to Fly *A Momentary Lapse of Reason*

Mason – The first demo that Dave gave me had the 'Learning to Fly' idea, it had the 'Dogs of War' idea; everything was potentially a good track and that's what the album launched from. 'Learning to Fly' actually started out more spiritually uplifting than it sounded when it was finished. I like it because every time I hear it, I hear my own voice doing this take-off.

Gilmour – There's an unfulfillable longing in the song, so it's not all joyful. Good Lord, I'd hate to admit to anything happy.

Roy Harper – Whereas Dave's got his pilot's licence and all that sort of stuff, I can operate a computer better than he can – because that's all I can afford.

Let There Be More Light *A Saucerful of Secrets*
Waters – We haven't done many tracks that had anything to do with science fiction at all. We did three: 'Astronomy Domine', 'Let There Be More Light' and 'Set the Controls'. It just depended what you read into it.

Let's Get Metaphysical *About Face*
Gilmour – I wrote out the chord structure and made a demo with a guitar line on it and I also recorded various melody lines that had come into my head. Michael Kamen, in arranging, used some of my melody lines and some of the guitar lines and incorporated them into the string parts. We had a click track and the strings were recorded first. We then did the guitar promptly afterwards.

There's nothing like the sound of a real orchestra standing in the room. Having a whole orchestra playing something you wrote and standing in that room when they play it is magic.

Let's Roll Another One
The original title for what became, at the BBC's insistence, 'Candy And A Currant Bun'.

Let's Split *Opel*
Waters – In spite of the fact that he was clearly out of control when making his two solo albums, some of the work is staggeringly evocative . . . It's the humanity of it all that is so impressive.

Libest Spacement
A not-overbright bootlegger secures the credit for this misinterpretation of Roger's announcement of 'Mr Nicholas Mason' at an Albert Hall concert in February '71. Having been applied to the instrumental introduction of 'Embryo', this has also been spotted as 'Libest Spacement Monitor' and 'The Librest Spacement'.

Lie For a Lie *Profiles*
Mason – I think the single is a real single, but there's a problem

in getting radio play over here. Let's face it, Radio One is the only station that counts, and they already have enough pressure on their playlists with real acts, like McCartney and Duran Duran, without odd spin-offs from ageing dinosaurs!

Living Alone
An unreleased Barrett song recorded in 1970. The tape is believed to be owned by Gilmour.

Long Gone *The Madcap Laughs*
Gilmour – I don't see Syd. His family don't think it's a very good idea that people from the glorious parts of his past see him. It upsets him too much.

Looking Through the Knotholes in Granny's Wooden Leg
Tour madness at the end of 1972 led Roger Waters to find new and exciting ways to introduce 'Echoes'. This was one; 'March of the Dambusters' was another.

Lost For Words *The Division Bell*
Waters – I have heard *The Division Bell*. Actually, I haven't heard all of it but I've heard most of it . . . I don't think I want to talk about this.

Gilmour – If he'd put all that time and energy into his own career instead of trying to fuck us up, he might be in a stronger position than he actually is.

Waters – Future and world welfare don't rest on a reconciliation between Dave Gilmour and myself.

Love On The Air *About Face*
Gilmour – I asked Pete Townshend for help because I was running short of time and even shorter of inspiration . . . I was very pleasantly surprised when I got the cassette back for 'Love On The Air'. I liked where he had put the line and how he had done the vocal. I had heard the vocal line in a completely different place and deliberately sent Pete a tape with no melody on it. It was just a completed backing track with no lines on it at all and no ideas as to what I thought the lyrics should be. He didn't have any

restrictions. Of course, in some places which I intended to be instrumental, he put words on. 'All Lovers Are Deranged' was the same situation, only I changed the placing of his melody and lyrics a bit.

Love Song *Barrett*
Wright – I can't imagine anyone liking Syd's albums. I mean, musically, they're atrocious. Most of the songs are great, but performed so badly. It was impossible to get any sound because of the state Syd was in at the time. At least it tells people how Syd was when he made them.

Love You *The Madcap Laughs*
Malcolm Jones – Lack of adequate rehearsal gave the Softs' performances a rather ragged aspect, for which I must take responsibility ... although I must add that over the years the erratic quality of these tracks has been what has endeared them to Barrett fans. I can't help feeling, though, that the Soft Machine themselves were not very proud of their contributions!

Robert Wyatt – We'd say, 'What key is that in, Syd?' and he'd reply 'Yeah' or 'That's funny.'

Lucifer Sam *Piper at the Gates of Dawn*
Barrett – 'Lucifer Sam' was another of those quite obscure pieces. It didn't mean much to me at the time, but after three or four months, it began to assume a precise meaning.

Lucy Leave
A likely fake from the 'King Bee' acetate.

Lucy Lee in Blue Tights
Mason – Our first composition together was a song called 'Lucy Lee in Blue Tights', or something like that. We recorded it, but it was never released.

This may have become 'Lucy Leave' ... but, then again, may not.

M

Mad Yannis Dance *Wet Dream*
Wright – I think most people would have expected me to do a sort of keyboard extravaganza, maybe similar to what I did on *Ummagumma*. I decided not to do that because there was something in me that I wanted to get out. Certainly, in the future, I would like to experiment with keyboards on an album.

Mademoiselle Nobs *Live at Pompeii*
A pastiche of *Meddle*'s already none too serious 'Seamus'.

Main Theme *More*
Gilmour – I can't remember how we did the film *More*, or why. I mean, I can't remember why we happened to meet the guy. But meet him we did, and we saw the film. We thought, Weeeellll . . . , you know, but we wanted to break into big-time movie scores, so we said, OK, we'll do it. And he gave us six hundred quid each or something (*sniffs*) and off we trotted and we did it.

Maisie *Barrett*
Barrett biographers have yet to discern if this was inspired by the 'Maisie' films from the 30s and 40s, or the *Perishers* cartoon strip. Could it be that they just don't care?

Malta *Profiles*
Mason – There's a hell of a lot of rock 'n' roll now, and it's a very broad spectrum. There's room for coexistence, from teeny-bop stuff to elderly rock legends such as myself.

Man, The
Waters – 'The Man' was the story of a day in the life of Everyman; you know, Sleep, Work, Play, Start Again. It suggested the sense of doing the same thing day after day; the routine. I was into that idea very early on. But the idea of personalizing it –

writing about the rock 'n' roller rather than, say, workers in a factory – cropped up later when I began to confront my own situation more and more directly.

'The Man' opened with 'Grantchester Meadows' and closed with an 'Embryo'-esque instrumental, both titled 'Daybreak' for the occasion (an example of the conceptual continuity that, in rather less prosaic guises, would become a motif of Waters' writing). In between were 'Work/Afternoon' ('Biding My Time', followed by an onstage tea-break), 'Doing It!' (a short drum solo that may explain why romance rarely figured on the Floyd agenda), 'Sleeping' (an instrumental not unlike *More*'s unloved 'Quicksilver') and 'Nightmare' ('Cymbaline').

Marooned *The Division Bell*
Gilmour – It's amazing how far I can bend those notes, isn't it?

Massed Gadgets of Hercules
A working title for the far more sensible 'A Saucerful of Secrets'.

Matilda Mother *Piper at the Gates of Dawn*
Alice Cooper – When this album came out, my band played it to death ... The original line-up lived with us for a while in Los Angeles. It was a, uh, weird time, I guess. Syd Barrett didn't speak for a fortnight. Good record, though.

Me Or Him *Radio KAOS*
Waters – Actually, 'Me Or Him' is rather a confused song, I confess; it's describing more Ben and Billy ... Benny and Billy (*laughs*), sounds like the Flowerpot Men. Benny represents the conscious self and the ego. He's really angry and getting pissed, smashing windows, teetering about on motorway footbridges ... he's the blundering half of these twins. Billy is the unconscious and within him lie the true feelings and within these feelings lies the power.

Mediterranean C *Wet Dream*
Wright – *Wet Dream* is a very personal album. It's not to say

that's what I always want to do. It was just the way I felt at the time.

Merry Christmas Song, The

An appalling, albeit cheerful, song performed by Nick Mason – assisted by Roger Waters and roadie Alan 'Psychedelic Breakfast' Stiles – for the *John Peel Show* in December 1975. A decade later, David Gilmour was accused of playing on a similarly puerile 'Christmas-on-45' type single by Holly and The Ivys; a charge he vehemently denied. 'Is nothing sacred?' pleaded the aggrieved axeman.

Mexico '78 *La Carrera Panamericana*

Gilmour – Lots of overgrown schoolboys getting together and having heaps of fun driving fast cars around Mexico. What more could you want?

Mihalis *David Gilmour*

Gilmour – 'Mihalis' is the name of my boat ... It's Greek for Michael. That's what it was called when I got it and, in Greece, they say it's bad luck to change it ...

Milky Way *Opel*

Malcolm Jones – He is pretty together there, isn't he?

Molly's Song

Performed by Doreen Chanter at the *KAOS* shows, this is the source of the lines 'Goodbye little spy in the sky / They say cameras don't lie / Am I happy, am I sad? / Am I good, am I bad?' in 'Four Minutes'.

Waters – There were sixteen songs, and eight on *KAOS*. The other eight certainly haven't been thrown out in disgust – but put to the side, possibly for use later. Some of them are very specific to this narrative, so they couldn't really be used for anything else ... I might put them out on an EP or something for people who were interested and wanted an appendix ... a few more pieces to the jigsaw.

Though mooted for *Amused to Death*, when that album was still envisaged as *KAOS II*, the song has appeared only as the b-side of the US 'Who Needs Information' single.

Pink Floyd

5.11 AM (Moment of Clarity, The)
The Pros and Cons of Hitch Hiking

Waters – In the moment of waking in the darkness, you suddenly feel that you've got the answer. Not a specific answer, but you suddenly feel as if you understand something you hadn't grasped before. You may not be able to put your finger on what that is either, but there's a real feeling of *Got It!* Sometimes it's about something specific in your conscious life, and I've even, on odd occasions, reached out and taken a pencil and paper and written down what it was. Of course, you wake up in the morning and it's gibberish. You think, what the hell was that all about? But none the less the moment is very powerful.

Money *Dark Side of the Moon*

Gilmour – Roger came in with 'Money'. I've still got his demo of it lurking around somewhere, of him singing it with an acoustic guitar. It's very funny. And we did it pretty well the same as the demo, apart from the middle section with all the solos and stuff, which we wrote and put together in the studio or in rehearsal. But we made up the cash register loop. We were always making tape loops.

There was this hilarious thing of having a studio control room with tape machines and mike stands all over the place with huge great loops of tape wandering all over the room and breaking and people treading on them and stuff...

Waters – The sessions for the album were very relaxed, but at the same time we were striving as hard as we could. I know we were jolly keen to have a hit record.

Wright – Capitol Records in America just said to us that they wanted to put a single out. We didn't think about it – we didn't think anything would happen ... and it just did, for some reason. Well, there's plenty of reasons, 'cos it's very good (and) it was on AM radio, whereas before we'd never been played on anything but FM.

Moonhead
An instrumental performed to complement the BBC's coverage of the

first manned Moon landing. It shares a basic theme with 'Daybreak', the final part of 'The Man', and can be found on bootlegs under the titles 'Corrosion', 'Labyrinth' and 'Trip on Mars'.

Gilmour – They used to ask us when they were about to land on the Moon or something; old whatshisface – Patrick Moore – in the studio and some experts. We'd sit at the back and they'd say 'Pink Floyd playing' and we'd just jam something which we'd make up on the spur of the moment . . .

Every once in a while I hear one of these old things being used on a documentary. I've heard them on the BBC and I think, what the hell is it? I know it's us, I know it's from the '60s, but I don't know where the fuck it comes from, or what it was, or what its title was. Hours of waffle.

More Blues *More*
'It is possible,' claimed Floyd biographer Rick Sanders, 'to see "More Blues" as a simplified history of the group. You take the best of the compulsive blues/rock riffs, open your head, dig in, see what comes out.'

Most Boring Song I've Ever Heard Bar Two, The
The inadequately dismissive working title for *A Saucerful of Secrets'* diabolical 'See Saw'.

Mother *The Wall*
Hills Road Journal, 1990

In 1976, an article was published in *Cantabrigian*, the Hills Road journal at the time, entitled 'The Piper at the Gates of Dawn'. The piece was concerned with Syd Barrett, 'the distinctive ex-Floyd musician, composer and mystery man' who attended the Cambridgeshire High School For Boys from 1957–1962. But what of Hills Road's second most famous Floyd figure, Roger Waters? Surely the composer of such masterpieces as *Dark Side of the Moon* and *The Wall* deserves attention? Therefore, our team of intrepid investigators (Tim Large, Mark Sheerin and Louise Reardon) decided to consult the nation's top authority on this man: Roger's mum.

'In 1954, at the age of eleven, he went to the Boys' High School on Hills Road, where he stayed until he was eighteen. I would have sent him to the Tech at sixteen if it had been the fashion to do so at the time. Syd had done so.

'The college was very different to what it is today, that's the impression I get now. Then it was very conventional. But it was a convenient place to send him and his brother John, living so close by. Syd lived in Hills Road and I liked them living at home with me.

'The staff included Mr Bilton and Mr Mills, who taught Roger physics. He took maths, physics and technical drawing at A-level, which led him on to studying engineering, but this was short-lived and he went into architecture, which he studied in London.

'He "tolerated" his schooling. His attitude was "You have to get on with it and make the most of it." He enjoyed sport in particular and was involved in much team work. He reached the First Eleven in cricket. He made some good friends – rather "wild" ones – but doesn't keep in touch, although a few old classmates ring me up now and again asking for his autograph for their families.

'He went to Morley Primary School and County School with Syd, but didn't really form a friendship until they were Regent Street Poly students. Syd was younger. I am good friends with his mother but I don't see her often as she lives on the other side of town.

'Roger was brought up in an unmusical and not very creative family, as his father – who *was* musical – was killed in the war. We possessed an old piano but it was rarely used. Roger had a mouth-organ, and at fourteen his uncle, my brother-in-law, gave him a guitar to play, and he started having some classical lessons. He had no musical influence or encouragement from college that I knew of.

'I'm not a great fan of Pink Floyd although I have got all his records and go to his concerts – with my earplugs! – as I enjoy the visuals. I particularly enjoyed the music he did for Bastille Day.

'At one point we both thought there might not be any future in the music business and from then on it was always very "iffy", as this kind of career is. After three years in architecture – he didn't even take his guitar – he decided to follow his musical instincts when some backing musicians made a proposal. It took a lot of sorting out, though, and he didn't start making money for a long while. Since, however, he has gained tremendously, financially.

'Roger thought Pink Floyd would finish when Syd left, because of his serious illness. They had made great efforts to get help for him. When Syd left, he was asked to continue writing for the group instead of performing. The last tour in America, Syd couldn't even remember going on.

'Roger now works on his own most of the time, having worked in the group for sixteen years. He has no regrets about his past or about splitting. He has released a solo album and is very proud of a song he wrote about Syd called "Shine On You Crazy Diamond". He was probably most proud of *The Wall*, most of which he wrote and now has the rights to. He has been asked to reproduce *The Wall* at the Brandenberg Gate, in view of the recent happenings in East Germany, but whether or not this will go ahead, we don't know.

'Syd is living in his mother's old house in St Margaret's Square at the moment, as far as I know, but will probably never be fully well again.

'I'm not particularly affected by Roger's career although I am proud of what he's done. I don't read the right papers to see any bad tabloid reports about him. I read the *Guardian*!

Mudmen *Obscured by Clouds*

Gilmour – None of us has ever been the best of friends. I have never been a close personal friend of anyone else in the band, and neither was Rick, really. Roger and Nick have at times been fairly close. We don't *not* get along, but we're working partners.

Mumbo Jumbo *Profiles*

Mason – I did most of the *Wall* film, actually. I'm the unsung hero of the band but I've been too modest to announce it until now.

Murder *About Face*

Gilmour – It's just a frustrated rage when people commit senseless acts like murder. Stealing someone else's life away makes me very angry. For example, when John Lennon got killed, I got incredibly angry. I still feel it sometimes: the cunt! Why did he do that?

There was one occasion when I was advised by the police to stay home because some 'fan' was on his way over from America with a gun in his pocket...

N

Narrow Way, The *Ummagumma*

Gilmour – We'd decided to make the damn album, and each of us to do a piece of music on our own. It was just desperation really, trying to think of something to do, to write by myself. I just went into the studio and started waffling about, tacking bits and pieces together – just bullshitted my way through. I got desperate at one point, rang Roger up and said, 'Please help me write the lyrics,' but he said, 'No, do 'em yourself.' I haven't heard it in years; I've no idea what it's like.

Near The End *About Face*

Gilmour – 'Near The End' is about being near the end of anything you like, really; about life I suppose is what it is. Each of the verses has a sort of double thing to it. The first verse is like talking to the person who's listening to the record; 'Will you just turn it over and start again?' means 'Will you just turn the record over and play it again?'. . .

The second one is about a girlfriend . . . the end of a relationship, and the third one is about the end of your own life, really: 'What once burned so bright is growing dim' is your own life spark, I suppose.

Everyone has a paranoia about getting old. No one wants to die. A lot of people say that I'm wrong . . . but I never believe them.

New Machine, A (pts I and 2) *A Momentary Lapse of Reason*

Gilmour – On the *Momentary Lapse of Reason* album, Nick's belief in himself was pretty well gone, and Rick's belief in himself was totally gone. And they weren't up to making a record, to be quite honest about it.

Waters – If you had a reasonably adept producer, Pink Floyd could go on for two hundred years after the original members were dead.

Gilmour – Maybe we should try that. Get some twenty-one-year-old kids in.

Nick's Boogie *Tonite Let's All Make Love in London*

An instrumental that, along with a lengthy take of 'Interstellar Overdrive', can be found on See For Miles' reissue of the *Tonite* ... soundtrack. Label boss Colin Miles told *Vox*: 'I think the most incredible find has to be twenty-four minutes of unreleased Pink Floyd. Peter Whitehead brings this seven-inch tape with all this green mould growing all over it and I thought, Oh dear, what can we do with that? But it was so tightly wound, the sound quality is absolutely superb.'

Nile Song, The *More*

In a dry run for later pairings like 'rail' and 'veil', this primeval rocker finds Waters rhyming 'Nile', 'smile', 'while', 'child' and 'wild', not to mention 'breezes' and 'pleases' and, most ambitiously, 'shadow' and 'window'. Intriguingly, the film *More* makes no reference to the world's longest river.

No Good Trying *The Madcap Laughs*

Malcolm Jones – 'No Good Trying' was positively impossible! Syd had, before the session, taken copy tapes ... which I presumed were to give to the musicians he was booking to learn ... I was wrong; he kept them!

Robert Wyatt – I liked the tunes on *Madcap* and the way he did them. We just started to feel our way round them when he said, 'OK, that's it.' So the final recording was like a sketch of a painting never completed. Dead punk when you come to think of it.

No Man's Land *The Madcap Laughs*

Waters – Syd didn't write after quite early 1968. His two solo albums are material that already existed at that point.

No Way *David Gilmour*

Gilmour – England is where I live. I don't want to move out and live anywhere else ... I'm not any keener on paying tax than anyone else is – well, not that amount anyway – so I have made a concession towards it and went abroad to make this record, because that will make the tax burden a little bit lighter. It will still be a high rate anyway, but it's just not worth selling. My freedom isn't for sale like that.

Nobody Home *The Wall*

Waters – Part of (Pink) wants help, but the part of him that's making his arms and legs and everything work doesn't want anything except to just sit there and watch TV.

Not Now John *The Final Cut*

Waters – It's a very schizophrenic song, because there's this one character singing the verses who's irritated by all this moaning abut how desperate things are, and doesn't want to hear any of it any more. There's part of me in that. Then there's this other voice which keeps harping back to earlier songs, saying, 'Make them laugh, make them cry, make them dance in the aisles,' which is from 'Teach'. So it's a strange song.

Gilmour – We more or less fell for a record company hype. Steve (O'Rourke) said that American radio stations wanted 'Not Now John' out as a single, and we just went along with it. The fact is it still says 'Fuck all that' because it's just a copy of the master with me and some backing singers shouting 'stuff' a bit louder than 'fuck'.

Nothing pts 1–24

The working title for the pieces recorded in 1971 that eventually emerged as 'Echoes'; hence 'Return of the Son of Nothing'.

Gilmour – We'd tell everyone the key, then they'd have to leave the studio while one person recorded something on one track of the tape machine. Then another person would come in and play on the same piece of tape without hearing what the other person had played. All of us did that. Awful, absolutely awful.

O

Obscured by Clouds *Obscured by Clouds*

Ron Geesin – One thing I didn't like about Pink Floyd music was that it lacked melody … which, of course, was an advantage in some ways, because the listener would provide the melodic lines as a thought process on top of the 'cloud layer' the group used to put out.

Octopus *The Madcap Laughs*

Robert Wyatt – I didn't notice that we (*Soft Machine*) weren't credited, but I'm sure we got paid, which is fairly novel. I played it a lot later, at home, until Elton Dean came from his room next door and asked me to stop playing 'that nonsense' and listen to more sophisticated music like Joe Henderson. Ever the sporting neighbour, I lost *Madcap*.

Daevid Allen – At the very beginning, Soft Machine and Pink Floyd were bracketed together a lot as being *the* psychedelic bands – although we were very different – so we crossed paths a lot. Mostly Syd Barrett sat around looking completely manic with staring eyes. In fact, it was very fashionable for everyone to sit around with staring eyes … like everyone was demented and totally out of their minds.

Barrett – I thought the Soft Machine were good fun.

Oenone

A quite pleasant, albeit not terribly interesting, instrumental out-take from the *Zabriskie Point* sessions. The title appears to be a rare flash of inspired bootleggery, and has inevitably appeared as 'Oneone'.

Old Faces

A Gilmour co-composition from Roy Harper's *The Unknown Soldier*. Guitar on the track, which is reminiscent of *More*, could be Dave.

A collection of great dance songs

Old Woman in a Casket
The working title of 'Scream Thy Last Scream', also listed as 'Old Woman With a Casket'.

On the Run *Dark Side of the Moon*
Alan Parsons – I dare say if it hadn't been for the way the Beatles had recorded, people like Pink Floyd, who are very much studio-based musicians, would not have turned out the way they did.

Gilmour – We created a kind of sound collage to show movement and travel . . . it was a very serious attempt to achieve a certain effect. We weren't lying spaced out in the studio, chucking anything together for the sake of it.

Waters – It's a bit like those young groups now, who I have no interest in at all . . . that get a Roland 808 out of the box, plug it in and it goes bum-petek, bum-bum petek . . . Oh wow! We're a band! Then they talk over it and it's called music . . .

Alan Parsons – *Dark Side of the Moon* was perfect fodder for American album radio at the time. It was very programmable. If a jock wanted to play two or three tracks one after the other, he'd had his work done for him because all the segues were carefully worked out within the grooves.

On the Turning Away *A Momentary Lapse of Reason*
Gilmour – It's a social commentary, I suppose – one can't say much more than that. We did argue at length about whether, in the last verse, one should get preachy, but in the end we said, let's preach!

Waters – I know that Gilmour has been scouring the ends of the earth to try and find somebody to write lyrics, for the last year. Maybe he gave up in the end and has written lyrics himself, I don't know.

Gilmour – The ideas for 'Learning to Fly' and 'On the Turning Away' came from Anthony Moore, a friend of mine. He came up with the basic idea and wrote the first set of lyrics, so I can't claim to have been the instigator of it – but as soon as I saw them, I said, 'That's perfect, that's exactly what we want.'

Waters – I know he spent a long time closeted on his own,

245

trying to write a single, which I think is unbelievable. Personally, I think it's an incredibly stupid thing to do. Certainly something that never happened when I was running the Pink Floyd.

One in a Million
An early live piece, also known – courtesy of cloth-eared bootleggers – as 'Rush in a Million' and 'Brush Your Window'.

One of My Turns *The Wall*
Waters – 'One of My Turns' is supposed to be his response to a lot of aggravation in his life, not really ever having got anything together. He's just splitting up with his wife and in response he takes another girl back to his hotel room . . . He's a bit dippy now.

Neil Peart, whose band Rush was one of several dubbed 'the next Pink Floyd', told *The Boston Globe*: 'So many musicians become victims of the "touring bubble", either through drugs or alcohol or just psychological imbalance, as in the case of Roger Waters. I really respect Roger as an artist, but his alienation soon became his only subject . . . He had to write about what he cared about the most – and, unfortunately, what he cared about the most was his own alienation.'

One of the Few *The Final Cut*
'The Few' was how Winston Churchill referred to the fighter pilots who won the Battle of Britain in World War II.

One of These Days *Meddle*
Waters – It's a poignant appraisal of the contemporary social situation.

Gilmour – For some reason, we decided to do a double track of the bass . . . The first bass is me. A bar later, Roger joins in on the other side of the stereo picture. We didn't have a spare set of strings for the spare bass guitar, so the second bass is very dull-sounding (*laughs*). We sent a roadie out to buy some strings, but he wandered off to see his girlfriend instead.

Waters – I was always fascinated by the very simple fact that if there's an echo delay going 'Gonk-gonk-gonk-gonk', you can go 'Gonk-ge-ge-gonk-ge-ge'; make rhythms with all the work being done for you by a simple delay device.

A collection of great dance songs

Gilmour – It just sounded very violent and, you know, we like a joke as much as anyone else ... It's an old thing for us. 'I'm Going to Cut You Into Little Pieces' and 'Be Careful With That Axe, Eugene' – they're similar sort of things, aren't they?

Waters – I think that the simplest sound effects are often the best. For example, just the sound of wind at the beginning of 'Cut You Into Little Pieces' is bloody effective.

One Slip *A Momentary Lapse of Reason*

Gilmour – Phil Manzanera's a friend of mine; most of the music for 'One Slip' came from him. We spent a couple of days throwing ideas around and this was the one that fitted the album best.

Manzanera – I know Roger, not as well as I know Dave, but I've always got on well with him. To be honest, though, after recording with Dave, I don't think Roger would want to work with me!

Gilmour – I personally get uncomfortable going out on choruses – to me, it's so much the pop formula that I try to avoid it. We didn't quite do it on 'One Slip', which was going that way. In the end we did a chorus, then went out with an instrumental.

Opel *Opel*

Waters – What was so stunning about Syd's songs was, through the whimsy and the crazy juxtaposition of ideas and words, there was a very powerful grasp of humanity. They were quintessentially human songs and that is what I've always attempted to aspire to. In that sense, I feel a strong connection to him.

Our Song *The Body*

Ron Geesin – I suppose some of the techniques I used could be seen as being rather dated now. But it was a great, fun piece to do. The collaboration between Roger and myself was also great fun. In some ways, I wanted to carry on and do another one with him. I felt we complemented each other well.

Out Of The Blue *About Face*

Gilmour – At some times I'm dealing with fairly depressing topics, but, at the same time, my idea is the music will be uplifting.

247

Maybe I've been around Roger Waters too long. It could be contagious!

Outside the Wall *The Wall*

Waters – That final song is saying, 'Right, well, that was it. You've seen it now. That's the best we can do.' That was us performing a piece of theatre about alienation. This is us making a little bit of human contact at the end of the show: 'We do like you really.'

Overture

Alan Parker – A prelude – a quite remarkable piece of music which, sadly, didn't quite work with the rather unusual, quiet beginning of the *Wall* film – sadly had to be left out.

P

Paintbox *Relics*
Wright – I think my singing's terrible.

Pan Am Shuffle *La Carrera Panamericana*
Mason – Five of us went into the studio, guys who were on the last tour, so we were an ensemble. We looked at the video and timed it. Then we'd say, 'Well, this part needs this sort of thing,' and we'd work it out. Dave would play a sequence of chords. He would pick up a musical idea, and the tempo would be set. Then the bass player would work out his part, and then the drummer would work out the drum part. And it just sort of came to life.

Paranoid Eyes *The Final Cut*
Waters – Just because something's going to be a lyric in a song that lots of people may listen to, doesn't mean that one should temper one's personal feelings any more than one would talking to somebody in a pub.

Party Sequence *More*
Wright – We did it because Barbet Schroeder wanted to use us. We didn't do it because it was about drugs.

Peace Be With You
In a 1988 *Penthouse* feature, Roger Waters claimed that among those approached by Gilmour for *Momentary Lapse* was Carole Pope, 'one of the finest contemporary Canadian songwriters'. 'The idea to contact me came from Bob Ezrin,' Pope told writer Timothy White. 'It was January of 1987 and they were looking for somebody to rewrite a bunch of Dave Gilmour's material, so I went over to England for a few weeks to lend assistance. Bob and David also asked me if I had any suggestions for concept albums in the Pink Floyd style. By the time I left England in February, they still couldn't decide what to do. They did have one song, though, which I thought was quite nice,

though it never surfaced on *Lapse of Reason*. It was a mid-tempo thing about Roger Waters, called 'Peace Be With You'. Seems strange that they didn't use it.'

Percy the Ratcatcher
The original title of 'Lucifer Sam'. A half-hour film by the Floyd, *The Life Story of Percy the Ratcatcher*, was scheduled for production in June '67.

Perfect Sense *Amused to Death*
Waters – 'Perfect Sense' came from thinking about the days of the Roman Empire, when they would flood the Colosseum and have fights between rival galleys. I've always been intrigued by this notion of war as an entertainment to mollify the folks back home, and the Gulf conflict fuelled that idea.

Piggy Back
An unreleased, early live track.

Mason – My memory of the Marquee, I have to say, is that we were not really Marquee material. I remember us being sort of demolished by people like Marmalade and proper bands with nice suits and all the rest of it. We would have been doing what can only be described as 'early Pink Floyd', which is rather abstract rhythm and blues, performing rather nasty operations on Chuck Berry material.

Piggy Got Stoned
A messy instrumental of dubious authenticity on the *Early Freakout Demos* bootleg.

Wright – We don't want people to be stoned out of their minds all the time when they go to hear us. We'd like to induce an experience without drugs. Anyone is free to have that kind of experience.

Pigs on the Wing *Animals*
Gilmour – I never expected *Animals* to sell as many as *Wish You Were Here* or *Dark Side*, because it's aimed at a narrower audience. There's not a lot of sweet, sing-along stuff on it!

Waters – I think the thing about *Animals* is that it didn't gel cohesively, either musically or conceptually, but perhaps that was good ... Three fairly angry songs about posturing and defensive ploys set between two verses of a love song to Carolyne, 'Pigs on the Wing'. The first verse poses the question, 'Where would I be without you?' and the second says, 'In the face of all this other shit – confusion, side-tracks, difficulties – you care. I know you care about me and that makes it possible to survive.' That is the first time that sentiment appears; the sense of having somebody, being with somebody.

Gilmour – I've never actually seen a pig flying past, so I wouldn't really know how to deal with it.

Pigs (Three Different Ones) *Animals*
Waters – I kept throwing that verse about Mary Whitehouse away. I've been throwing that verse away for about eighteen months but I never managed to write anything else. I kept coming back to it and changing it, and it worried me a lot all the time ...

She doesn't really merit the attention but she is really a cry ... and she is a terribly frightened woman, isn't she? Terrified. Why does she make such a fuss about everything if she's not motivated by fear? Why doesn't she just get on with everything? She's frightened that we're all being perverted.

Asked, in 1987, if he thought of Mrs Thatcher while singing 'Pigs' on the *KAOS* tour, Waters replied, 'I confess I do.' He added that 'someone else' came to mind during the first verse, although this should obviously not be construed as a reference to his legal sparring partners of the time.

Gilmour – *Dark Side of the Moon* and *Wish You Were Here*, I am fairly in sympathy with. *Animals*, I could see the truth of, though I don't paint people as black as that.

Pillow of Winds, A *Meddle*
Gilmour – Most of the early stuff I find embarrassing. It's all part of growing up and being British.

Pink
An unreleased, early live piece.

Pink Floyd

Mason – Audiences weren't ready for the psychedelic stuff we used to play. We weren't ready for it either. We couldn't play it.

Pink's Song *Wet Dream*

Wright – I went to a private school, a dreadful private school, to do theory and composition. That was while I was going to architecture school as well, and after that I went to the London College of Music. Someone used to stand there and he obviously didn't beat my hands if I went wrong, but it was a bit of a joke. I used to learn pieces off by heart, and then play them and pretend I was sight-reading. And, of course, he caught me out. He said, 'Right, stop and go back four bars,' and I didn't know where I was.

Playing Games

Gilmour co-composition and possible cameo on Roy Harper's *The Unknown Soldier*.

Point Me at the Sky *single*

Waters – That was the last of the unknown singles. I don't know why we did it. It was a constructed attempt and it didn't happen. But we will be releasing another one – it can't do any harm.

Poles Apart *The Division Bell*

Polly Samson – It's about Syd in the first verse and Roger in the second.

Gilmour – The significance of Syd in the modern-day Pink Floyd is vastly over-emphasized. I don't think it's nearly as important a thing as some people seem to think. However, he was a fantastic talent.

Post War Dream, The *The Final Cut*

Waters – My father died in the last war and I feel that I personally may have betrayed him, because we haven't managed to improve things very much.

Peter Jenner – I really don't want to hear about him, and his whinging on about how his dad died and his guilt feelings about Syd. I mean, he's just done that over and over again . . .

A collection of great dance songs

Pow R Toc H *Piper at the Gates of Dawn*

Mason – How 'Pow R Toc H' started was just one geezer would go up to the microphone and go, Ba-boom-chi-chi, Ba-boom-chi-chi, and everyone picked up on it and put the other things in it and then the drums picked up and that was more or less that . . .

Powers That Be, The *Radio KAOS*

Waters – This generation of Reaganite teenagers who are rock 'n' roll fans – what can you say? It upsets me that any young, or old, people feel like that. That they can be conned into thinking the bombing of Tripoli is a good thing. You only have to look at it rationally for a minute and a half to realize that it did nobody any good at all except possibly Reagan. I feel huge anger at the perpetration of such a monstrous piece of terrorism purporting to be anti-terrorist. It's such doublethink. Real George Orwell.

Priväte Persön *Identity*

Wright – I'm not interested in electronics for (their own) sake; if you turn this knob you get this sound – why it happens I don't know.

Profiles (pts 1–3) *Profiles*

Mason – I've certainly enjoyed working with Rick . . . I think it's useful and important to change the people you work with. You get so stuck in certain patterns. You know: Roger will do this and Dave will do that and . . . well, you can go and make the tea, Nick!

5.01 AM (Pros and Cons of Hitch Hiking, The)
The Pros and Cons of Hitch Hiking

Waters – Some of the ideas have come from my own dreams and also there are bits and pieces of other people's dreams. In fact, the third verse of the album's title track talks about standing on the wing of an aeroplane, looking down at the eastern seaboard of the United States and Yoko Ono being there, and telling me to jump; that everybody's got to die some time and the manly thing to do is to end it all now.

Pink Floyd

That dream belongs to Andy Newmark, the drummer. He came in one day and over lunch in the pub he told me about this dream and I thought, that's a good dream, I'll try and fit that in somewhere. So I did.

Q

Quicksilver *More*

Wright – We didn't really like the film. It's hard to say what I thought of our music in *More* since I didn't hear it with the film, but apparently it works quite well. As an album I don't really much like it.

R

Radio Waves *Radio KAOS*

Waters – The lyrics are clearly ironic: 'AM, FM, weather and news, our leaders had a frank exchange of views'; but there was no irony intended in the music.

Rain in the Country

An unreleased instrumental out-take from *Zabriskie Point.*

Mason – It was a terrible experience. Antonioni was a right bastard.

Raise My Rent *David Gilmour*

Gilmour – Favourite guitar solos? I like what I did on 'Raise My Rent'. That was sort of an excuse to go on a 12-bar blues.

Rats *Barrett*

Jerry Shirley – 'Rats' in particular was really odd. That was just a very crazed jam and Syd had this lyric that he just shouted over the top . . .

Raving and Drooling

Waters – We were about to do a British tour and had to have some new material . . . 'Raving and Drooling' was something I'd written at home.

Reaction in G

An instrumental piece – supposedly 'about' having to play 'See Emily Play' in Scotland – from 1967.

4.47 AM (Remains of Our Love, The)
The Pros and Cons of Hitch Hiking

Gilmour – I like Eric, and what he does, a lot. I consider him to be a strange choice. If I'd been in Roger's shoes, I wouldn't have turned to him. I don't know if he's trying to replace me or find something else.

A collection of great dance songs

Waters – When I was a kid, I used to buy records by Billie Holiday and Bessie Smith. Leadbelly, too – blues records, mainly. My first love is American music from the beginning of the century. And, of course, when Eric Clapton is on the album, that can only increase it. He's peerless ... At the end of side one, I said to him, 'Play like Floyd Cramer.'

We really enjoyed making this record. We love that country blues from the end of the '20s and the '30s so much. It's a very strong feeling that we all share.

Remember a Day *A Saucerful of Secrets*
Robert Lindsay, *Sunday Telegraph*, 25 August 1991

Although there have been many stage performances that have affected me, moved me and, indeed, changed my life – or rather my attitude to life – there is one particular night and one particular performance that I remember more than any other.

In a magical, hippy night, in the summer of 1975, the Pink Floyd appeared on a makeshift stage in the grounds of Knebworth House, witnessed by me and seventy thousand others. We had waited throughout a glorious summer's day while various other bands played; then, as if God had stage-managed the event, a spectacular sunset lit up the skies, as the sun disappeared behind the auditorium. The air was heady with the smells of barbecues, incense and dope.

All the other artists had finished their acts; through the silence, a bass line began to demand everyone's attention. Two war planes, a Hurricane and a Spitfire, roared over the crowd and up into the sky, where they simulated a dog-fight. They were up there for five or perhaps ten minutes – weaving, spiralling, diving down over our heads; the bass line started up again. Then another aeroplane, a huge life-size model, appeared at the back of the amphitheatre and crashed onto the stage. Now everyone knew that we had launched into *Dark Side of the Moon*, Pink Floyd's great and immortal album. Seventy thousand and one people went wild with delight as Pink Floyd themselves appeared; what masters of theatre!

Pink Floyd

They weren't just four great musicians; they would have made the ancient Greeks proud. They certainly had the spectators gasping in absolute awe. One felt so small and yet, at the same time, so huge with all this going on and being a part of such a great crowd of people witnessing an incredible spectacle.

As an actor, I have experienced a certain power over an audience, but it had always been through the strength of the narrative and suspension of belief; nothing could have prepared me for this. Pink Floyd had literally wrenched *Dark Side of the Moon* from their audience's imagination and transported it onto that makeshift stage, one summer's night at Knebworth. In its way, it was almost a religious event. Pink Floyd and that summer's night gave me the inspiration to continue and they took my youth with them. I shall always be in their debt.

Return of the Son of Nothing
The working title for 'Echoes'.

Wright – We went into the studios in January to put down a lot of ideas and called them all bits of 'Nothing', which is where the title comes from. It's twenty-two minutes long and is a piece we can do live without any of the problems of 'Atom Heart Mother'.

Rhamadan
Malcolm Jones – This was a long, boring track, lasting about eighteen minutes, which Syd (or at least, I have always presumed it was his playing) had made ... It featured several conga drum overdubs, with no apparent theme or direction.

Rhoda *Profiles*
Rick Fenn – We both write the pieces, but I suppose, because I play the more melodic instruments, I possibly come up with more thematically. Basically, we just toss it all around together.

Richard's Rave-Up
A track recorded in February '68. This may be a working title for a piece on *Saucerful*, but is more plausibly an instrumental later incorporated into that album's title track.

Andrew King – You could never tell with Rick what number he

was playing; it always seemed to be the same. We used to call it the 'Rick's Fry's Turkish Delight Lick'.

Rooftop in a Thunderstorm Row Missing the Point, A
A poem published in the Sydzine *Terrapin*. The existence of a track of the same name has been neither confirmed nor even rumoured.

Round and Around *A Momentary Lapse of Reason*
At just over thirty seconds, the live version on *Delicate Sound of Thunder* is the shortest track ever released by Pink Floyd.

Run Like Hell *The Wall*
Waters – After 'Run Like Hell', you can hear an audience shouting 'Pink Floyd!' on the left-hand-side of your stereo, and on the right-hand side or in the middle you can hear voices going 'Hammer!' This is the Pink Floyd audience, if you like, turning into a rally.

This track marked the only point during the *Wall* show in which Waters would regularly address the audience. As the inflatable pig bobbed overhead, he would declare 'Home piggy home' or 'He's an old pig but he's a big pig,' then dedicate 'Run Like Hell' – or 'Run Like Fuck' – to the paranoids, psychopaths or disco freaks in the audience.

Waters – It's actually a sort of disco tune, really, isn't it? It's just supposed to be this kind of crazed rock 'n' roll band doing another sort of 'oom-pah' number.

Alan Parker – Our point was always that if Hitler was around today, the first thing he'd ask Albert Speer to do would be to get a really good rock 'n' roll group at Nuremberg. It would be part of the trappings.

4.33 AM (Running Shoes) *The Pros and Cons of Hitch Hiking*
On the *Pros and Cons* tour, 'Running Shoes' included an unrecorded third verse, celebrating 'the feel and the flavour of dark teenage skin'. Lest anyone miss the point, a three-screen film backdrop spelled out Y-E-S and S-E-X.

S

San Tropez *Meddle*

Waters – *Atom Heart Mother* and *Meddle* are half good. I like 'Atom Heart Mother' and 'Echoes' themselves, but we made a right mess of it on the other sides.

Saucerful of Secrets, A *A Saucerful of Secrets*

Waters – 'A Saucerful of Secrets' allowed you to think of anything that you wanted and, because it had echo, people thought it was science fiction, but it could be anything.

Wright – We all believed it was going to be one of the best things we'd ever put on to record – which I think it was at that time ... Parts of 'Saucerful' on *Ummagumma* came from the Birmingham gig, which we put together with the Manchester stuff ... but the stuff on the album isn't half as good as we *can* play.

Mason – I don't write much myself. I do what I can. I can't really write songs but I certainly put forward my suggestions on arrangements of other people's material. It's in this capacity that I am credited on some of the Floyd's songs.

Gilmour – I still think it's great. That was the first clue to our direction forwards from there. If you take 'Saucerful of Secrets', the track 'Atom Heart Mother', then 'Echoes' – all lead quite logically towards *Dark Side of the Moon*.

Scarecrow, The *Piper at the Gates of Dawn*

Wright – Just listen to Syd's songs, the imagination that he had. If he hadn't had this complete breakdown, he could easily be one of the greatest songwriters today. I think it's one of the saddest stories in rock 'n' roll, what happened to Syd. He was brilliant – and such a nice guy.

Scream Thy Last Scream

The proposed, but abandoned, follow-up to 'See Emily Play': occasionally covered, often acclaimed and incessantly bootlegged.

A collection of great dance songs

Sea Shell and Soft Stone *The Body*
Waters – It would be absolutely wonderful if I could write beautiful love songs that make people feel wonderful and warm inside . . .

Sea Shell and Stone *The Body*
Geesin – I dashed forth with me goods and Roger did four songs. I actually did all the fill-in bits, funny spluttering noises, then classical cello and guitars; the strain nearly exploded my mind – maybe it did explode my mind, but we did it.

Seabirds
Despite appearing in the *More* film, this up-tempo number inexplicably failed to make it on to the album.

Waters – We did the *More* soundtrack as a sort of personal favour for Barbet. He showed us the movie – which he'd already completed and edited – and explained what he wanted; and we just went into the studio and did it. I don't really like working under that sort of pressure, but it can help you by focusing your ideas.

Mason – It was a good exercise, as Barbet Schroeder was a really easy person to work with.

Seamus *Meddle*
Gilmour – I was lucky to have a very broad base of stuff that the radio played and my parents played and my friends liked. It went through very wide spheres of folk music to show music to old acoustic blues – Leadbelly, Bill Broonzy . . .

See Emily Play
Barrett – Singles are always simple . . . The whole thing at the time was playing on stage (but) obviously, being a pop group, one wanted to have singles.

Wright – Although it sounds a bit gimmicky, hardly any special effects were used. Take that 'Hawaiian' bit at the end of each verse: that was just Syd using a bottleneck through echo. The part that sounds speeded up, though, was speeded up! John Woods, the engineer, just upped the whole thing about an octave. On stage, we have to cut that particular bit out, but then I don't think the audience minds if our reproduction isn't 100 per cent accurate . . .

I don't think the success of 'See Emily Play' has affected us personally. Sure we get more money for bookings, but the next one could easily be a flop. When I first heard the playback in the studio, I had a feeling it would go higher than it did, but I'm not complaining.

David Bowie – Pink Floyd got a hit, and for a few months they were moderately overground. And Syd just didn't want any part of that, so he opted out. And I understood why. I thought, Yeah, right, they're being accepted. Nobody wants that (*ironic laughter*).

Gary Brooker of Procul Harum was played the song in a 'Blind Date' singles review: 'The Pink Floyd – I can tell by the horrible organ sound. It's much better than "Arnold Layne".'

See Saw *A Saucerful of Secrets*

Gilmour – We were just an R&B band, churning out Bo Diddley and Chuck Berry hits, and then we saw *The Magic Roundabout* and never looked back.

Seems We Were Dreäming *Identity*

Wright – The people in the village expected a whole load of freaks to arrive when they heard we'd bought the house. They thought the whole band would be staying and there'd be hundreds of groupies roaming around . . . Certainly, when I went into the country, people would actually come down to the house expecting to see Gary Glitter prancing about nude in the swimming pool . . .

Set the Controls for the Heart of the Sun
A Saucerful of Secrets

Peter Jenner – 'Set the Controls . . .' was the first song that Roger wrote that stood up against Syd's songs, which was significant at that time.

Waters – 'Set the Controls . . .' is about an unknown person who, while piloting a mighty flying saucer, is overcome with solar suicidal tendencies and sets the controls for the heart of the sun.

Gilmour – Even in those days, recording tended to be a few

people playing, and then dropping in overdubbing afterwards. There are tracks on *Saucerful of Secrets* that Syd played on and I played on later. 'Set the Controls for the Heart of the Sun', I think I played a bit on.

Waters – I managed to get hold of a book of Chinese poetry from the late T'ang period – and I just ripped it off. Except for the title: I've no idea where that came from. It came from . . . within me. (*Karl Dallas has identified the title as a quote from William S. Burroughs.*)

The KLF – The live half of *Ummagumma* is essential to both of us. 'Set the Controls for the Heart of the Sun' is the centrepiece for the whole of the Floyd's career.

Waters – The live LP was supposed to be a sort of: 'Here's the live LP. It's the last time you'll hear these tracks performed live, so say goodbye.' But the public treated them as though they were new tracks and this resulted in the fact that we've been playing three of them ever since.

Several Species of Small Furry Animals Gathered Together in a Cave and Grooving With a Pict *Ummagumma*

Waters – That was a very light-hearted and easy exercise. It's really just speeding up and slowing down tape, and using a bit of echo and imagination. It's just voices and me beating on myself with my bare hands . . . In fact, if you slow it down, you'll hear it's somebody gibbering – probably me.

Playing this at 16 r.p.m. does indeed transform some of the high-pitched vocals into Gilmour, while Waters marvels, 'That was pretty avant-garde, wasn't it?' At 45 r.p.m., Waters reappears on a tape loop, saying 'Bring back my guitar, bring back my guitar . . .'

The 'poem' was improvised in the studio by Waters, and later parodied by Ron Geesin on his 'To Roger Waters, Wherever You Are'.

4.41 AM (Sexual Revolution)
The Pros and Cons of Hitch Hiking

Waters – One of the great paradoxes of the design of human beings is the disparity between the hopes and aspirations of men and women ... presumably based on the separate biological functions in terms of human survival: that man has been designed to go out and screw everything he can in order to populate the world and that we should multiply and spread.

It appears, from my limited experience, that, by and large, women are far more interested in providing a safe place within which to rear children and, if possible, keep the hunter there, hunting for them; which may all be very simplistic and I'm sure that I shall be attacked by all kinds of women and probably men too, all over the world, but ... so what.

Eating and sleeping and 'effing' are like 'it', really, at a fundamental level. All the other intellectual, sociological, anthropological, historical, der-der-der stuff is very *Interesting!* and *Exciting!* and can be *Elevating!* and *Challenging!* and all those things. But compared with making love, it's small time.

She Took A Long Cold Look *The Madcap Laughs*

Gilmour – I did those albums because I liked the songs; not, as I suppose some might think, because I felt guilty taking his place ... I was concerned that he wouldn't completely fall apart. The final remix on *Madcap* was all mine as well.

She Was A Millionaire

Demoed at the recording of *Piper*, this song (also known simply as 'Millionaire') is thought to have been tackled again during Syd's penultimate set of sessions in June 1970. Neither version has been released, officially or otherwise.

Barrett – *Piper at the Gates of Dawn* ... was very difficult in some ways, getting used to the studios and everything. But it was fun; we freaked about a lot. I was working very hard then; there's still lots of stuff lying around from then, even some of the stuff on *Madcap*.

Sheep *Animals*

Gilmour – I think there's lots of hidden or dry humour in things we've done. Half of it is absolutely there, like the 'Lord's

Prayer' bit on 'Sheep', but people take our lyrics so seriously that they don't see it. (*The prayer actually parodies the 23rd Psalm.*)

Waters – I think one of the *Animals* songs stands up: 'Sheep.' It was my sense of what was about to come down in England and it did with the riots in Brixton and Toxteth ... It had happened before in Notting Hill in the early '60s – and it will happen again. There are too many of us in the world and we treat each other badly. We get obsessed with things – products – and if we're persuaded it's important to have them, that we're nothing without them, and there aren't enough to go round, the people without are going to get angry. Content and discontent follow very closely the rise and fall of the graph of world recession and expansion.

Gilmour – 'Sheep' came closest to inclusion (*on the 'comeback' tour*) because I had a lot to do with making it come out the way it did and I feel quite proud of it. But Roger sang it and I don't think I could sing it with the same particular venom.

Shine On You Crazy Diamond *Wish You Were Here*
Vanetta Fields – When I first worked with Pink Floyd, I didn't like *Dark Side of the Moon* very much. But, playing with them for a few months, I really got into it, and then I agreed to record the *Wish You Were Here* album with them.

Gilmour – My argument, when we went to do *Wish You Were Here*, was to try to get some of the feeling and musical power of 'Echoes' with the lyrical power of *Dark Side of the Moon*.

Waters – I wrote that song, above all, to see the reactions of people who reckon they know and understand Syd Barrett. I wrote and rewrote and rewrote and rewrote that lyric because I wanted it to be as close as possible to what I felt – and, even then, it hasn't altogether worked out right for me. But none the less there's a truthful feeling in that piece ... that sort of indefinable, inevitable melancholy about the disappearance of Syd. Because he's left, withdrawn so far away that, as far as we're concerned, he's no longer there.

Gilmour – It is sad. Syd's story is a sad story romanticized by people who don't know anything about it. They've made it fashionable but it's just not that way.

Waters – It's too long ago to remember exactly why I was thinking about Syd ... I think it was a guitar line of Dave's that sparked me off; a very plaintive phrase you hear at the beginning of 'Shine On'. It's actually the signature tune from the radio show *Take It From Here*. You can't tell from the album, but in terms of my lyrics, it is the first use I make of memories of childhood; the juxtaposition and interplay between memories of childhood and feelings I have now.

Gilmour – It sounds like Peter Green? Thank you (*laughs*) – we try! Yes, it's obviously largely based in blues stuff. I've got a background in that; psychedelia and blues coming together is obviously a large part of what I do, I suppose.

In one of the less celebrated instances of Floyd's music being appropriated by film-makers, 'Shine On' appears in a soft-porn flick called *La Marge* (*The Streetwalker*), featuring *Sticky Fingers* cover star Joe Dallesandro. The song was also chosen as a 'Desert Island Disc' by disgraced TV presenter Frank Bough, who applauded it as a 'very good piece of pop music' which 'goes to the soul'.

Short and Sweet *David Gilmour*

Roy Harper – This is a celebration of life – the quality – on whatever level ...

Gilmour – (Harper) is one of those people who never want to compromise anything. He often takes things a lot further than I personally would, in the way he performs, but I like it. I like and admire the way he does things: his courage, getting up there and doing it that way ... his honesty and openness in the way he puts over his own life on stage. I think he's very much more talented than a lot of people who've been more successful than he has; maybe because people are frightened of that sort of thing that he does and the kind of honesty he puts over. I think it scares a lot of people off.

Show Must Go On, The *The Wall*

Waters – The idea is that they're coming to get (Pink) to take him to the show because he's got to go and perform. They realize that something is wrong, but they're not interested in any of his problems. All they're interested in is the fact that there are however many thousand people there, all the tickets have been sold and the show must go on, at any cost to anybody. You cancel a show at short notice and it's expensive.

Backstage 'at the tight-lipped Pink Floyd's very exclusive ligerama following their series of concerts at New York's Nassau Coliseum', an undercover *Melody Maker* columnist asked one notable guest for his opinion of *The Wall*. The paper subsequently reported that 'Mr Warhol was tersely noncommittal: "I always felt that The Velvet Underground was a good psychedelic group."'

Waters – I'm sure there were a hell of a lot of people who came to the show and went away thinking, what the fuck was that all about? And aren't interested anyway. There's no reason why everybody should be interested in the same things I am, after all.

Siam *Fictitious Sports*
Mason – It's a sort of new wave *King and I*.

Signs of Life *A Momentary Lapse of Reason*
Mason – The boat was one of the earliest things we started with as a sound effect because it's such a romantic sound; so clear when we recorded it.

Gilmour – The guitar and whistling answers was actually a demo that I did in '77 or '78. We had to replace the actual guitar, but the backing chords are from an ancient thing I did.

Small Theme *La Carrera Panamericana*
Mason – Racing is dangerous. But I've lost more friends through rock music than I have through motor racing.

Smiles for Miles
A song apparently recorded for, but omitted from, *Amused to Death*.

Snowing
An unreleased early live piece.

Mason – What's hard to get over now is just how bad we were! What we were doing was different, but, my God, it was bad!

So Far Away *David Gilmour*

Gilmour – That's a short moment in my life when I felt pretty desperate ... I had doubts as to whether or not to put it on, to use it, because it felt a little too close to me, too personal and that's a nervy thing to do. That's one of the things I find it hard to do. But I've worked with other people and they've played me their demo songs and there's been one or two of these songs that have been like that – very close, personal – and I say 'We should do this' and they say, 'No, I can't do it.' We haven't done it and the whole album at the end has felt to me like they left something out that they should have put in there. It's not anything for them to worry about and no one else is going to think the worse of you for it.

John Lennon's a great example of someone who *does* do it and Paul McCartney is a great example of somebody who doesn't (*laughs*). Paul McCartney always seemed ... frightened of exactly that, of letting anything of his true self out, which is a shame because there probably is a true self in there somewhere.

Sorrow *A Momentary Lapse of Reason*

Gilmour – It's the first thing I think I've written with the words first. Most of 'Sorrow' got put down the day after I wrote it; the vocal of the verses, the background guitars, the drum parts and the lead guitar. The solo was done first take ... I never got around to doing it again.

Ezrin – We hired a twenty-four-track truck and a huge PA and brought them inside LA Sports Arena ... We piped Dave's guitar tracks out into the arena and re-recorded them in 3D. So the tracks that originally came from a teeny little Gallien Krueger and teeny little Fender ... sound like the Guitar From Hell.

Southampton Dock *The Final Cut*

Fish – What I find really disgusting is that the most powerful comment on the Falklands, Pink Floyd's *The Final Cut*, didn't reach as many people as it should have. You know why? Because everyone was told it was sooo unhip to like anything by the Floyd.

Waters – I love all that 'Southampton Dock' stuff, that little section – I'm really proud of that.

Spanish Piece, A *More*

Mason – Our music is quite well integrated into the film; like every time anyone switches on a radio or is in a bar with a jukebox or anything, it's the Pink Floyd which comes out.

Waters – We were told one bit had to be coming out of a radio in a Spanish bar so we had to do something that suggested that. In the middle of it, Dave tried to make the sort of speech noises you'd expect to hear.

Speak to Me *Dark Side of the Moon*

Waters – God, I resent giving that to him (*Mason*) now. 'Cos he had nothing to do with it . . . it was like a gift. It was all right at the time.

Fish – When I'm really pissed up, once I start talking about *Dark Side of the Moon*, just walk away!

Stay *Obscured by Clouds*

Wright – *Obscured by Clouds* is a bit simpler than *Ummagumma* or *Atom Heart Mother*, because of the limitation of writing for movies, but we put in a lot more time on it than we did on *More*, and we're a lot better at getting out our musical ideas now.

Stoned Alone

Possibly an alternative title for 'I Get Stoned'.

Mason – As far as I can remember, neither myself, Rick or Roger were taking anything at that time. On the other hand, we didn't do badly for drink. Later on though, things changed and, looking back, I recall that we all had experiences with drugs at one time or another.

Stop *The Wall*

Waters – At the end of 'Waiting for the Worms', the aggression gets too much for him and he says, 'Stop!' I don't think you can actually hear the word 'stop' on the record, or maybe you can. It's very quick . . . and then he tries himself, if you like.

Strange Rhythm *Identity*

Wright – The great thing about the Fairlight is that every time you go back you learn something else. We had to get control over it though, because it would have been very easy just to have ended up making funny noises. We spent several weeks sequencing and scripting everything, but it was all worth it in the end.

Summer Elegy *Wet Dream*

Wright – There is a lot of stuff that I do reject, not for myself, but for the band . . . there are lots of things in the Pink Floyd's music that I don't like – and I don't like them because there's four of us doing them. It's a compromise. Obviously, I do like a lot of the stuff we're doing or I wouldn't be in the band.

Summer '68

Wright – My lyrics are really bad and they're not saying anything that's important. A couple of songs I haven't minded being put out, in terms of lyrics, like 'Summer '68'. Although I don't think that the lyrics were good, they did at least say something that, I felt, was a real genuine feeling and therefore that's cool.

Sunset Strip *Radio KAOS*

Waters – I accidentally tuned into the FM radio station KMET. They had this bizarre spot called The Fish Report, which was a strange, fanciful and very surreal sports-fishing report about the beaches in and around LA. It was complete gibberish from beginning to end: real Monty Python. It made me realize my superior European overview of this culture was quite wrong.

Sunshine

Although Malcolm Jones' *The Making of The Madcap Laughs* suggests that this was an early version of 'Remember A Day', it is now thought to be a working title for part of 'Matilda Mother'. Hey, this stuff is *important*!

A collection of great dance songs

Swan Lee (Silas Lang) *Opel*

Peter Jenner – I only did a couple of sessions (in 1968): it was reasonably together in a fairly wacky way – at least there were songs and things.

Sysyphus *Ummagumma*

Wright – We all played alone on our pieces. I thought it was a very valid experiment and it helped me. But I think Roger feels that if we'd all worked together it would have been better.

Gilmour – Rick wanted to do a solo piece, because he was the one who tended to grumble the most about the musical direction we were going in, and all that sort of stuff. He said he wanted to make *real* music.

Mason – Rick always used to maintain that he'd been to music school; which he had, but only for a year. And he was pretty lethargic about that . . .

T

Take It Back *The Division Bell*
Mason – The biggest problem now for a number of people, including ourselves, is to try and avoid getting locked into this cycle of spend a year making a record, then go on tour for a year and a half, then go mad, then wait until the money runs out or the accountants run off with the cash, then start again. It would be better now to find other ways of doing it, to pace it in a different way, and do some slightly different things.

I suppose it's back down the job centre; see if they've got anything else for legendary drummers . . .

Take Up Thy Stethoscope And Walk
Piper at the Gates of Dawn
Barrett – Sometimes we just sort of let loose a bit and start hitting the guitar a bit harder and not worrying quite so much about the chords.

Waters – It's stopped being sort of third-rate academic rock; started being . . . sort of intuitive groove, really.

Teach
The working title for 'One of the Few', whose protagonist, said Waters, 'is the same personality from *The Wall*, the teacher . . . It gives him a *raison d'être*. It explains some of his feelings that didn't get explained in *The Wall*. That was a very thinly sketched character, who didn't have any real reason for being as horrible to everybody as he was. Well, I'm giving him a reason now.'

Terminal Frost *A Momentary Lapse of Reason*
Gilmour – 'Terminal Frost' and 'A New Machine' are both things that I had lying around pretty well complete for some time; at least, I think, a couple of years. 'Terminal Frost' is very similar to what it was as a demo. But there was a long period of time where

A collection of great dance songs

I thought I might get words for it and turn it into a song. In the end it decided for itself that it would remain the way it was.

Terrapin *The Madcap Laughs*
This reappeared on Barrett's *Peel Sessions* EP, of which the Strange Fruit label's Clive Selwood told *Record Collector*: 'It was difficult to find Syd, but once I'd found his brother, who handles his business, that was fine ... We also had to have the approval – as we always do – of the other musicians involved. We had to track down Jerry Shirley, who was then working with the new version of Badfinger in the States, and also ask Dave Gilmour. I understand that Syd himself is alive and quite well, has a happy life, spends a lot of time working in the garden and has a decent income from his songwriting royalties. So he's probably got a better life than any of us!'

Of the five songs that Syd performed on the session, only 'Terrapin' came from the album that he was presumably supposed to be promoting.

Theme From An Imaginary Western
The chord sequence on which 'Atom Heart Mother' was based.

Waters – We were rehearsing somewhere or the other; Dave played that riff and we all listened to it and thought, Oh, that's quite nice. But we all thought the same thing, which was that it sounds like the theme from some awful Western.

It had that kind of heroic, plodding quality – of horses silhouetted in the sunset. Which is why we thought it would be a good idea to play on that really; cover it in horns and strings and voices ...

There's No Way Out Of Here *David Gilmour*
Gilmour – Ken Baker is in a group called Unicorn that I produced a couple of albums for ... It was a track on one of their albums (*Too Many Crooks*) that I found suited my mood when I was making my album; we tried it out and it worked well.

Thin Ice, The *The Wall*
Waters – After 'In the Flesh?' we start telling a story which is about my generation.

Pink Floyd

Three Wishes *Amused to Death*

Waters – I was casting around for somebody to play lead on this record and Jeff Beck's been in the back of my mind for a long time, so I called his people up and said, 'Might he be interested?' And they said, 'Weeell, he might be ...'

So we went through a big shadow-boxing thing and it ended up with me sending a cassette of four or five of the songs to a studio so Jeff could listen to them. I didn't go, because it's awful to have that embarrassing thing of Jeff Beck sitting there and he goes, 'Well, it's interesting,' (*laughs*) – you know, gets in the car and goes home.

Beck – I was never a Floyd fan, never even been to a gig. I knew they had the biggest-selling record of all time, but I didn't know any of the songs off it, never thought there was any common ground. They were a visual act with all that back-projection and crashing airplanes. What a show. It seemed a bit humiliating to think one turns up with just an amp, not even a helicopter of your own that drops bombs or anything.

Tide is Turning (After Live Aid), The *Radio KAOS*

Gilmour – I listened to one side of *KAOS*, the first side, then I heard 'The Tide is Turning', which I liked, on the radio. I haven't listened to the other side.

It's not really to my taste, most of it. It's all done with machines, too disco-ey for me. But I'm obviously biased. You shouldn't really ask me about it.

Fish – It's nice and positive ... As an album, I really love *Radio KAOS*; what I've got out of it. But you've gotta really study his stuff. It ain't something you can just put on and get exactly what it was about from first-hand.

Waters – Between Ian Ritchie and myself, we really fucked that record up. We tried too hard to make it sound modern. Also the part where Billy pretends that he's just started the Third World War I now find faintly embarrassing, and I dislike the backing vocals on 'The Tide is Turning'.

Mason – I actually thought that *Radio KAOS* had some great tracks on it and was a good record.

A collection of great dance songs

Time *Dark Side of the Moon*

Mason – I like certain things on *Dark Side of the Moon*, such as 'Time', which I did with Rototoms. We tried it with things like boobams – very small, tuned drums which are usually made with a two-inch tube, so it's almost like a xylophone – but the Rototoms were just the right sort of thing. That was knocked off very quickly, or relatively quickly; maybe three days instead of three weeks.

Waters – Listening back, the thing that most surprised me was how long the intro to 'Time' is. I got the feeling that there was a serious lack of panic about losing the listeners' interest.

Gilmour – There are bootlegs of us doing *Dark Side of the Moon* a long time before we ever started recording it and the differences are unbelievable ... 'Time' was, like, half the speed. I think the vocal was me and Rick singing in harmony, very low. It sounded terrible.

Waters – I was twenty-eight years old before I suddenly realized that I wasn't going to wake up one morning and find that, now, my life was going to start. I realized that it was happening for a long, long time without me noticing it.

The term 'quiet desperation' is from pioneering conservationlist Henry David Thoreau's *Walden* (1854). The song's cultural ties are further strengthened by a naked guitarist singing the opening lines in soft-porn movie *The Joy of Mykonos*.

Alex Paterson (The Orb) – One of the biggest shocks of my life was when I went to Chicago in 1988. I'm going, 'I've come here for a dance revolution. Where's Derrick May? Where's Fingers Inc? The first thing I heard in the car was "Time" by Pink Floyd.

House music producer Marshall Jefferson was also blown away. 'Man, I love rock 'n' roll!' he told a startled *NME*. 'I started off with rock 'n' roll: Pink Floyd, Led Zep, Deep Purple, Hendrix, Cream, Procul Harum – sheeyut! All them groups, man. The soloing and shit! When I do my rock 'n' roll group it's gonna be a double album and there's gonna be soloing that'll knock your head off. Believe it, man, believe it!'

Mr Jefferson is currently sharing a room with Alex Paterson at the George Clinton Home for Dispossessed Dance Gurus.

Too Much Rope *Amused to Death*

Waters – When we recorded the album, I would sometimes rehearse vocal takes by impersonating Bob Dylan. That line originally read, 'Each man has his price, my friends,' so make of that what you will. As a joke, I sang 'Bob' instead and Pat insisted that we left it in. So although it was unintentional, I'm happy that it's there for Bob Ezrin. I hope he appreciates it.

Towers Of Faith *When The Wind Blows*

Waters – (Clare Torry) is just . . . magical.

Trial, The *The Wall*

Gilmour – I think it was written by Bob (Ezrin) with the immediate intention to do it with an orchestra, although we did demos of it with synthesizers and stuff.

Waters – Bob Ezrin would be prepared to argue with me about things. It's no good arguing with me in the studio and saying, 'I don't like that'; you've got to explain why you don't like it and why we should do it a different way. Bob is articulate and quite able to do that, so we had a good, lively relationship making the record. He was a very good musical and intellectual sounding-board for me, 'cos he's very bright and quite tough as well. We could sit and talk about what it was about *ad nauseam* – which was absolutely invaluable, because I don't think anybody else in the band had any idea of what it was about, and I don't think they were very interested. In fact, I know they weren't interested.

True Story

A Gilmour co-composition on Roy Harper's *The Unknown Soldier*, with guitar by Dave.

Harper – Dave Gilmour was talking about *Dark Side of the Moon* having sold twenty-four million and went on to say that *Wish You Were Here* had sold eighteen million or something. It was a business conversation. I mused for a minute over the silliness of it all and I said, 'You know something, Dave? I've never had a silver record.' I was just emphasizing the gap. He turned to me and said, 'That's because you're a tosser, Roy.'

A collection of great dance songs

Twelve-Eight Angel

A Gilmour co-composition from The Dream Academy's *A Different Kind of Weather*, featuring Dave on vocals, guitar and bass synth. Renamed 'Angel of Mercy', the song was released as a single, and reviewed by 808 State's Martin Price: 'As soon as that came on I thought it sounded like Pink Floyd and sure enough Dave Gilmour has produced it.'

Two of A Kind

From Barrett's *Peel Sessions* EP, this song is officially credited to Syd but is believed to be the work of Rick Wright.

Two Suns in the Sunset *The Final Cut*

Waters – That was a thought I had, driving home one night, thinking we all sit around and talk about the possibility of accidents or – as I put it in the song – people just getting so bloody angry that finally somebody pushes a button. Well, the song's all about that moment when suddenly it happens ... It's very easy to go, 'Oh yes, well, there may be an accident and the holocaust might happen,' without having the feeling of what it might be like. And that's why it says in the song, 'Finally I understand the feelings of the Few,' which is supposed to be a reference to the bomber and the gunner ... my dad, and all the other war casualties. That song, I suppose, in a way is going back to the second song where there's a line, 'A warning to anyone still in command of their possible futures: take care.'

Mason – I was going to play on it and then more or less said, 'Let's not get too precious about this, let Andy Newmark do it the way you want it done, rather than me spend weeks trying to get it absolutely stylistically right.' It still doesn't seem that important to me.

Waters – I've always been a fan of Andy Newmark's playing. I saw him at a Roxy gig in the south of France and was deeply impressed.

U

Until We Sleep *About Face*

Gilmour – On the demos for the album, I played fretless bass myself on all the songs because I like the sound and I can play it enough to do demos ... There is a Fairlight synthesizer doing the bass part on 'Until We Sleep' but other than that, it's all fretless.

Untitled

Curiously unclaimed by A. Bootlegger, this is a Barrett song; probably a working title for 'Let's Split', recorded in 1970.

Up the Khyber *More*

Mason – I look back and wish that I'd done things differently or better; you know, kept time! 'Oh, it's meant to go like that, it's meant to speed up!'

Us and Them *Dark Side of the Moon*

Gilmour – For me, personally, the periods of writing *Dark Side of the Moon* were not at all creative. I was definitely going through a bad patch – which is reflected in the writing credits, where I don't seem to get an awful lot.

Alan Parsons – It was literally a fight to get the delay effect on 'Us and Them'. We spent a tremendous amount of time hooking up Dolby units and realigning machines at the wrong speed to accomplish that effect.

Peter Jenner – Roger was always one of the good guys. There's a story that he bought almost a whole street of houses and got them as nice sheltered subsidized accommodation for old people. Which he did without brandishing it from the rooftops as to what a good thing it was. He just did it. And if that is true, which I've every reason to suppose it is, it was a terrifically good thing to do with his money.

V

Variation
An early 'Great Gig in the Sky', as found on several 1972 bootlegs.

Vegetable Man
An unreleased (but much-bootlegged) gem from August '67.

Peter Jenner – Syd was around at my house just before he had to go and record and, because a song was needed, he just wrote a description of what he was wearing at the time and threw in a chorus that went, 'Vegetable man, where are you?'

Vera *The Wall*
Waters – This is supposed to be brought on by the fact that a war movie comes on TV – which you can actually hear. Mentioning no names! (*It's actually* The Dambusters.)

'Vera Lynn was the Forces' Sweetheart in England. We all have songs about the soldiers going away. In 'Nobody Home', he skips back to 1968 . . . and now he's going all the way back to the war.

Violent Sequence, The
An instrumental, composed for *Zabriskie Point*, which evolved into 'Us and Them'.

Mason – There was a lot of news film, of cops and students fighting it out, all with no soundtrack apart from this very lyrical piano thing which Rick played as a solo. Antonioni never used it.

Gilmour – We couldn't understand it when Antonioni said, 'Ees not quiiite riiight for thees beet.'

Waters – We did a concert at the University of California just after all the campus violence. The administration had closed the school but we did our concert, which was very nice. It was sad to note that the students had really got themselves organized in readiness for violence: there were field dressing posts available for casualties.

Students here attempt to live out a situation that doesn't exist. I feel strongly about English students who wreck debates when they should accept it as a medium of communication.

Vöices *Identity*

Wright – Obviously, we hope to be successful, sell a few records and go on the road . . .

W

Waiting for the Drummer
A one-off, light-hearted jam on the *KAOS* tour.

Waiting for the Worms *The Wall*
Waters – You hear a voice through a loud hailer. It starts off going 'Testing, one, two' or something, then 'We will convene at one o'clock outside Brixton Town Hall.' It's describing a march towards some kind of National Front rally in Hyde Park; the NF are what we have in England, but it could be anywhere in the world. If you listen very carefully, you might hear 'Lambeth Road' and 'Vauxhall Bridge', you might hear the words 'Jew boys' or 'Somewhere we may encounter some Jew boys.' It's just me ranting on.

Walking on the Other Side
Allegedly, an unreleased track from the *Division Bell* sessions.

Watching TV *Amused to Death*
Waters – I had been watching the pictures taken from (Tiananmen) Square, in the days leading up to the massacre, and I was struck by how articulate they were – at least, the ones who spoke English.

It was interesting to see ... the flowering of the new individual freedom within the repressive nature of the Communist regime. So when they murdered them it was a cruel blow and I wept. I was terribly upset ...

Waves *Wet Dream*
Wright – I wanted to feature saxophone on this album because I played the saxophone myself for a bit, but not successfully. The music I first listened to that made me decide that I wanted to be a musician was back in the days of Coltrane, Miles Davis and Eric Dolphy. If you like, they are my heroes, funnily enough, and not keyboard players.

I liked the sound of the sax that the Floyd had, so obviously I tried to get that kind of sound. I originally wrote 'Waves' for the saxophone, and he (Mel Collins) played it so well that I brought him on to another couple of tracks.

Waving My Arms In The Air/I Never Lied To You *Barrett*

Barrett – I have lots of undeveloped things lying around. I'm still basically like I've always been – sitting around with an acoustic getting it done. I never get worried about my writing.

'Waving My Arms In The Air' reappeared in set-lists by Syd's short-lived Stars enterprise. 'I don't know where the tapes are,' drummer Twink told Barrett fanzine *Opel.* 'I think all of the gigs were recorded, and Syd recorded the rehearsals ... just on a cassette. The other ones were recorded on a really professional set-up by a guy from America based in Cambridge.' None of this material has surfaced on bootleg, although a recording of Syd's 6 June 1970 gig at London's Olympia (accompanied by Gilmour and Jerry Shirley) has been erroneously credited to Stars on occasion.

We Won the Double

A tongue-in-cheek working title for 'Echoes', inspired by Arsenal Football Club's triumph in the 1971 league and FA Cup tournaments.

Wearing the Inside Out *The Division Bell*

Wright – On *The Division Bell*, there were things I thought could have been better. I think there was material that should have been on that wasn't on. This is always the case when more than one person is working. So on my own album, I can do what I really believe should be on the album. Not necessarily better – it may be worse; because I need Dave to say, 'No, that's no good,' and Dave needs me to say, 'No, that's not so good.'

Gilmour – Rick is happy to sail off on his yacht and be part of this thing and earn very good money out of it. He doesn't like shouldering responsibility, so it's a very good arrangement.

Welcome to the Machine *Wish You Were Here*

Waters – The idea is that the Machine is some underground power and therefore evil, that leads us towards our various bitter destinies. The hero's been exposed to this power ... and it informs him that all his actions are Pavlovian responses ...

In fact, he doesn't exist any more, except that he has the feeling deep down inside himself that something just isn't right. That's his only reality. So he goes off, leaves the machinery and enters the room, the world. The doors open and he realizes it's true: the people there are all zombies. That's not very serious, you see ...

The song? Oh, it's all that stuff about buying guitars and punishing your ma ... It's kind of self-explanatory. We don't have to talk about those lyrics, *surely*.

Wervin' *Fictitious Sports*

Mason – I don't feel that I'd like Pink Floyd to suddenly adopt a rather jazzy style – it's just something I'd like to investigate with some other musicians.

Carla Bley – The lighter stuff like my work on *Fictitious Sports* was received very coldly by the jazz community. It completely disappeared in America.

What Do You Want From Me? *The Division Bell*

Gilmour – A lot of the lyrics were the result of a collaboration between myself and my girlfriend, Polly Samson ... and some, unfortunately, came after moments of lack of communication between us. The title 'What Do You Want From Me?' came out of exactly one of those moments.

What God Wants – or, to put it another way: ### Less fun than watching TV
Charles Shaar Murray, *Weekend Telegraph*, 29 August 1992

There are many ways to spot a puritan élitist demagogue, but one reasonably reliable method is to watch for those who instinctively distrust pleasure, particularly the pleasure of others. They can be found in roughly equal proportions on the left and the right of the political spectrum.

Take Kingsley and Martin Amis. England's most celebrated literary father-and-son team are divided by ideology, but umbilically linked by their distaste for the working classes. Amis *père* dislikes them because they are vulgar and ignorant and sometimes vote Labour, Amis *fils* because they are vulgar and ignorant and often vote Conservative.

Had he been blessed with a rudimentary sense of humour and rather more verbal fluency than he actually possesses, Pink Floyd's former leader Roger Waters might well be pop's Martin Amis. Waters is consumed with disgust and world-weariness; his species is clearly a great disappointment to him.

His new single, 'What God Wants', is a trailer for the album *Amused To Death* (released next week); said album's title is derived from that of the American academic Neil Postman's book *Amusing Ourselves To Death*, a blast of loathing for the consequences of television's dominance over the printed word.

Thus the video for 'What God Wants' depicts a selection of real and – um – animated animals watching television. However, its own argument is demolished because instead of depicting the crazed TV evangelists, patriotic double-think and voyeuristic war-as-entertainment footage against which 'What God Wants' quite cogently rails, we watch Waters and his studio guest Jeff Beck performing the song. The music is standard post-Floyd Waters: a steady, clumping beat, ominous synthesizer chords, a choir and a squibbling guitar.

The title of the song, incidentally, may provide a wry twist of amusement for Waters' former colleagues in Pink Floyd. When Waters resigned, he not only insisted that the group disband, but also attempted to injunct the others from continuing without him on the grounds that anything in which he was not the dominant participant couldn't possibly be authentic Pink Floyd. Waters had clearly forgotten that his own tenure as Pink Floyd's helmsman began only when the group's original visionary, the theoretically irreplaceable but chemically challenged Syd Barrett, retired after the group's first few hits. Led by guitarist David Gilmour – who had replaced Barrett in 1968 – Pink Floyd continued, outselling Waters' own solo efforts and outperforming the last couple of Pink Floyd albums. In this case, what God wanted he didn't get.

A collection of great dance songs

What Shall We Do Now?

Waters – It's just about the ways that one protects oneself from isolation by becoming obsessed with other people's ideas – that it's good to drive a powerful car or be a vegetarian; adopting somebody else's criteria without considering them from a position of really being yourself.

At this level the story is extremely simplistic. I hope that, on the other levels, there are less tangible, more effective things that come through.

Although the song appears in the *Wall* movie and was triumphantly disinterred by Bryan Adams at Berlin in 1990, it was omitted from the original *Wall* album.

Gilmour – A double album is something that I've rarely ever liked from other people in the past, but I think *The Wall* works. The only problem we had was reducing it down from a triple to a double (*laughs*). Towards the end, we were actually cutting chunks out of songs to fit the time.

Waters – We just axed 'What Shall We Do Now?' and left the lyrics because they helped to tell the story. There's a list of things to do, which I'm quite glad isn't on the album now because it's rather banal.

What's the New Mary Jane

A cacophonous Beatles out-take reputed, by entrepreneurial bootleggers, to feature Barrett. There is absolutely no evidence to suggest that this is so.

When the Tigers Broke Free *single*

Having been rejected from *The Wall*, this also failed to make it to the final cut of *The Final Cut.*

Waters – The rest of the guys in the band criticized its inclusion on the grounds that it was too personal to me. It's very specific about the time and place and so on, and therefore it would have made it clear that *The Wall* was about me.

Gilmour – I think there's a lot of it that's irrelevant to me. I don't feel that a lot of the things that happened to me in my earlier years – some of which weren't so wonderful – adversely affect my life to the extent Roger feels some of those things affected his life ... That's his viewpoint and he's perfectly entitled to it, but I don't subscribe to it.

Waters – I think there are things in my story that have helped my creativity. Your father being killed, for instance, is one of the best things that can happen to a kid if he's going to write poetry or songs.

When You're In *Obscured by Clouds*

Mason – I thought the LP was an amazing improvement on the film music, and I thought the film music was really good. But then again, I thought the same about *More*.

John Martyn – I've got all the Floyd records, and when they were at their height, they used to come to see me play in America. I never used to go to theirs, though. I was never allowed in.

Who Needs Information *Radio KAOS*

Waters – That's about the tabloid press and how they have ceased to be about the dissemination of news information; particularly the Murdoch press in England – newspapers like the *Sun* and the *Mirror*. All you get is gossip, tits and ass.

Wined And Dined *Barrett*

Gilmour – He would never do those songs twice the same, ever. He'd change the chords and his way of singing them and everything ... extraordinary. But it would take forever with him, because he just wouldn't do it the same twice, so he kept getting it wrong. So you'd be lifting vocal lines off and moving them to a different place on the tape and stuff. Just the method of working was so difficult ... and I don't think he had as many good songs as we had for *The Madcap Laughs*.

Wish You Were Here *Wish You Were Here*

Gilmour – When it sounds like it's coming out of a radio, it was done by equalization. We just made a copy of the mix, knocking out all the bass and most of the high top so that it sounds radio-like. The interference was recorded on my car radio and we put that track on top of the original. It's all meant to sound like the first track getting sucked into the radio with one person sitting in the room playing guitar along with the radio.

A three-month correspondence in *Classic CD* magazine eventually identified the introductory orchestral snippet as an extract from Tchaikovsky's Fourth Symphony. That hardly explains the preceding reference to Schumann, but, hey, this was the '70s.

Waters – In a way it's a schizophrenic song. It's directed at my other half, if you like ... the battling elements within myself. There's the bit that's concerned with other people, the bit that one applauds in oneself; then there's the grasping, avaricious, selfish little kid who wants to get his hands on the sweets and have them all. The song slips in and out of both personae so the bit that always wants to win is feeling upset and plaintively saying to the other side, 'Wish you were here.'

Sam Brown – My ideal evening? Light some candles in the bathroom, put *Wish You Were Here* on the stereo, then get in the tub with a large Campari and orange.

Dave Mustaine (Megadeth) – Great headphone music, great for unwinding to after sex or after a show. Or after a sex show. Preferably all three. Do you need downers to enjoy this album? Well, I've never really been into downers. I was into heroin. It was only later I realized that music sounds just as good when you're sober. In fact, it sounds even better, 'cos I know what line is coming next.

Wolfpack *Barrett*
Reputedly Syd's favourite track from *Barrett.*

Barrett – (The songs) have got to reach a certain standard and that's probably reached in *Madcap* once or twice and on the other one only a little – just an echo of that. Neither of them are much more than that.

Womb Bit, The *The Body*
Geesin – I had bad staggers of the brain by then, and took to the seaside to play with pebbles.

Wondering and Dreaming
A working title for part of 'Matilda Mother'.

Pink Floyd

Word Song *Opel*
Also known as 'Untitled Words' or simply 'Words'.

Barrett – It would be terrific to do much more mood stuff. They're very pure, the words ... I feel I'm jabbering.

Wot's ... Uh, the Deal *Obscured by Clouds*
Mason – We were very satisfied with our music, and I can't really lay the blame for the failure of the film on anyone in particular ... Barbet Schroeder has a very particular style which doesn't really appeal to me. His characters are quite dry and discover themselves slowly.

Wouldn't You Miss Me *Opel*
An alternative version of 'Dark Globe'.

Waters – If our hobby is to be interested in ... whether Syd did this or did that, or what colour shoes he wore on 18 March 1967 or whatever, who am I to say that's obsessive? Some people collect stamps! It's better than watching Ninja Turtles on TV, in my view. Being a Syd Barrett fan seems to me to be a perfectly legitimate and reasonable way of spending your spare time.

He was a very interesting man. He wrote some fantastic songs. There's a body of work; unfortunately it is complete. There won't be any more, I don't think. He was a visionary, he was an extraordinary musician, he started Pink Floyd ... well, Syd and I started the band together, but if he hadn't been there, nothing would have happened. I'd be working for an architect ... I might be my own boss by now – I probably would – but I would not be doing the work that I'm doing, I don't think. He was the key that unlocked the door to rock 'n' roll for me.

X

A sadly neglected character in the Pink Floyd canon.

Y

Yet Another Movie *A Momentary Lapse of Reason*

Gilmour – It's hard to explain 'Yet Another Movie'. It's a more surrealistic effort than anything I've attempted before. I've tended to stick within personal experience and reality very much; but I have a desire, without getting into fiction and little stories about other people – which I generally don't care for – to find a broader base to write things about ... I'm very fond of it but I don't even know what all of it means myself!

Mason – It's one of my favourites on the album; I think just because of the way it was recorded. It was an unforgettable occasion: this enormous studio with more drums than I've ever seen in my whole life. We had Jim Keltner's kit, my kit, Steve Forman the percussion player with all his stuff, and two of these people known as 'drum doctors', who are ultra-specialist drum people. They set the drums up, tune them and so on; bring you seven snare drums and say, 'Which one do you think you would like to use for this?' Just the power and the sound of all that air being moved by these drums ... real 'drum city' in there that day!

In the past, we've used musicians other than the group, even if they haven't always been credited: it doesn't mean that I'm not playing on all the tracks. On 'Yet Another Movie', all three of us played together – the percussionist, Jim Keltner and me. We drummed in unison but, at other times, I kept the rhythm while the others played fills. It's a different approach which benefits the music.

You Know I'm Right *About Face*

Gilmour – It started off being about a girl, a relationship. I'd done the first verse ... and someone looked at it and said, 'That's about Roger, isn't it?' And it absolutely wasn't, at that point. But that had blown it, because I'd still got to write the rest of the song.

There are some little jokes in there, but that's all it is . . . things we've argued about.

You (The Game part II)
From Roy Harper's *The Unknown Soldier*, with co-writer Gilmour on guitar and Kate Bush on vocals. The track is a sequel to the Gilmour-starred 'The Game (parts 1–5)' on Harper's HQ.

Young Lust *The Wall*
Waters – When I wrote this song, the words were quite different. It was about leaving school, wandering about town, hanging around outside porno movies and dirty bookshops and things like that: being very interested in sex but too frightened to get involved. Now it's completely different. That was a function of all of us working together on the record, particularly Dave Gilmour and Bob Ezrin.

Ezrin – One thing we went for with the vocals was an 'acting' quality. For example, Gilmour – who's very sober by nature – sang screaming on 'Young Lust' in a way he hadn't sung for years.

Waters – 'Young Lust' is a pastiche young Brit. It reminds me very much of a song we recorded years and years ago called 'The Nile Song'. Dave sings it in a very similar way and I think Dave's singing on 'Young Lust' is terrific. I love the vocals, but it's meant to be a pastiche of just any rock 'n' roll band out on the road.

Alan Parker – Pink Floyd had always been the thinking man's rock 'n' roll.

Waters – Actually, there were almost no Pink Floyd groupies anyway. They miraculously divined that this was not a band that was really worth pursuing.

Your Possible Pasts *The Final Cut*
Waters – By the time we had gotten a quarter of the way through making *The Final Cut*, I knew that I would never make another record with Dave Gilmour and Nick Mason. We just didn't agree on anything any more.

Mason – It's still a Pink Floyd album. I don't think it's our best, but I don't suddenly start going through the ancient catalogue and going, 'Well, that's really a Pink Floyd album and that isn't,' and 'That's really a Dave Gilmour album and that's Roger Waters...'

Z

Zip Code *Profiles*

Mason – If you think I'm going to get Phil Collins in just so I can ponce about the front of the stage with a tambourine, you're very much mistaken!

Oh, by the way . . .

Chris Welch

Floyd Joy

Melody Maker, 19 May 1973

O Floyd – wherefore art thou? What lies yonder – on the dark side of the moon? Madness they do say, and present death. In their seventh year together, paranoia and fear seem to haunt their music, despite or perhaps because of success.

Much of the Pink Floyd's latest album (actually over a year old in terms of studio time) reflects the pressures and obsessions that afflict the itinerant rock musician. Without the lifestyle, there would not be music; and without the music, the lifestyle could not be supported.

Mad laughter and sane voices intermingle in the Floyd's measured, timeless compositions, and it would be easy to read into the characters of the men who make up one of the most original and fulfilling of groups a kind of omniscience.

Fans – and journalists – can and have been disappointed, or surprised to find that the Pink Floyd are but human. Their output is not prolific, they have been known to repeat material at concerts, they have yet to announce details of any plan to save the world and what is more, they operate and enjoy taking part in a moderately successful football team.

Time wasted, the curse of money, ambitions unfulfilled, these are all matters that concern the Floyd, and form the basis of many of their musical ideas. They are not esoteric subjects and should be easily assimilated without recourse to mystical interpretation.

Yet even today, the Floyd occasionally feel misunderstood. But they can also feel a tremendous satisfaction in the knowledge that the band said to be 'finished' when Syd Barrett left them all those years ago has reached a peak that is impressive even in this age of supergroups.

Acceptance of the Floyd's poised and delicate music has never been greater. On their last American tour they casually sold out massive venues from coast to coast; *Dark Side of the Moon* has taken world charts in its stride, while their forthcoming London concerts at Earl's Court – for charity – sold out as quickly as tickets could be passed over the counter.

The Floyd have doubtless earned an attractive penny in their time, but unlike many other successful artists they do not wallow in riches.

Roger Waters lives in a modest house in Islington, where his wife bakes pots in the garden shed. And while David Gilmour lives on a farm in the country, it is through his own efforts that the establishment has been made habitable. He might boast an ornamental pool in the garden, stocked with gaily coloured fish, but he dug it himself.

It was to this rural retreat that I drove one sunny day last week, wending through the fields of Hertfordshire, made fearful by juggernauts wallowing on S-bends and locals driving dented grey Cortinas at speed.

Arriving at the village at the appointed hour, a further sixty minutes were spent following the conflicting directions of rustics pushing bicycles. Still lost, I consulted a map that seemed to have been drawn up in 1932.

Hurling this aside, my gaze perceived a fissure in the hedge opposite. It seemed scarcely possible that I was parked outside the Gilmour estate and had passed it innumerable times in the last hour.

Such was the case. In a secluded courtyard an Alsatian stood guard and a venerable old horse clomped about. A youth in faded blue jeans and straggly black hair appeared like Heathcliffe at the cottage door. 'Mr Gilmour's abode?'

'Yes, indeed. Come in and have a cup of tea. It will calm you.' My motorist's fury began to abate, as I drank in the ornate but tasteful decor. Low beams, a jukebox here, woodcarvings there – since taking over the abandoned Victorian farmhouse a couple of years ago, the guitarist had worked hard at improvements.

When he moved in, there was no electricity or heating, and he lived rough as he created an open-plan living area, constructed a music room, dug the aforementioned pool and cleaned out stables for Vim, his retired brewers' dray horse. He had even permitted himself the luxury of a swimming pool, following the satisfactory sale of many of the Pink Floyd albums.

Then came Nemesis, not in the shape of a writer to Mailbag, but a man from the council, only minutes before my arrival. He had presented a copy of the council's plans to build a housing estate on the surrounding green-belt land, and to compulsorily purchase great chunks of the Floydian paradise.

'We'll have to pack our bags and move,' he said with hopeless resignation. Our eyes turned to megalopolis creeping over the horizon, the threatening blocks of Harlow, poised ready to march.

We toyed with ideas to build a wall of fire around the premises, to be touched off at the instant the bulldozers arrived, and I suggested sowing landmines in Vim's meadow. Eventually we decided it would be more cheering to speak of the Pink Floyd.

For the benefit of new reader George Loaf (12), it should be explained that the group was born in 1967 during the heady days of flower power and UFO. Mr Gilmour replaced the legendary Syd Barrett on guitar, who had written such chart hits as 'See Emily Play'.

The Floyd went through a bleak period when they were written off but quietly drew about them an army of fans, and went about their creative work, wholly unmoved by the shifting fortunes and fashions that affect their contemporaries.

They are a proud, pioneering and somewhat detached group who sometimes look upon the cavortings of some of their fellow groups with faint dismay, not out of sour grapes, but from purely aesthetic considerations.

But first, what had the Floyd been doing these last few months, and how long had it taken them to conceive *Dark Side of the Moon*, which I believed was their best yet?

'We did the American tour,' said Dave. 'We only ever do three-week tours now, but that one was eighteen dates in twenty-one days, which is quite hard. We started recording the LP in May last year, and finished it around January. We didn't work at it all the time, of course. We haven't had a holiday in three years and we were determined to take one. On the whole, the album has a good concept . . .'

Isn't it their best yet?

'I guess so. A lot of the material had already been performed when we recorded it, and usually we go into the studio and write and record at the same time. We started writing the basic idea ages ago, and it changed quite a lot. It was pretty rough to begin with. The songs are about being in rock 'n' roll, and apply to being what we are on the road. Roger wrote "Money" from the heart.'

Money seemed to be a touchy subject for musicians and fans alike. Were the Floyd cynics?

'Oh, no – not really. I just think that money's the biggest single pressure on people. Even if you've got it, you have the pressure of not knowing whether you should have it, and you don't know the rights and wrongs of your situation.

'It can be a moral problem, but remember the Pink Floyd were broke for a pretty long time. We were in debt when I joined and nine months afterwards I remember when we gave ourselves £30 a week, and for the first time we were earning more than the roadies.'

For a band that relies on creating moods, good sound was essential for the embryo Floyd.

'We hardly had any equipment of our own. We had a light show, but we had to scrap it for two years. We've had lights again for the last couple of years, but in the meantime we developed the basic idea of the azimuth coordinator.

'We did a concert at the Festival Hall with the new sound system, and none of us had any idea what we were doing. I remember sitting on the stage for two hours feeling totally embarrassed. But we developed the ideas, and it was purely down to setting moods and creating an atmosphere.'

To digress, what did Dave think of Hawkwind, the newest prophets of the UFO tradition?

'I don't ever listen to them, but they seem to be having jolly good fun,' said Dave without the trace of a smile.

What about the Moody Blues?

'I'm not too keen on the Moody Blues. I don't know why – I think it's all that talking that gets my goat. It's a bit like Poets' Corner.'

Dave did not want to be drawn on the subject of rivalry, but he did admit to hearing with pleasure that an expensive piece of equipment belonging to another group had collapsed. The group had recently tried to poach the Floyd's road crew.

Looking back over his six years or so with the group, what milestones did he see in their development?

'There haven't been any particular milestones. It's all gone rather smoothly. We've always felt like we have led some sort of a cult here, but in America it's been slow but sure. This year in the States it's been tremendous, but I can't say why – specifically. We have been able to sell out ten- to fifteen-thousand seaters every night on the tour – quite suddenly.

'We have always done well in Los Angeles or New York, but this was in places we had never been to before. Suddenly the LP was number one there and they have always been in the forties and fifties before.

'No – success doesn't make much difference to us. It doesn't make any difference to our output, or general attitudes. There are four attitudes in the band that are quite different. But we all want to push forward and there are all sorts of things we'd like to do.

'For Roger it is more important to do things that say something. Richard is more into putting out good music and I'm in the middle with Nick. I want to do it all, but sometimes I think Roger can feel the musical content is less important and can slide around it.

'Roger and Nick tend to make the tapes of effects like the heartbeat on the LP. At concerts we have quad tapes and four-track tape machines so we can mix the sound and pan it around. The heartbeat alludes to the human condition and sets the mood for the music, which describes the emotions experienced during a lifetime. Amidst the chaos – there is beauty and hope for mankind. The effects are purely to help the listener understand what the whole thing is about.

'It's amazing ... at the final mixing stage we thought it was obvious what the album was about, but still a lot of people, including the engineers and the roadies, when we asked them, didn't know what the LP was about. They just couldn't say – and I was really surprised. They didn't see it was about the pressures that can drive a young chap mad.

'I really don't know if our things get through, but you have to carry on hoping. Our music is about neurosis, but that doesn't mean that we are neurotic. We are able to see it, and discuss it. The Dark Side of the Moon itself is an allusion to the moon and lunacy. The dark side is generally related to what goes on inside people's heads – the subconscious and the unknown.

'We changed the title. At one time, it was going to be called *Eclipse*, because Medicine Head did an album called *The Dark Side of the Moon*. But it didn't sell well, so what the hell. I was against *Eclipse* and we felt a bit annoyed because we had already thought of the *Dark* title before Medicine Head came out. Not annoyed at them, but because we wanted to use the title. There are a lot of songs with the same title. We did one called "Fearless" and Family had a single called that.'

Did the Floyd argue among themselves much?

'A fair bit, I suppose, but not too traumatic. We're bound to argue because we are all very different. I'm sure our public image is of hundred per cent spaced-out drug addicts, out of our minds on acid. People do get strange ideas about us. In San Francisco we had a reputation from the Gay Liberation Front: "I hear you guys are into Gay Lib." I don't know how they could tell ...'

As a guitarist Dave had been somewhat overshadowed by the Floyd's strong corporate image. But his virile, cutting lines are one of their hallmarks and a vital human element. Did he ever fancy working out on a solo album, or forming a rock trio?

'I get all sorts of urges but really nothing strong. Put it down to excessive laziness. No, I don't do sessions, I don't get asked. Any frustrations I might have about just banging out some rock and roll are inevitable, but are not a destructive element to our band. I have a lot of scope in Pink Floyd to let things out. There are specially designated places where I can do that.'

In the past the Floyd have been subject to criticism, not the least appearing in the *Melody Maker*. How do they react to that?

'React? Violently! People tend to say we play the same old stuff – that we do the same numbers for years. We don't. We are playing all new numbers now, except for "Set the Controls for the Heart of the Sun". The Who are still playing "My Generation" and nobody complains about that.

'We can take criticism when it's valid. But we are only human and we can only do so much. Sometimes it surprises me when we play really well, and spend some time on presenting a special show, like we did at Radio City in New York, and we get knocked.

'Some people dislike the basic premiss of what we are all about. Then their criticism is a waste of time. For someone to criticize you, who understands you, and can say where you have fallen down – that's valid.

'There are some people who come to our shows with no real interest in what we are doing, don't like the group, so they don't like the concert. We put all the bad reviews into a little blue book.'

This time Dave was smiling (Geo Loaf, please note: musician's joke. Gilmour does not really have a 'little blue book'. He was speaking lightly, in fun).

'I remember after Michael Watts did his piece on us, we all gave him a complete blank in an aeroplane. It wasn't deliberate. We just didn't recognize him. But he made some snide remark in the *MM*, so we sent him a box with a boxing glove inside on a spring. Nick got them specially made. But it wasn't taken in good humour. Syd Barrett would never have done a thing like that. All very childish really.

'We don't get uptight at constructive reviews, but when somebody isn't the smallest piece interested in what you are doing, then it's no help to them or to us. We did get uptight at what Mick

Watts said – it was very savage. But you can't stay angry for long. We tried to turn the feud into a kind of joke with the boxing glove. You've got to have a sense of humour,' said Dave, scowling into his tea.

'There's humour in our music, but I don't know if any of it gets through.'

As a key member of a band with its gaze fixed firmly on the future, it seemed unlikely Dave would want to reminisce, yet he was happy enough to recall their origins.

'Nick has got a date sheet ten yards long with all the gigs in red ink – every one since 1967. It's quite extraordinary when you look at the gigs we got through – four or five a week.

'We couldn't do that now, not when you think of the equipment we carry. The roadies have to be there by eight in the morning to start setting up. It's a very complicated business. Things still go wrong, but we virtually carry a whole recording studio around with us, all the time.

'In 1967, no one realized that sound could get better. There was just noise, and that's how rock and roll was. As soon as you educate people to something better, then they want it better – permanently. PAs were terrible in those days – but we've got an amazing one now.

'Before we do a gig, we have a four-page rider in our contract with a whole stack of things that have to be got together by the promoter. We have to send people round two weeks beforehand to make sure they've got it right, otherwise they don't take any notice.

'There have to be two power systems, for the lights and PA, otherwise the lighting will cause a buzz through the speakers. Usually a stage has to be built – to the right size. We've got eleven tons of equipment, and on our last American tour it had to be carried in an articulated truck.

'Oh yes, it's the death of rock and roll. Big bands are coming back.

'There was a long period of time when I was not really sure

what I was around to do, and played sort of back-up guitar. Following someone like Syd Barrett into the band was a strange experience. At first I felt I had to change a lot and it was a paranoiac experience. After all, Syd was a living legend, and I had started off playing basic rock music – Beach Boys, Bo Diddley and "The Midnight Hour". I wasn't in any groups worth talking about, although I had a three-piece with Ricky Wills, who's now with Peter Frampton's Camel.

'I knew Syd from Cambridge since I was fifteen, and my old band supported the Floyd on gigs. I knew them all well. They asked me if I wanted to join when Syd left, and not being completely mad, I said yes, and joined in Christmas '67.

'I later did the two solo albums with Syd. God, what an experience. God knows what he was doing. Various people have tried to see him and get him together, and found it beyond their capabilities.

'I remember when the band was recording "See Emily Play". Syd rang me up and asked me along to the studio. When I got there, he gave me a complete blank.

'He was one of the great rock and roll tragedies. He was one of the most talented people and could have given a fantastic amount. He really could write songs and, if he had stayed right, could have beaten Ray Davies at his own game.

'It took a long time for me to feel part of the band after Syd left. It was such a strange band, and very difficult for me to know what we were doing. People were very down on us after Syd left. Everyone thought Syd was all the group had, and dismissed us.

'They were hard times. Even our management, Blackhill, believed in Syd more than the band. It really didn't start coming back until *Saucerful of Secrets* and the first Hyde Park free concert.

'The big kick was to play for our audiences at Middle Earth. I remember one terrible night when Syd came and stood in front of the stage. He stared at me all night long. Horrible!

'The free concerts were really a gas. The first one had five thousand people and the second had a hundred and fifty thousand. But the first was more fun. We tried to do two more singles around this time, but they didn't mean a thing. They're now on the *Relics* album.'

Where lay the future for Floyd?

'God knows. I'm not a prophet. We have lots of good ideas. It's a matter of trying to fulfil them. It's dangerous to talk about ideas, or you get it thrown at you when you don't do it. We have vague ideas for a much more theatrical thing, a very immobile piece we'd put on in one place.

'Also we want to buy a workshop and rehearsal place in London. We've been trying to get one for some time.

'No, we don't want our own label – but we do have our own football team! We beat Quiver nine–one recently, and now there's talk of a music industries' cup. Oh, and we played the North London Marxists. What a violent bunch. I bit my tongue and had to have stitches.'

So that's what lies on the dark side of the Moon – a pair of goalposts. But the Floyd will be all right – as long as they keep their heads.

Tony Dron

Track record

Penthouse, December 1984

Set the controls for the heart of the sun, I was thinking to myself: who is Nick Mason? I've met Nick many times over the past few years but until *Penthouse* asked me to seek him out I had not realized how little I actually knew about him. One of the most successful rock musicians of all time, and I had been thinking of him as one of the good blokes in motor racing.

That's Nick's easy style: he fits in, gets involved in things and does well at them but there are many sides to the man. Bar a few weeks, it's twelve years since the band wrapped up *Dark Side of the Moon*, and about the same time since Nick's first motor race. He's had sixteen great years in the music business in all and the ideas are still coming fast and good. He's raced all kinds of motor cars from vintage Astons to the latest 225 m.p.h. Group-C Porsches, and he's got five Le Mans races under his belt. He has built up one of the best restoration and preparation businesses for historic race cars in the world, with customers in Europe, Japan and the States. It suddenly dawned on me: just who is this guy? Thinking fast, I finally found a 50p bit and stuck it in the machine in front of me. A second later your intrepid reporter had his ticket and was on his way to Kentish Town to find out.

Up a narrow cobbled alley off the Highgate Road is Morntane Engineering, specialists in every aspect of thoroughbred Aston Martin race cars. Prop.: N. Mason. Outside the door was a new 1,000 c.c. motorbike, one of the latest BMW K-series machines. I rang the bell, impressed.

'Very impressive,' said Nick as he opened the door, 'every other sod gets lost trying to find this place. Let's go up to the office.'

While Nick went off to get our afternoon tea, I looked around his office. There was a file marked 'N. Mason – Inland Revenue';

an enormous framed poster of a superb painting by an Italian artist showing Fangio in his 1955 Maserati, in a full-blooded drift with modern single-seater racers crashing in his wake; dozens of model cars in glass cases, which on close inspection I realized made up a full set of Ferrari works racing cars; bound volumes of *Motor Sport* and *Thoroughbred and Classic Car*; modern office equipment; and loads of files all stacked neatly.

'No bound volumes of *Penthouse*?' I asked as Mr Mason brought the tea in himself. 'Can't keep them. The mechanics always pinch them.' Nick smiled and sat down, the same as ever: relaxed without losing his good manners, easy-going without being complacent, confident but never showing off.

These days Nick likes to fit in a day's private flying as often as possible. 'Really it's an excuse to go to Elstree for breakfast. No, seriously, when Jonathan Palmer rings up and asks me to join him in the chopper to go to Silverstone, I can say, "Sure, great, I'll bring my logbook and get some hours in."

After school, Nick studied architecture, already reflecting his interest in style, and while at college he met up with some friends to form the Pink Floyd.

The music business became totally consuming and although one member of the band did leave early on, the Pink Floyd developed a near ideal working relationship as they struggled together for success. 'Keeping that relationship going is more difficult after success has been achieved,' says Nick, 'But I think we kept going so well because after that break into commercial success, we grew apart a bit in our private lives and followed our own ways. Roger and Dave have both done solo albums and tours and I have gone into film music. I'm doing an NVC video film for TV right now: it's about musicians with other interests.

'Some people think the Pink Floyd as an idea is a bit of a dinosaur nowadays and, sure, it's a major operation to make a record or go on the road. But we never tried to second-guess public tastes, just went on to the next good sound. It goes on like that: busy for a time, then not much happening for a while, like now, with Roger, as the writer, the dominant force. Anyway, what's

wrong with having a few dinosaurs around? It would be a shame
to let them become extinct!

'If I've done my part well that gives me great pleasure. Like with
the Dorset Racing Association's Lola in my first Le Mans in '79; I
was just one of the drivers, but we won the Index of Performance
and came second in class. I got very involved with the team and
the whole Le Mans experience.

'Out on the circuit at night, the experience was magical: the
sheer speed, the lights of the fairground as the car just about took
off under the Dunlop bridge and then swooping down to the Esses.
The smell of brake pads and then the incredible Mulsanne straight.
In the pits, the team spirit was marvellous. You'd finish your stint
and come in to hand over the car, and with every hour that went
by, the excitement in our pit grew. Then you'd walk out to the
back of the pits for a rest, hearing the French commentator and
the roar of the engines – and smelling frying onions from hundreds
of barbecues. The best day at Le Mans is the Friday, though, with
practice over the night before. You can walk around and be lazy
with nothing to do as a driver.'

That must be his one day's rest a year! Is there anything he
regrets having been unable to do?

'Yes, I'd like to spend more time with my children. I've got two
young daughters who go to the local comprehensive. I'm really
pleased to see them as often as I can, but I miss a lot of what they
are doing with so many races at weekends in the summer and so
much work.

'I'd like to spend more time here at Morntane. At first I would
come in and work on my own car, but I don't suppose I've touched
one of my super set of Snap-On tools in three years. I used to
enjoy that. Derek Edwards, who runs the place for me full time,
would come over and help me out and say things like, "Jesus, no
wonder you were in trouble: some animal's used Araldite on these
bleeding studs." And I'd mutter, "Hmm, animals" – not letting on
I'd done it five years before.'

His thoughts on modern cars?

'I like good modern style but there's no single perfect car, though for me the Porsche 928 comes near. Fantastic machine. And I love Ferraris, though I don't think they're so practical for everyday use. I like the way the Porsche is so modern but has the traditional front-engined, rear-wheel-drive layout. I don't go much on walnut dashboards in new cars: that's false traditionalism.

I've been trying out a Renault 25 recently and that's a stylish modern car. It talks to you, and that's great. You know, this Dalek voice says, "The-bonnet's-open, you-are-low-on-fuel, the-engine-tem-perature-is-high,   we're-not-going-to-make-it-on-this-one-Nick, we'll-be-walking-after-this-corner."

'Normally I drive a little Renault Gordini, which is the best thing around town, apart from the bike, of course.'

Finally, I asked Nick how he viewed himself as a race driver.

'Oh, not so seriously. I started out with the thought that it's a good idea to have a faster car than anyone else! Unlike the real professionals, I like to take a bit of time – like five years! – to work up to a good lap time, but I think I'm probably quite a good amateur. I just like motor racing, full stop. I can take the old Aston Martin Ulster to Oulton Park and crack the lap record, think I'm Jack the Lad. Then I can get in the Canon Porsche 956 and it's magic; the sheer speed and power. So long as I do a good job and everyone in the team is pleased, then I'm happy. In the long run, I'd like to run a really good Formula One or Group C team myself.

'Have I made myself seem like the man who never smiles?'

Anything but that, I replied, with total honesty. With that, Nick donned his crash helmet and black leather jacket and sped off into the London night on the big Bee-Emm. The rock 'n' roll rebel on the roaring bike has turned forty, but he wears it well.

Caroline Boucher

Waters in the pink

Disc and Music Echo, 8 August 1970

Roger Waters is bass guitarist, vocalist, gong-banger and on-stage extrovert with the Pink Floyd. At times he seems rather menacing, and other times rather obnoxious and self-indulgent. Off stage you feel guilty for prejudging him. He is a reserved, pleasant, very intelligent and home-loving person with a slightly brusque manner which tends to recede as he relaxes.

'This,' he explains, 'is because I'm frightened of other people. I don't think I know anybody at all who isn't frightened of other people. People know that if you lower your defences, someone jumps on you. I find myself jumping on people all the time and regretting it afterwards – blowing your horn at other people in the car; small things like that are all part and parcel of everything getting more uptight.'

Meeting him at his Islington home with his lovely wife Jude, it seems hard to relate Roger to the legendary Pink Floyd, foremost of the psychedelic bands, and revered to the extent of being a cult in France. There's even a shop in Paris named Ummagumma after their last album, and they've been presented with awards for their contribution to modern music.

Right now the Floyd are at the peak of their career – constantly in demand, able to fill any large concert hall or get a festival field on its feet – because after four years they're still unique, untouchable and good.

Roger is incredibly modest about the whole thing. When they started, he says, there were other bands in America doing what they were doing far better. Their phenomenal success in France still somewhat bewilders him.

Roger was born in Great Bookham, Surrey, and moved to Cambridge when he was two. He went to school there, didn't like it particularly and, when he left, came down to London to do architecture at the Regent Street Polytechnic.

'I'd had a guitar in Cambridge, but I never really played it much. Nick and Rick were both there doing the same course and we had a kind of blues group when we were in our second year. Then Syd came up to London – he'd lived round the corner from me in Cambridge but I didn't really know him very well because he was a couple of years younger than me. And there was another guy from Cambridge, Bob Klose, on lead guitar.

'We played together occasionally. We'd go out and do £10 gigs and play at people's parties, and we bought some gear and gradually got a bit more involved.

'We were called Pink Floyd pretty early on, and then at some point we stopped adhering rigidly to the twelve-bar blues thing, and just started improvising round one simple root chord. I think Bob leaving had a lot to do with us stopping playing blues; he was a man with a great wealth of blues runs in his head, and when he left we hadn't anyone who had any blues knowledge, so we had to start doing something else.

'Syd took over as lead guitar, and I'm sure it was the noises that Pete Townshend was making then – squeaks and feedback – that influenced Syd, so we started making strange noises instead of doing the blues. We did something at the Marquee one afternoon and Pete Jenner and Andrew King heard us and rang us up and said we should do it professionally, but as we were all about to go on holiday, we said, "No, ring us in the autumn." Which they did, and became our managers.'

This was late in 1966 – and the start of UFO, held in those days at All Saints Hall, Powis Gardens. It cost 2s. to get in, and the Floyd made £6 the first week. They did four weeks there and by the last week the hall was packed full. In February 1967, Pink Floyd went professional and Roger left college, having done five of the seven years in the architecture course. While they were semi-pro, they'd managed to scrape together a couple of hundred pounds and went into a studio to record 'Arnold Layne', which was a hit.

'Then we did "See Emily Play", and a year followed doing

ballrooms and clubs. We went down terribly badly because everyone expected us to do "Emily" and we didn't – we were doing lots of other stuff off the first album. We were incredibly bad and we knew what we wanted to do but we couldn't do it. The whole Floyd sound wasn't an intellectually contrived thing; it was just improvising the sounds and the sounds suggested the lyrics.

'The idea of a light show came when we did a gig at the Essex University and someone showed a film on the wall next to us while we were playing. We thought that was rather good. Then we discovered how to do it with bubbles and oils at Powis Gardens when a bloke came down with some.

'Everything we've done we've done because it seemed like the obvious thing to do next. There was a great glut of those sort of things shortly after that time, but they'd been doing light shows, et cetera, in America before us, far more efficiently and better.'

After their two hit singles and the unsuccessful tours which lost them a lot of money, things began to get rather bad with the Floyd. Syd left while they were beginning to make the second album, *Saucerful of Secrets*, and Dave Gilmour joined them.

'It was a very bad period. People were saying we'd had it. I don't think any of us thought so, but it was just a question of coping with the Syd situation. The original idea was that Syd should stay on and write songs but not do live gigs, but it became obvious that that wasn't going to work at all. But with Dave joining, it became a group again, and since then it's been good all the way.'

Now Roger lives in a pretty terraced house in Islington which he bought for just over £8,000, including a huge studio at the end of the garden. He and Jude are doing the house up gradually – at the moment they're living mainly in the basement – and have divided the studio; a sound-proofed part for Roger, complete with a superbly ancient harmonium, and the larger studio for Jude to do sculpture, at which she's very good. At the moment she's teaching art and sculpture, but gives up at the end of this term. Recently Roger bought her a huge kiln for her pottery.

'I don't want him to start doing pottery himself though,' she admits, 'because he's so good at everything, he'd probably be better than me.' Roger, however, is determined to do some sculptures of his family of Burmese cats – George, Abie and four kittens.

Also in the corner of the studio is a bag of golf clubs that Roger's rather hesitant at owning up to. Jude says he likes to play golf at every available spare moment, but gets a bit embarrassed about it. Roger grudgingly admits to playing 'about twice a month, if that', with Ron Geesin.

Roger and Jude got married a year ago and had known each other for about fourteen years – Jude was literally the mythical 'girl next door'.

'Being married, I think, makes things much simpler,' says Roger. 'It makes it easier to cope with what's important and what isn't; it sorts out your priorities. A family is the most important thing in life – even if only in terms of one's biological function of having kids, which is all life's really about, because I can't believe in life after death or any of that stuff.

'Assuming that fact, you ask yourself: "What else is there in the world?" The answer is a lot of people and a few trees and grass and cows and things, and there's you sitting in the middle of it, alive for an unspecified period of time.

'And so, assuming you haven't just accepted that life is all about getting a good job and buying Rolls-Royces, you're faced with trying to sort out what it's all about so you can then decide what to do to fill in your life.

'And it seems to me that what is important is to cope as best you can with the rest of the people, primarily because I think people are more important than trees and grass. So although it would be simpler to sit in a shed in a wood and wander about in the dew, I choose the alternative and I haven't even really begun to find out how to relate myself to the rest of the world and the people and what to do about them, so I'm nowhere really.

'But I do have a kind of nagging optimism about the possibility of people coming together. It would appear that most of us can agree on some things, like saying nobody wants war. One of the exciting things about pop is that it's a new media and a vehicle for communication with a very relevant percentage of young people in the world, whereas the other media – like radio and TV – are much more involved with the system.

'I think there are thousands and thousands of people in this country, let alone the rest of the world, who could and would be doing the kind of thing that I'm doing and the rest of the Floyd is doing if it wasn't for the way the system is geared. I really believe that everybody needs a creative outlet. Obviously quite a lot of people find it in their work – I'm not suggesting everyone should be rock 'n' roll musicians – but a hell of a lot of people go to school and the great boot comes down on top of them and they never get out from under it again.

'My school was all for getting me to university – no reasons. If you asked why, they'd say it was to get a degree, and a good job. They don't tell you it's in order to be better equipped to cope with your environment.

'I could have been an architect, but I don't think I'd have been very happy. Nearly all modern architecture is a silly game, as far as I can see. Anyway, to get on in architecture you either have to have a daddy who is in the business, say the right things at the right times, or be a whiz-kid. I'm happier the way I am, and I can always build a house for myself one day if I want to.

'I just hated being under the boot so much I got out. But I think a lot of people can cope with being under it much better than I can. Take people who decide to become accountants, for example. I don't believe people sit down and say, "Wow, wouldn't it be great to become an accountant and work out how to get money off people's taxes for the rest of my life?" I believe they go into accountancy because it's bloody well paid.

'I think my music could do things for other people because I like it, and music does things for me. If Berlioz pottered through the garden gate, I'd sit back and look at him for hours because I get a great buzz out of his and a lot of other music. I can't sit down and make a piece of music and not play it to anyone or just listen to it myself and say, "Gosh, it was good." Music is a very real way of communicating with people, communicating emotions, and must be used as such – because we have such highly sophisticated

315

defences these days that there are not many ways of communicating left.'

As a group, Pink Floyd get on well together, but they don't meet much socially. When they're not on the road, they rarely see each other. Roger says this is the best way – either a group is so close that the relationship is almost telepathic, which is very rare, or, if not, the best alternative working relationship is to be quite apart.

Doing albums takes them a long time – they're working on one at the moment – because of their numerous tours. Sometimes individuals get ideas for songs and present them to the rest of the group to work out; sometimes they just set up the gear and work from scratch.

'The defensive barriers that are apparent in a small group of people who work together are almost heavier than everyday contact with the general public. Like people in shops, which is a very easy situation because they can't really hurt you or you them; but in a small group, you feel more susceptible. The individual pieces we did on *Ummagumma* weren't really very soul-baring and difficult to show each other, because we'd agreed before we started that we'd do it like that and just come up with the finished product.

'*Ummagumma* was a gamble which I think paid off. It would have been a better album if we'd gone away, done the things, come back together, discussed them and people could have come in and made comments. I don't think it's good to work in total isolation.'

The Floyd have also done two film scores: *More*, which they did in ten days flat, and *Zabriskie Point*, from which director Antonioni cut out a lot of their music, which upset them. Now there is an offer of another film which they hope to do later this year in the Canary Islands.

'I personally like films. I think I get more out of going to the cinema than going to the theatre. But that's the other thing we want to do – something in the theatre, probably using some film and actors moving about.'

Roger's main aim at the moment is to continue the struggle of finding the best means of communication.

'I wonder if there's anything to say which I'm capable of

articulating. There's words, obviously, but unless you know someone very well, so you're not at all frightened of them, it's very hard
to communicate with words. But we don't say what we mean half
the time. We say either what sounds right, or what the other
person wants to hear or any number of things.'

How long the Floyd will last Roger can't envisage. Certainly at
the moment they have a very good work relationship, and he sees
no reason why they shouldn't get together when they're forty if
something interests them, and there's enough of interest to them
at the moment to keep them together for a very long time.

Life after Floyd
from A to Zee

Evening Standard, 27 March 1984

Rick Wright, founder member of Pink Floyd, is gradually putting his past behind him after his unhappy split with the group. The keyboards player has just released his first single, 'Confusion', under the name Zee with colleague Dave Harris.

Here is Rick's style:

Homes – An early Victorian house in Bayswater. I used to live in a large house near Cambridge, but I didn't want to sit in the country and vegetate. I also have a house near Grasse in the South of France. I have a forty-five-foot yacht called *Gala* moored in Rhodes. It's my one luxury. I am thinking of chartering it out to honeymooning couples.

Food – I go to the Kalamaras, a Greek restaurant off Queensway. But I have gone off posh restaurants. I cook very simple things like fish and salad.

Clothes – I buy things about once a year in a big blitz. The last one was mainly at Jones in King's Road. I spent about £500. I like casual, but well-cut clothes.

Car – I have a Lotus Esprit Turbo and a ten-year-old Ferrari Boxer which is sitting in the garage. It's like brand new. I was persuaded to buy it by Nick Mason.

Family – I have two children: Gala, fourteen, and Jamie, twelve. They are at boarding school in Hertfordshire. My divorce came through a few months ago. It was friendly, but it was still emotionally quite traumatic. I have come through it and I feel very good and positive. My girlfriend Franka is Greek. She was a model and used to run a night club; now she designs clothes.

Hobbies – Collecting antique Turkish and Persian carpets.

What is so incredible is the work that goes into them. One carpet can take one family two generations to make. I have about thirty. I also love sailing; it is very therapeutic.

Pink Floyd – I left the Floyd with great relief. I am proud to have been a member of the band. We were rather faceless and it became a thing that no publicity was good publicity. Our business advisers couldn't understand it, because we could have sold more records and done more work. But we put our families first. Looking back, I think that it is a good and reasonable way to work.

Music – I like Talking Heads, Steely Dan. Mainly I listen to a lot of radio, usually Capital and Caroline when the signal is not too bad.

Dave Thompson

The madcap laughs

Pandemonium!, 3 Marach 1995

He's been immortalized as the Crazy Diamond, and Pink Floyd live still bid him shine on. He's been touted as a principal influence by everyone from Julian Cope to Robyn Hitchcock; he's been covered by David Bowie and Love And Rockets; and according to the legend to which he ascended twenty-five years ago, he's as nutty as a fruitcake and grows mushrooms in his basement.

Welcome to the world of Syd Barrett.

It's strange seeing Floyd still flouncing about; when Roger Waters filed his acrimonious divorce papers, it would have been a brave man indeed who would argue that the band could carry on without their leading light – carry on and flourish. *The Division Bell* may not be a patch on *Ummagumma*, but it's still obvious Floyd and there's gold in them grooves. And besides, it's not as if Pink Floyd haven't been beheaded before. When Barrett quit (or was he pushed? Or did he simply turn into a periscope and donate his toad to medical science?), the doomsayers were saying their doomy-bits then, because Barrett was the singer, the guitarist, the writer, a wizard and, before even Todd Rundgren, a true star.

'Arnold Layne' was Pink Floyd's first single, a Barrett mini-epic about a pervert who stole ladies' underwear off the washing line. Then came 'See Emily Play', 'Apples and Oranges' and, smack in between, *Piper at the Gates of Dawn*, Pink Floyd's first album and a disc which history has so frequently reassessed that the last I heard it was rated above *Sgt. Pepper* as the most influential album of 1967.

Damn right it was. Forget lovely Rita, meter maid, a day in the life and fixing a hole, *Piper* introduced demon cats ('Lucifer Sam') and walking scarecrows ('Scarecrow'), demented nursery rhymes ('Bike') and ... and ... oh, and just in case you were wondering where Space Rock came from, 'Astronomy Domine' and 'Interstellar Overdrive'. Roger Waters may have gone to the dark side of the Moon, but without Barrett's example during his own musical apprenticeship, he'd have been lucky to reach the other end of the street.

Barrett and Floyd parted ways during the taping of *Saucerful of Secrets*, the Floyd's second album. You can hear the hewing, on album and more especially on bootleg; the last songs Barrett recorded with the Floyd, 'Vegetable Man' and 'Scream Thy Last Scream', remain in the official vault, say Floyd's office, because it wouldn't be doing Syd any favours to let them be released. Booting him out of the band, on the other hand . . .

Barrett recorded two solo albums following his departure from Floyd, *The Madcap Laughs* (1969) and *Barrett* (1970). Both are locked in the twilight world of Syd's own supposedly burgeoning insanity, both are trapped within their own legend. Fiercely idiosyncratic, locked into songs which either stride purposefully towards pure pop immortality ('Octopus', 'Late Night', 'Terrapin' . . .) or else bumble and tumble into their own unsteady laps ('She Took a Long Cold Look', 'Feel', 'It Is Obvious'), your biggest regret upon hearing them today is that you didn't hear them when they first came out, before all the Syd Is Mad mythologizing began, and the albums could be accepted on their maker's own terms.

If you want any sort of modern comparison, compare the reviews of *Nirvana Unplugged*, back when the TV show first aired . . . then the ones which greeted the posthumous album. First time out, we were all in agreement, Kurt seemed relaxed, happy, playful. But now, 'Oh, the sense of foreboding, the fear in his eyes . . .' Madness (followed by twenty-five years in self-imposed exile) may not be quite as extreme as death, but the gulf between Truth and Hindsight is just as harsh.

Nowhere is this better illustrated than with *Opel*, a 1988 collection of *Madcap/Barrett* out-takes, and *Crazy Diamond*, the 3CD boxed set which gathered up both of Barrett's real albums, plus *Opel* and another nineteen dodgy off-cuts. Both released to finally assuage the continued demand for 'new' Barrett material, but all the vaults held was a handful of unheard songs, out-takes, run-throughs and rehearsals.

So that's what we got, and yes, they're a mess. But don't pay any attention to the critics who reckon you can chart Syd's disintegration from the ramshackle state of his unfinished songs. Grab a Beatles studio bootleg, and hear what they used to sound like when they were caught unawares. Were they insane as well?

Barrett's state of mind can never be divorced from his music. It can, however, be disregarded. Barrett at his best (the first Floyd album and Cleopatra's *Octopus* compilation for a cheap introduction; *Madcap* and *Barrett* for the more adventurously inclined; the *Magnesium Proverbs* bootleg for the real arcane fanatic) remains one of the most individual, exciting and unpredictable songwriters of his or any other generation, a weaver of words whose very enunciation was pregnant with visions.

He sings of gigolo aunts and you can see them parading, of wolfpacks and rats, and you see them as well. And then there's 'Octopus' itself, lost in the woods with cackling sails and dream dragons, and that strange self-fulfilling prophecy as the madcap laughs in the bare middle eight.

Maybe Barrett was the madcap (well, John was the walrus), but after a quarter of a century of rock inactivity, he's making more money now than he has ever in the past. Floyd have just remastered *Piper* for CD, and still trot out Syd-nuggets when they tour ('Astronomy Domine' was a recent UK b-side). There's a Floyd tribute album on the way, and Syd cops most of the writing credits; there's even a tribute to Syd Barrett himself, which is still ticking over, though it's really not that good.

But most of all, there's the legend of a young man who had everything and let it all slip away, only to find he had even more at the end.

Don't believe the legend. If the madcap's still laughing ... he's laughing at you.

Ken Langford

Which one's really Pink?

The Amazing Pudding, November 1993

When the suits of the record industry began to see profit potential in our young heroes, they were ill prepared for the enigmatic monicker 'Pink Floyd'. 'OK, which one of you guys is Pink?' asked the besuited gravy train engineer, with a certain look in the eye and an easy smile.

After some embarrassed umming and ahhing it was probably explained that there was no real Pink, that it was just the name of the band. But as the question persisted, so did it find its place among the lyrics of 'Have A Cigar'.

Pink finally found life as the hero of the *Wall* epoch. Having accepted this drone-faced friend as 'the' Pink, fans were shocked in 1987 to be presented with a choice of Pinks, the biggest character controversy since the Walrus.

I was even called Pink by friends, owing to a certain obsession of mine. But there is a true Pink, known primarily on a trivial basis by hard-core Pink Floyd fans. In fact, there is a Floyd too. Let's meet the men behind the beloved, 'warm comfy' name.

Miles' *Visual Documentary* introduced most fans to Pink Anderson and Floyd Council. We were invited to believe that the name 'appeared to [Syd] in a vision', although Miles continues: 'Actually, it is taken from the Georgia bluesmen Pink Anderson and Floyd Council who Syd had a record of.'

Barrett biography *Crazy Diamond* provides a more detailed account. Syd had travelled to Cambridge from London, looking for a front-man for his band, Leonard's Lodgers. The trip 'failed to unearth a singer, but he did return with a new name for the band. As he patiently explained to Bob Klose, he had a couple of records by two grizzled Georgia bluesmen named Pink Anderson and Floyd Council. How about putting the two Christian names together?

'Later he would often claim that the peculiar name was transmitted to him from an overhead flying saucer.'

Nicholas Schaffner's *Saucerful of Secrets* refers briefly to the two 'Georgia bluesmen', adding only the years of their births and deaths.

That is all of the readily available information on the men whose names have passed our lips Lord knows how many times. Precious few fans have taken the time to actually seek out their music. For those who have, it can be discouraging to discover that Floyd is virtually unheard of, even amongst blues aficionados. Four years of actively seeking his music turned up only a tape of one song. Finally, in May 1992, I located and purchased his complete catalogue. Pink isn't quite as obscure, but is not well known. Here, then, is the most comprehensive profile of the two men.

Pink Anderson was born in Lawrence, South Carolina, on 12 February 1900, and was raised in Spartanburg in the north-western part of South Carolina.

He first went on the road at age fourteen, employed by a Dr Kerr of the Indian Remedy Company. In the early 1900s, pitchmen such as this would travel from town to town with a 'medicine show'. Musicians attracted attention to the cart, from which the 'doctor' would sell a most miraculous elixir, available today only for the paltry sum of one dollar-step-right-up.

Pink travelled with Kerr until 1945, when the good doctor retired. In the early days Pink sang a little, danced and told a few jokes: 'I couldn't play nothing but "bastopol" tuning when I started on guitar. You know, "John Henry" and songs like that.'

In 1916 Pink met Simmie Dooley, a blind singer much older than himself, living in Spartanburg. With Simmie he became a blues singer. When Pink wasn't out with the Indian Remedy Company, he and Simmie played at picnics and parties in small towns around Spartanburg, like Woodruff and Roebuck.

Pink's musical life with Simmie was very different from his stage life. They'd go into the woods to practise, usually with a bottle of corn whiskey to help their throats, and Simmie would sing the songs over and over until Pink got the chords. Sometimes Simmie would cut a switch and hit at Pink's hands if he kept missing a change.

Pink recalled playing at a country club party, after he'd spent the entire day sitting on a log in woods behind the golf course trying to learn the chords for 'The Stars And Stripes Forever'. His hands were so swollen from Simmie's switch that he could hardly play.[1]

With Simmie, Pink made his first recordings: two sides for the old Columbia 1400 series, made in Atlanta in the late '20s. Columbia tried to get him into the studios again without Simmie, but Pink refused, and it was not until the early '50s that Paul Clayton heard him playing at a fair and recorded him again, doing a group of his favourite medicine show tunes.

After Dr Kerr's retirement in 1945, Pink worked less and less, preferring to stay near his home in Spartanburg. He kept a small guitar, washboard and harmonica trio working until 1957, when heart trouble forced him into retirement.[2]

After Simmie's death in December 1960, Pink made a few recordings, including his appearance in a film called *The Bluesmen* (1963). Otherwise, he mainly played for friends, and taught songs to his son. Pink died in 1974.

Note that while all of the Pink Floyd books refer to Pink as a Georgia bluesman – possibly because his early recordings were cut in Atlanta – he is in fact a son of Carolina. Furthermore, his singing is said to characterize a style associated with the red clay hills of the western Carolinas. One of his album covers states: 'A singer from the flat glare of the sun on the Mississippi Delta seems to shout his anger and his pain, while a singer from the Carolinas seems to sing with a melancholy shrug . . .' His singing is said to be comparable to Blind Boy Fuller, a more well-known Carolina singer.

According to bluesman Paul Geremia, who opened for Pink at a series of dates shortly before the latter's death, he was unaware of the Floyd's appropriation of his name: 'I don't think I even realized that till after he was dead.'

1. Notes from *BV 1038*, Samual B. Charters
2. Ibid.

Geremia had sought out Pink in the early '70s: 'He was living in very poor conditions in a little house that cost him $50 a month.' That was two-thirds of Pink's retirement income. To supplement it, Geremia said, 'He was running card games at his house, and selling booze to people, moonshine, or whatever he could get.

'It's too bad. The guy was a real important person, culturally speaking, and he was virtually ignored. Even his neighbours had little inkling that he was a musician.'

Floyd Council was born 2 September 1911 in Chapel Hill, North Carolina – again, not Georgia. He began his career playing in the streets of Chapel Hill in the mid-'20s with musical brothers Leo and Thomas Strowd; the latter is said to have taught him a great deal.

Floyd occasionally worked with Blind Boy Fuller in the '30s, which may have led to his first recording sessions. In late January 1937 he was heard by ARC Records scout John Baxter Long, playing alone on a street in Chapel Hill. It was Long who had first brought Fuller to NYC to record in July 1935.

Long invited Floyd to join Fuller on his third trip to New York. Floyd agreed, and a week later the three travelled to the city. Accounts leave it uncertain as to whether Floyd was intended to be a solo or backing musician, but his recorded legacy seems to suggest the latter.

During his second visit to New York in December, Floyd was used as a second guitar only. His solo tracks were later issued under the name 'Blind Boy Fuller's buddy'.

Floyd was also promoted as 'Dipper Boy Council', and 'The Devil's Daddy-in-Law'; these were probably the invention of record companies, not genuine nicknames.

In a 1969 interview, Floyd recalled having recorded twenty-seven titles. The documented tracks are: six as a soloist; seven backing Fuller; two, unissued, from December 1937, featuring blues harmonica legend Sonny Terry; and three, again unissued, from late in his career with another harp player.

Floyd performed around Chapel Hill through the '40s and '50s, both with Thomas Strowd and on his own; playing at country clubs, the Elks Home and on local radio, where he is said to have often sung non-blues material.

Floyd slowed and eventually stopped playing, owing to an unspecified illness dating from 1963. In the late '60s, a stroke partially paralysed his throat muscles and slowed his motor skills. These debilitating handicaps aside, he is said to have been quite sharp mentally.

Floyd moved to Sanford, North Carolina, where he died in June 1976. His final recordings, made in August 1970, did not, apparently, merit release. Floyd is none the less remembered by older musicians in Orange County NC as one of the area's best guitarists.

The curious Pink Floyd fan who seeks out the recordings of these men will find gritty Negro blues, which – while not irrelevant to rock and roll – is unfamiliar to most modern music fans. Lest we forget, however, the likes of John Mayall, Eric Clapton, the Rolling Stones and Syd Barrett cherished this music, and it is an important root of modern rock.

I can find no evidence that Pink and Floyd ever recorded together, met, or even heard of each other. Nor does it appear they ever shared the same vinyl, such as a compilation. I conclude that the pairing of these names was totally random.

Copyright Permissions

Every effort has been made to contact copyright holders for the pieces used in this book. Authors or publishers who have not been credited are invited to contact Sidgwick & Jackson.

Barrett, Syd: 'Blind Date'. Reprinted from *Melody Maker* (22.7.67).

Bennun, David: 'The Division Bell'; *Melody Maker* (16.4.94). Reprinted by permission of the author.

'Sid Beret': 'Writing on the wall for Floyd'. Reprinted from *NME* (11.11.78).

Boucher, Caroline: 'Waters in the pink.' Reprinted from *Disc and Music Echo* (8.8.70).

Burchill, Julie: 'Another Brick in the Wall pt. 2'; extract taken from *The Virgin Rock Yearbook 1980*, copyright © 1980 Julie Burchill. Published by Virgin Publishing Ltd.

Christgau, Robert: extracts from *Rock Albums of the '70s* (Da Capo Press, 1981). Reprinted by permission of the author.

Cocks, Jay: 'Pinkies on the wing'; *Time* (25.2.80). Courtesy of Time Inc.

Cook, Richard: 'Over the wall and into the dumper'; *NME* (19.3.83). Reprinted by permission of the author.

Dallas, Karl: 'Floyd's soundtrack becomes new album'; *Melody Maker* (August 1982). Reprinted by permission of the author.

Dann, Trevor: 'Faded Pink'; *Sunday Telegraph* (May 1984). Reprinted by permission of the author.

Dellar, Fred: extract from 'Rock'; *Hi-Fi News & Record Review* (August 1981). Reprinted by permission of the author.

Dron, Tony: 'Track record'. Reprinted from *Penthouse* (December 1984).

Erskine, Pete: 'Dirty hair denied'; *NME* (11.1.75). Courtesy of IPC Magazines.

Farren, Mick: *Ummagumma*. Reprinted from *International Times* (*c.* October 1969).

Copyright Permissions

Lindsay, Robert: 'A night to remember'; adapted from *Sunday Telegraph* (25.8.91). Reprinted by permission of the author.

MacDonald, Douglass: 'Now that's what I call music!'. Reprinted from *The Amazing Pudding* (November 1987).

Mehlman, Lisa: 'The trouble with Pink Floyd's hits'. Reprinted from *Disc* (November 1971).

Middleton, Richard: extract from 'Pop Music and the Blues' (Victor Gollancz Ltd, 1972). Reprinted by permission of the author.

Mikhlick, Sergey (trans. Oleg Muhkin): 'The post-war Dream.' Reprinted from *The Amazing Pudding* (April 1992).

Miles: '*A Saucerful of Secrets*'; *International Times* (8.8.68). Reprinted by permission of the author.

Moines, Des: '*Wet Dream*'. Reprinted from *Sounds* (4.11.78).

Mulligan, Brian: 'Waters' view – just too black to be credible'. Reprinted from *Record Business* (19.7.82).

Paytress, Mark: extract from 'Floyd Shine On'; *Record Collector* (January 1993). Reprinted by permission of the author.

Peacock, Steve: 'A pre-season report on Pink Floyd'; *Sounds* (17.8.74). Reprinted by permission of the author.

Peel, John: 'A saucerful of dollars'; *Evening Standard* (4.8.88). Courtesy of Solo Syndication.

Rose, Bernard: 'Wind of change'. Reprinted from *Sounds* (7.2.87).

Rowntree, John: 'Rock'. Extract reprinted from *Records and Recording* (November 1975).

Scarfe, Gerald: extract reprinted from *Scarfe by Scarfe* (Hamish Hamilton, 1986). Reproduced by permission of Penguin Books Ltd.

Shaar Murray, Charles: extract from 'Less fun than watching TV'; *Weekend Telegraph* (29.8.92). Reprinted by permission of the author.

Shipston, Roy: 'Are spacemen Floyd on the way back to Earth?'. Reprinted from *Disc & Music Echo* (22.11.69).

Smith, Debbi: 'The Pink Floyd is London's answer to West Coast Sound'. Reprinted from *GO* (4.8.67).

Thompson, Dave: 'The madcap laughs'. Reprinted from *Pandemonium!* (March 1995).

Copyright Permissions

Index

Several of the songs include times at the beginning (e.g. '4.30 AM'). For indexing purposes, the alphabetical order is derived from the words in brackets after the times. This corresponds with entries in the book's 'A–Z' section.

Ayers, Kevin, 33
azimuth coordinator, 35, 135, 300

'Baby Blue Shuffle in D Major', 191
'Baby Lemonade', 53, 191
Badfinger, 273
Bailey, John, 26
Baker, Ken, 273
'Ballad of Bill Hubbard, The', 191
Banks, Pete, 225
Barrett, 54, 214, 286, 287, 305, 321, 322
Barrett, Winifred, xiii, 238, 239
Beach Boys, 305
Beatles, xi, 10, 28, 35, 37, 39, 45, 60, 88, 245, 285, 322
Beck, Jeff, 145,.274, 284
Bedford, David, 98
'Beginning, The', 227
'Behold the Temple of Light', 227
Bennun, David, viii, 156–7
Berlin Philharmonic, 140
Berlioz, Hector, 315
Berry, Chuck, 34, 250, 262
'Beset By Creatures of the Deep', 183, 227
Beyond the Valley of the Dolls, 210
Beyond the Wildwood, 322
'Biding My Time', 191, 234
'Big Theme', 191
'Bike', 11, 192, 320
'Bike Song, The', 192
'Birdie Hop', 192
'Bitter Love', 222
Blackberries, 93
'Black Ice', 192
Blackhill Enterprises, 23, 28, 39, 40, 71, 73, 305
Bley, Carla, 114, 196, 223, 224, 283
'Blue Light', 192–3

'Blues (Improvisation/Jam)', 193
Blues Magoos, 49
Bluesmen, The, 325
Blyton, Enid, 195
'Bob Dylan Blues', 193
Body, The, xv, 183, 193, 247, 261
'Body Transport', 193
Bolan, June (née Child), 39
Bolan, Marc, 24, 160
Bomb Culture, 40
'Boo to You Too', 193
'Boom Tune', 194
'Boppin' Sound, The', 194
Bough, Frank, 266
Bowie, David, 49, 88, 208, 262, 320
Boyd, Joe, 24, 25, 35, 39, 71, 194
'Brain Damage', 87, 194
'Bravery of Being Out of Range, The', 194
'Breathe (*Dark Side of the Moon*)', 195
'Breathe (*The Body*)', 194
Brezhnev, Leonid, 176
Briggs, Raymond, 172, 209
'Bring the Boys Back Home', 195
Britannia Row, 109, 119, 120
'British Submarine, The', 186
British Winter Tour '74, 101
Brooker, Gary, 262
Broonzy, Bill, 261
Bros, 160
Brown, Arthur, 33, 71
Brown, Sam, 215, 287
'Brush Your Window', 246
Burchill, Julie, xi, 187
'Burning Bridges', 195
Burroughs, William S., 263
Bush, Kate, xii, 291
Butler, Bernard, 198
'By Töüching', 195
Byrds, 49

Index

Index

Index

'Malta', 233
'Man, The', 233–4, 237
Mann, Thomas, 195
Manning, Barbara, 158
Mansell, Nigel, 144
Mantler, Michael, 114, 196
Manzanera, Phil, 247
'March of the Dambusters', 231
Marillion, 209
Marmalade, 250
'Marooned', 156, 234
Marquee club, xiii, 27, 70, 250, 312
Martyn, John, 286
Marvel comics, 32
'Massed Gadgets of Hercules, The', 234
'Matilda Mother', 234, 270, 287
May, Derrick, 275
Mayall, John, 26, 327
'Me Or Him', 234
Meddle, 12, 16, 56–7, 68, 70, 74, 77, 81, 98, 162, 203, 215, 233, 260
Medicine Head, 302
'Mediterranean C', 107, 234–5
Meine, Klaus, 224
Mercury, Freddie, 151
'Merry Christmas Song, The', 235
'Metamorphosis', 46
'Mexico '78', 235
Middle Earth, 19, 37, 305
'Mihalis', 235
Miles, Barry, 24, 31–2, 46, 323
Miles, Colin, 242
'Milky Way', 52, 53, 235
Miller, Glenn, 195
Mills, John, 172
Milton, Jake, 26
Mitchell, Joni, 140
Mitchell, Juliet, 174
'Molly's Song', 235

'5.11 AM (The Moment of Clarity)', 236
Momentary Lapse of Reason, A, 5, 6, 10, 15–17, 135–7, 152, 156–7, 241, 249–50, 290
'Money', xiv, 4, 15, 16, 87, 98, 116, 155, 183, 236, 300
Monroe, Marilyn, 31
Monty Python, 270
Moody Blues, 301
'Moonhead', 236–7
Moore, Anthony, 204, 245
Moore, Patrick, 237
More, 69, 169, 171, 198, 217, 223, 233, 234, 242, 244, 255, 261, 269, 286, 316
'More Blues', 227, 237
Morrera, Tom, 111
Morrison, Brian, 73–4
Morrison, Van, viii, 148
Morrissey, x
'Most Boring Song I've Ever Heard Bar Two, The', 237
'Mother', 175, 237–9
Mother's, 161, 208
Mothers Of Invention, 46, 49
Move, 38
MTV, xi
'Mudmen', 239
'Mumbo Jumbo', 239
Munoz, Mason, 142
'Murder', 240
'Murderistic Woman', 228
Murdoch, Rupert, 286
Murray, Pete, 222
Mustaine, Dave, 287
'My Generation', 303

'Narrow Way, The', 47, 191, 227, 241
'Near The End', 241

Index

'Reaction in G', 256
Reagan, Ronald, 115, 176, 194, 211, 253
'4.47 AM (The Remains Of Our Love)', 256
'Rebel Rebel', 88
Red Hot Chili Peppers, 226
Reed, Lou, 160
Reeves, Jim, 48
Relics, 306
'Remember A Day', 257, 270
'Return of the Son of Monster Magnet', 46
'Return of the Son of Nothing', 243, 258
Revolver, 88
'Rhamadan', 258
'Rhoda', 258
Richard, Keith, 37
'Richard's Rave-Up', 258
Ring, The, 140
Ritchie, Ian, 221, 274
'Roadrunner', 27
Robbins, Harold, 195
Rock Et Folk, 211
Rockettes, 112
Roeg, Nicholas, 86
Rolling Stones, xi, 28, 88, 94, 228, 327
Romeo, Max, 107
'Rooftop in a Thunderstorm Row Missing The Point, A', 183, 259
Rose, Bernard, 172–73
Rotten, Johnny, 187
'Round and Around', 259
Roundhouse, 30, 72
Rowe, Keith, 25
Roxy Music, 277
'Run Like Hell', 127, 259
Rundgren, Todd, 320
'4.33 AM (Running Shoes)', 259

Rush, 246
'Rush in a Million', 246
'Russian Missile, The', 186

Samson, Polly, xii, 252, 283
San Francisco Oracle, 32
'San Tropez', 260
Sanborn, David, 131
Sanders, Rick, 237
Saucerful of Secrets, xiv, 12, 46, 72, 73, 93, 152, 194, 237, 258, 263, 305, 313, 321
'Saucerful of Secrets', 31, 45, 46, 77, 160, 227, 234, 258, 260
Saucerful of Secrets (Schaffner), xi, xiii, 324
Savoy Brown, 34, 98
'Sawdustland', 169–70
'Scarecrow, The', 260, 320
Scarfe, Gerald, 131, 164–5, 177
Schenker, Rudy, 224
Schoenberg, Arnold, 174
Schroeder, Barbet, 171, 179, 217, 233, 249, 261, 288
Schumann, Robert, 287
Scorpions, 224
'Scream Thy Last Scream', 38, 245, 260, 321
'Sea Shell and Soft Stone', 261
'Sea Shell and Stone', 261
'Seabirds', 261
'Seamus', 204, 233, 261
'See Emily Play', 11, 35–6, 38, 43, 71, 228, 256, 260, 261–2, 299, 305, 312, 313, 320
See For Miles records, 242
'See Saw', 46, 237, 262
'Seems We Were Dreäming', 262
Selwood, Clive, 273

Index

Index